MW00424730

Voices from the Dust

OTHER BOOKS AND BOOKS ON CASSETTE
BY S. KENT BROWN:

From Jerusalem to Zarahemla

Finding God at BYU

Mary and Elisabeth: Noble Daughters of God

Voices from the Dust

BOOK OF MORMON INSIGHTS

To Bishop Eickbush -
In gratitude for your service.

S. KENT BROWN

Covenant

Covenant Communications, Inc.

Cover image *King Benjamin Addresses His People* by Gary Kapp © Intellectual Reserve, Inc.
Cover design copyrighted 2004 by Covenant Communications, Inc.

Published by Covenant Communications, Inc.
American Fork, Utah

Printed in Canada
First Printing: April 2004

12 11 10 09 08 07 06 05 04 10 9 8 7 6 5 4 3 2 1

ISBN 1-59156-478-6

ACKNOWLEDGMENTS

No book passes through the hands of just one person. That situation is certainly true for this volume. Over a period of years, many have helped. And I owe all of them my heartfelt thanks. One of the most important has been Patricia Ward, my administrative assistant. As she shepherded draft after draft through her computer, she was burdened with trying to figure out my sometimes complicated marks on a page. My gratitude also goes to Shauna Humphreys, whose encouragement and fine editing were important ingredients in the final product. Over a period of years, student assistants have checked and gathered sources for me. These good-spirited, capable individuals include Bryan Johnston, David Elkington, Taylor Mammen, Levi Smylie, Jocelyn Sparks, Melanie Fillmore, and Reed Larsen.

Friends and associates have willingly read and critiqued drafts of the studies that appear in the book. My appreciation goes to Ashley Crandall, Blair Van Dyke, Richard Wellington, George Potter, and Steve Gilliland. The same can be said about a few students from my classes who have willingly commented on my efforts. A couple of teenaged neighbors, Aaron and David Pinegar, read chapters to see whether I had aimed my language too high. I turned to our five children and their spouses for critique, and they graciously gave it. (This was payback, in a measure, for all of the red marks that I scribbled on their high school and college papers.) And Andy Livingston graciously drew the map of the possible routes from Jerusalem to the Red Sea.

Naturally, I would not have finished anything without the support of my beloved Gayle who read the final version of these chapters as well as some earlier versions. Thank you all.

In memory of
Orpha and Phyllis

TABLE OF CONTENTS

INTRODUCTION

Jerusalem in 600 B.C. was a city riven with social and political fissures. The city witnessed the precipitous descent of its citizens from supporting a series of important, rejuvenating religious reforms under King Josiah (640–609 B.C.) down to the haughty rejection of the Lord's last-ditch effort through Jeremiah to save the city from the barbarous cruelty of Nebuchadnezzar's soldiers by freeing enslaved Israelites from the well-appointed homes and estates of the wealthy (see 2 Kgs. 23:1–25; Jer. 34:8–22). During the twenty-two years between the death of Josiah and the crushing capture of Jerusalem by the Babylonians (609–587 B.C.), the Lord raised up "many prophets" to warn Jerusalemites and the people of Judah that their disobedience to prophetic counsel and their disdainful disregard of the sacred character of the temple would mean destruction (1 Ne. 1:4).[1] One of those whom the Lord touched was the man Lehi, who had "prayed unto the Lord, yea, even with all his heart, in behalf of his people" (1 Ne. 1:5). Lehi thus became one of the Lord's mouthpieces in His ever intensifying effort to turn the tide of roaring, rampant wickedness. It did not succeed.

In the days before Lehi's divine calling, Zedekiah, whose birth name was Mattaniah, had been installed as a puppet king by the Babylonians in 598 B.C. Thus, in the midst of religious and political uncertainties gnawing at Jerusalem sat the weak and indecisive

Zedekiah, unable to control factions that had grown up among the city's elite. Although the factions were weakened when the Babylonians took hostages from their numbers at Zedekiah's enthronement, they still raged against one another, even murdering opponents. The moral malaise in the city, which followed the deflating of the religious reforms initiated by Josiah twenty-five years earlier, revealed itself in the hatching of plots and the commissioning of death squads. In fact, one suspects that Lehi's kinsman Laban, who the record says was out "by night" with the "elders of the Jews," had been involved in a clandestine meeting with trusted associates, thus tending to confirm the presence of extremism within the society, an extremism that one detects in other sources.[2] (See 2 Kgs. 24; 1 Ne. 1, 4.)

While the Lord left other prophets—notably Jeremiah and Habakkuk and Zephaniah—as a slowly collapsing bulwark against the evil tide in the city, He directed Lehi and his wife Sariah to lead their family out of Jerusalem. For Mormon, the main compiler and editor of the Book of Mormon record, Lehi and Sariah held their own charm and attraction because they were the founders of his civilization. Yet there is more. A thousand years later, Mormon watched as his own fellow citizens ran pell-mell into the jaws of certain destruction because they chose wickedness over righteousness (see W of M 1:1; Morm. 6:1–22), and it seems amply evident that the fate of deviant Jerusalem stood as the grand but horrifying example to Mormon of the Lord's two-fisted justice against His wilfully aberrant people.

Although Lehi and his family were not witnesses to the sudden, terrifying fall of Jerusalem, he had prophesied of this event more than once (see 1 Ne. 1:18; 10:3; also 17:22, 43). And after arriving in the New World, he sought to know, and then learned by revelation, "that Jerusalem is destroyed; and had we remained in Jerusalem we should also have perished" (2 Ne. 1:4). This combination of Lehi's prophecies about God's frightening justice upon the city, and his later, inspired assurance that it had occurred, would have stood as a major proof for people like Mormon that God will exact punishment upon His proud, disobedient people.

Not surprisingly, while Jerusalem presses itself upon readers of the Book of Mormon from beginning to end, so does the Redeemer. Most who spend time in the pages of the Book of Mormon come away with schooled impressions about the Redeemer and His wondrous work among us. Indeed this forms the major focus of the book from its earliest pages. Nephi, the first author, pushes the Redeemer onto the stage both by narrating his own vision about the Messiah and by quoting his father's words about the coming Redeemer.[3] Moreover, Mormon, the chief compiler and editor of the work, shaped the final version of the record to bring the Redeemer into a clear light for readers. For instance, at the end of his own account, he writes poignantly about those who squandered their chance to come to Jesus:

> O ye fair ones,
> how could ye have departed from the ways of the Lord!
> O ye fair ones,
> how could ye have rejected that Jesus,
> who stood with open arms to receive you! (Morm. 6:17)[4]

On another level, yet closely linked to the theme of the Messiah's redemption, Jerusalem emerges as a symbol of the Redeemer's work, and thereby a symbol of mercy and hope. As the Book of Mormon opens, Jerusalem and its inhabitants are hopelessly flawed. Even so, Lehi learns prophetically that, after Jerusalem's "iniquity is pardoned" (Isa. 40:2), her people "should return again . . . [and] should be brought back out of captivity . . . [and] should possess again the land" (1 Ne. 10:3). After punishment and dispossession come the sweet fragrances of mercy and restoration.

In a second example, Lehi's fifth son, Jacob, learns from an angel that when the Messiah shall "come among the Jews . . . they shall crucify him. . . . Wherefore, because of their iniquities . . . they . . . shall be scattered among all nations" (2 Ne. 10:3, 6).[5] This is not the end of the story. In Jacob's continuing words, "When the day cometh that they shall believe in me, that I am Christ . . . they shall be gathered in . . . from the four parts of the earth" (2 Ne. 10:7–8). Here we witness again the pattern of divine punishment and merciful restoration. It is a pattern of redemption and fits tightly with the more visible message about the Redeeming Christ and His work. Moreover, it involves Jerusalem where the Messiah will die and where, in the words of Lehi, through the miracle of miracles, He "should rise from the dead" (1 Ne. 10:11).

In fact, it is through the eyes of Moroni, son of Mormon, that we see what Mormon saw as he looked back through time to the fall of Jerusalem. Though he knows that the restoration of the Jews back to Jerusalem is still a long time off, Moroni, the final custodian of the record, turns compassionately to the city and, borrowing Isaiah's language, pleads that she "arise from the dust . . . and put on [her] beautiful garments . . . that the covenants of the Eternal Father . . . may be fulfilled" (Moro. 10:31; Isa. 52:1; 54:2). As Moroni knows, the redemption of Jerusalem, and the creation of her counterpart, the New Jerusalem,[6] will signal that God's redemptive power is real and that His mercy is genuine. Jerusalem, the fallen and abandoned, is also the hope of the future.

The six studies in this volume also share a common focus on persons who made a remarkable difference in Book of Mormon history. Beginning with the all-important founding generation of the Lehite peoples and their epic journey across Arabia, and ending with the last known survivor of the Nephite-Lamanite wars of the fourth century A.D., these studies attempt to set both heroes and heroines of the Book of Mormon narrative within their times, bringing their world to life.

Hints exist that the memory of the journey of Lehi and Sariah was kept alive among Book of Mormon peoples for hundreds of years, after the two of them had kept their traveling party together through one of the harshest climes on earth (see Mosiah 2:4). Nephi's narrative of that trek in 1 Nephi 2–18, though sparse, offers a photograph of Arabia in the early sixth century B.C. Some parts of the photograph are clear, other parts are out of focus. But recent research has begun to bring into focus the unclear elements of the journey, placing the party of Lehi and Sariah against a known Arabian backdrop.

Studies on the speech of King Benjamin have grown in number during recent years, but his speech and its formal coronation setting are so rich that they invite students to reinvestigate their depth and breadth. Besides, the coronation of his son Mosiah draws us into the world of Old Testament royalty.

One of the least studied sagas in Book of Mormon history is the mission of the four sons of King Mosiah to the Lamanities, their enemies. Not only are the successful actions of the four men and their companions worth serious study, but this story opens one of the few windows that peers onto the culture and civilization of the Lamanite people, including their social, educational, and governmental institutions.

The visit of the Risen Jesus to people in the New World stands without parallel in ancient literature. The exploration of His three-day visit seeks to illumine important dimensions of the Savior's stay among the Lamanites and Nephites, which resulted in an almost 200-year era of peace and prosperity. Such an era has never been seen in any civilization before or since.

Moroni stood where no one has ever stood. In one day, after the utter annihilation of his people, he became a fugitive rather than a trusted citizen, a hunted man rather than a faithful church member, an outcast rather than a general. As a Nephite survivor, he was completely alone. Yet, through it all, he remained true to his faith and rose above debilitating cynicism, continuing and finishing the record that his father Mormon had been editing.

In all, these studies take Book of Mormon students into places where few studies have ventured, probing possibilities, that enrich our understanding of people who made a difference, who kept their faith, and who believed that God had orchestrated events in their lives.

Incidentally, I have taken the liberty of prefacing two of the studies with fictional introductions—the section that deals with the mission of Mosiah's sons and the section on Moroni—in an effort to place them meaningfully into plausible, living contexts. The reader will judge whether I have succeeded on this count, and on all the rest.

NOTES TO THE INTRODUCTION

1. See 1 Ne. 1:4; also 2 Chron. 36:14–16; for overviews, consult John Bright, *A History of Israel,* 3rd ed. (Philadelphia: Westminster Press, 1981), 324–27; S. Kent Brown and Richard N. Holzapfel, *Between the Testaments: From Malachi to Matthew* (Salt Lake City: Deseret Book, 2002), 3–6.
2. See the summary of Bright, *A History of Israel,* 328–31.
3. For Nephi's vision of the Messiah, see 1 Ne. 11:13–34; 12:6–7; for Lehi's dream, see 10:4–11.

4. The arrangement of these verses is that of Grant Hardy. See his *The Book of Mormon: A Reader's Edition* (Urbana: University of Illinois Press, 2003), 566.

5. Lehi also knows about the scattering that follows the Messiah's death, as well as a subsequent restoration. After narrating the slaying of the Messiah and then His resurrection (see 1 Ne. 10:11), he speaks of "the house of Israel, that . . . should be scattered upon all the face of the earth" as well as the fact that these people "should be gathered together again" (1 Ne. 10:12, 14). See also Nephi's words in 1 Ne. 22:12.

6. The Risen Savior spoke of the New Jerusalem (see 3 Ne. 20:22; 21:23–25) as did Moroni (see Ether 13:2–8, 10).

Out of Jerusalem

CHAPTER ONE

Propelled steadily by the Lord's warnings, Lehi and Sariah led their family out of Jerusalem and into the desert of Arabia, beginning an exodus that would be celebrated in story and song for a thousand years (see Mosiah 2:4). But their story would remain unknown to the wider world for more than two and one-half millennia, until the translation of the Book of Mormon. While spending months, perhaps longer, at a base camp near the northeastern arm of the Red Sea, the family briefly kept contact with their estate at Jerusalem through the four sons, Laman, Lemuel, Sam, and Nephi. Twice these sons had to go back the more than 250 miles to the city at the behest of the Lord: the first time to obtain a scriptural record inscribed on metal plates of brass, and the second time to persuade another family, that of a man named Ishmael, to join them in their quest for a "promised land." After the Lord directed the party to move deeper into the desert, they packed up their tents and "provisions" and crossed the "river Laman," never to return again to Jerusalem, effectively cutting themselves off from hearth and home (see 1 Ne. 16:11–12).

LEHI'S FIRST VISIONS

It all began at a rock, probably a prominent landmark. The limestone crust that lies just at the earth's surface in Jerusalem has given a generally stony appearance to the region for millennia, with rocks and pebbles strewn everywhere over hills and across fields. Here the Lord prodded the man Lehi into taking his first steps toward becoming a prophet when Lehi saw a heaven-sent pillar of fire dwelling on that rock, and he also "heard much" (1 Ne. 1).

Exhausted, Lehi returned to his home. Owing to the military strength of the kingdom of Judah at the time, it was possible to build one's home outside the walls of the city. And that is apparently where Lehi's estate lay.[1] His fatigue after this intensely spiritual experience mirrored that of Ezekiel, his contemporary in Babylon, who spent a week recovering from his own first vision (see Ezek. 3:15). While lying on his bed, a second vision burst upon Lehi's consciousness, transporting him as it were to the large throne room of God, which was filled with uncounted "concourses of angels in the attitude of singing and praising their God" (1 Ne. 1:8). In a word, the vision had borne Lehi into the council of Jehovah, a body into which, as scripture records, several of Lehi's contemporaries and predecessors had entered, even if for a brief moment, to receive instructions from the Lord. Among those who carried prophetic messages a century or so before Lehi's time were Isaiah, who spoke of his visit to this council (see Isa. 6), and Amos, who referred to its purpose (see Amos 3:7). Of Lehi's contemporaries, Jeremiah, whom the Lord called as a "prophet to the nations," heard the complaints of the Lord that false prophets had claimed to be privy to the secrets of this council but were not (see Jer. 23:18, 23; 29:8–9).[2]

Lehi's vision differed from that of others in that he saw "One descending out the midst of heaven," followed by "twelve others." Although there is no evidence that Lehi at this moment recognized the individual as the future Messiah, the book that the heavenly one brought to Lehi prophesied openly of the coming One. As Lehi read the words of the book aloud—"he read, saying"—he also learned that the city of Jerusalem was in danger of destruction, verifying the message that Jeremiah had been repeating for almost thirty years (1 Ne. 1:9–13).[3]

Lehi's visions brought two results. First, it put him and his family on notice that the future of the city was in dire straits, potentially affecting their lives, just as it had already affected others who had paid attention to Jeremiah's warnings and also those of Habakkuk. For indeed there must have been people like Lehi who were scandalized by the low spiritual climate in the city and had moved away.[4] Second, Lehi responded to the Lord's directives by going public, raising a voice of warning to citizens of the city, a warning that included a condemnation of "their wickedness and their abominations." Reaction was sharp. People of the city at first "did mock him," and then grew "angry with him," and finally "sought his life." (See 1 Ne. 1.)

In order to save Lehi's life, and ultimately the lives of his family, the Lord ordered them to leave—permanently. Taking the bare essentials, the family carried only "provisions, and tents," the tents being carried by pack animals—camels or possibly donkeys—because of their weight. All of their moveable wealth they left behind, striking out generally south and east "into the wilderness," not yet knowing their destination. (See 1 Ne. 2.)

TO THE RED SEA

The family's exact route to the tip of the northeastern arm of the Red Sea remains unknown. At least four options lay before them.[5] They could depart eastward down through the Jordan valley, passing just south of Jericho and north of the Dead Sea, and climb the hills of Moab until they reached the well-trodden King's Highway where they would turn south. A second path would have taken them farther east, beyond the King's Highway, where a dusty desert road ran south toward the Red Sea. Another route ran south from Jerusalem, one spur descending steeply eastward into the Jordan valley from Tekoa, birthplace of the prophet Amos, leading travelers to the Ein Gedi oasis and then to a trail running south. A second spur of this southbound road would have taken them through Hebron toward Arad, eventually leading them into the Jordan valley some twenty-five miles south of Ein Gedi. By any route, the Red Sea lay almost 200 miles away. They continued on another "three days"—a ritually significant number.[6] After arriving in the area south of modern-day Aqaba, the family found itself about 250 miles from Jerusalem, virtually a two-week walk from the city, including Sabbaths. Here they set up their camp. (See 1 Ne. 2.)

Lehi inaugurated their home away from home by building "an altar of stones" in accord with the specifications of the Mosaic law, erecting it from field stones. He then "made an offering unto the

Possible Routes for Approaching the Red Sea

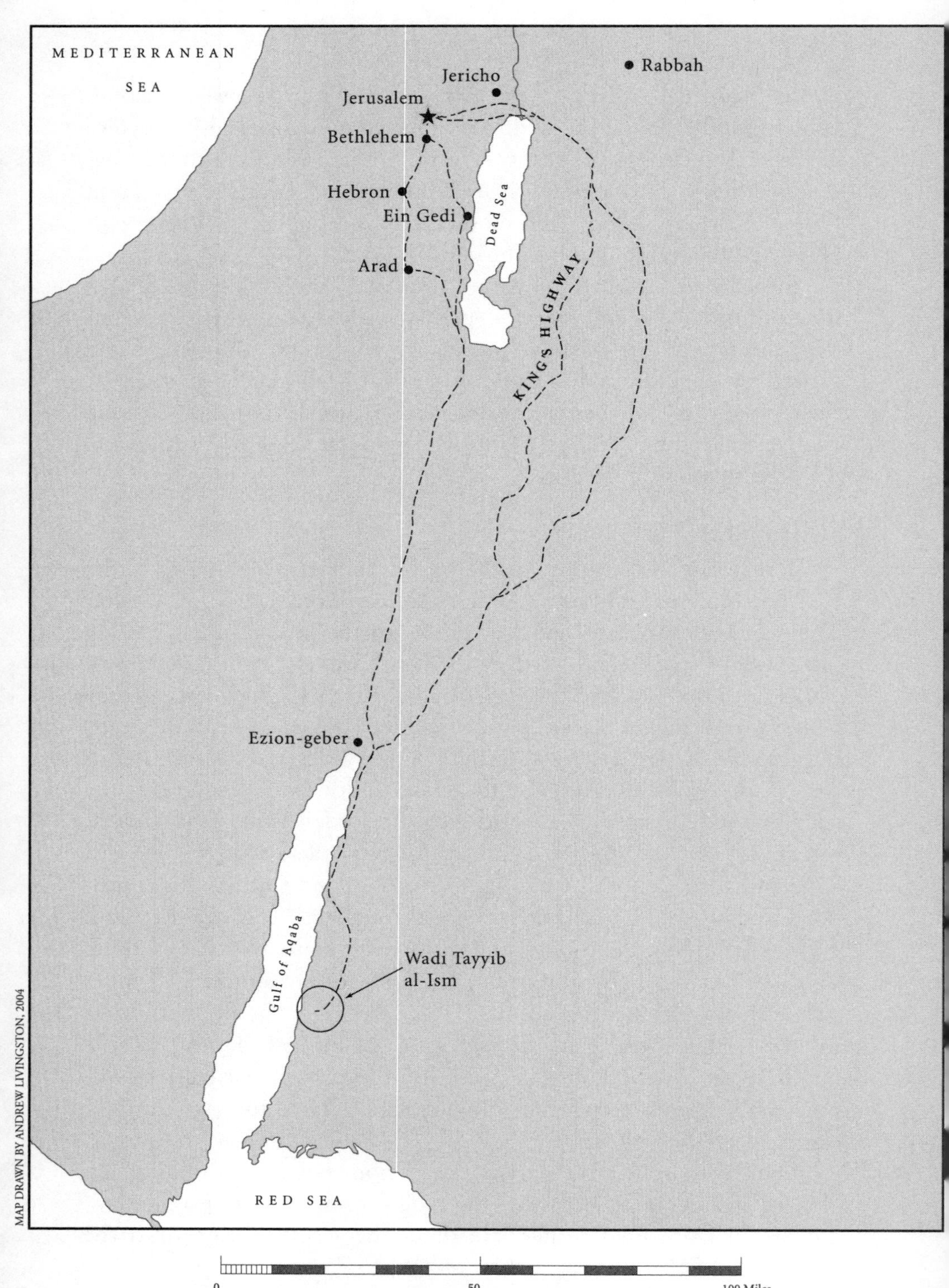

Lord, and gave thanks." By his actions he showed himself faithful to the requirement that a person sacrifice a peace offering for safe journey, whether on land or on sea (see Ps. 107:4–8, 19–32). A question remains, however, whether he had brought animals for sacrifice—unlikely, since none are mentioned—or whether he purchased animals from a local herdsman by trading precious "provisions" that the family had carried. Whatever the case, the sacrifice would have cut deeply into the family's supplies, supplies that could not easily be replenished, underscoring of course Lehi's determination to put the Lord first in family affairs.[7] But not all agreed. Lehi's two older sons "did murmur against their father," exhibiting a widely known characteristic of certain desert peoples.[8] (See 1 Ne. 2.)

The location of the camp has long been a matter of discussion. Assuming a travel rate of fifteen to twenty-five miles per day, the family reached a point between forty-five and seventy-five miles south of Aqaba in their three days of travel after arriving at the northeast tip of the Red Sea, which would locate them in one of two promising spots. First, it is possible that they walked into the valley called Wadi Al-Ifal, which they could have reached after traversing the east shore of the Red Sea southward toward a small range of impassible mountains, and then ascending southeast through the corridor formed by the Wadi Umm Jurfayn. A trade route passing through this part of the country connected southern Arabia with Gaza on the Mediterranean Sea. If in fact they set up camp in the Wadi Al-Ifal, they would have pitched their tents in the area of the oasis now known as Al-Bad', where there were wells and, very occasionally, a seasonal stream.[9] Located about thirty miles north of the seashore in a valley that collects winter and spring runoff from a number of higher canyons, Al-Bad' oasis sits between nearby rocky hills rising to the east and west, with any runoff water passing southward through the valley that gradually widens to a breadth of twenty miles where it meets the Red Sea.

A more promising candidate for the camp is Wadi Tayyib Al-Ism, which lies west and slightly north of Al-Bad' in the range of mountains that cuts off a traveler moving south along the seashore from Aqaba. The distance from the northeast tip of the Red Sea to Wadi Tayyib Al-Ism, where a year-round stream bubbles up, is about seventy-five miles, a distance that Lehi and his family could have traveled in "three days." Not only does the valley feature a flowing stream that spawns an oasis in the mountains, but the steep canyon walls form an impressive, narrow, three-and-one-half-mile valley that runs westward down to the coastline of the Red Sea.[10] (See 1 Ne. 2.)

In each case, because of the distance of the oasis from the shore—at least thirty miles at Al-Bad' and three and one-half miles at Wadi Tayyib Al-Ism—Lehi and his party would not have known, without exploring, that the stream ran all the way to the sea. But after learning that the water flow reached the Red Sea, Lehi "called the name of the river, Laman" and said to this son: "O that thou mightest be like unto this river, continually running into the fountain of all righteousness." Then, referring to the solid, steep hills that framed the valley, Lehi spoke to Lemuel: "O that thou mightest be like unto this valley, firm and steadfast, and immovable in keeping the commandments of the Lord." Thus Lehi drew on two of the more important geographical features of the landscape—the stream and the valley—to drive home his desire that his two older sons be faithful to the Lord's commands. (See 1 Ne. 2.)

THE FIRST RETURN TO JERUSALEM

A test for the sons soon reared its head. Through Lehi, the Lord asked that they return to Jerusalem to the house of a relative named Laban "and seek the records" that he held. These records, inscribed on metal plates of brass, contained the early parts of the Bible—in Nephi's words, "the record of the Jews and also a genealogy of [Lehi's] forefathers." Fortunately for the enterprise, Lehi's youngest son, Nephi, had already received a spiritual assurance that his father was acting under the direction of the Lord. And Nephi had successfully communicated this assurance to Sam, the brother just older than himself. But the two eldest, Laman and Lemuel, were again showing signs of resistance. Evidently, they agreed to go because it meant returning home. (See 1 Ne. 3.)

The return trip of 250 or so miles to Jerusalem must have been uneventful because Nephi does not comment on it. It was after they arrived that matters began to unravel. In a first attempt to obtain the plates, Laman went to visit Laban by himself and, when he broached the subject, was tossed out. A second attempt failed even more miserably. Lehi's sons decided to try to purchase the record by carrying all of the family's moveable wealth—"our gold, and our silver, and our precious things"—to a second interview with Laban. This time Laban sent his thugs after them, falsely accusing them of theft—and he kept their precious possessions for himself, showing himself to be the real thief. (See 1 Ne. 3.)

After this close call, while hiding in one of the many small caves that dot the valleys surrounding Jerusalem, the oldest brothers angrily argued that their father's directive had brought them too close to serious harm. Seeing Nephi and Sam as embodiments of their frustrations, they began to beat them "with a rod." The beating caught the notice of heaven because only an angel's intervention stopped it. When he had jerked the brothers' attention to himself, the angel stressed that the plates were still a priority. So the brothers worked on another plan while Laman and Lemuel were still smarting from the angel's rebuke. (See 1 Ne. 3.)

The youngest, Nephi, was to sneak into the city under cover of darkness to see what he could see. Unexpectedly, he stumbled onto Laban who, in a quiet street, was lying facedown in a drunken stupor. Nephi seemingly did not know what to do, although he was trying to be sensitive to impressions from the Spirit. Noticing the fine work of Laban's sword, he drew it from its sheath and held it up in the moonlight to admire it[11] when, with a rush, the sickening feeling swept over him that he should use it on Laban. Try as he might, he could not expel the intensifying impression that he was to take Laban's life with the sword. Three times, each with more force, the Spirit bore the thought into Nephi's mind until the words came audibly: "Slay him, for the Lord hath delivered him into thy hands." Even though the thought made Nephi recoil—"I shrunk and would that I might not slay him"—he killed Laban so that his descendants would not "dwindle and perish in unbelief." In the Lord's view, it was "better that [Laban] should perish."[12] (See 1 Ne. 4.)

But the emotional pressures of that night had not ended for Nephi. He knew that he still had to get his hands on the plates. So he carefully undressed Laban and then dressed himself in the dead man's clothes. What now? He did not have to wait long. While walking toward Laban's home, he met Laban's servant, Zoram, whom he must have met in Laban's house. As Zoram's position of trust demonstrates, he was an Israelite working as an indentured servant. Dressed as Laban, Nephi attempted his best imitation of Laban's voice and asked to see the record on the plates. Evidently not suspecting foul play, Zoram led Nephi to the record in "the treasury," a building that remains unknown. In Nephi's company, Zoram carried the record out of the city directly toward the hiding place of the brothers, chatting nervously all the while. The brothers, thinking Nephi to be Laban, panicked and bolted, only stopping when Nephi called out in his natural voice. It was now Zoram's turn to panic. Nephi, large for his age, seized Zoram, held him fast, and with an oath extracted a promise that Zoram would go with them to their father's camp. Zoram must have been relatively young, perhaps in his late teens, for he was not yet married. Moreover, it was important that Zoram not return to his duties since others would see him as a traitor to his master for allowing the plates to be taken. Besides, Laban's death would be discovered in the morning, complicating everything. Further, someone in Laban's household would remember the earlier visits of the brothers and, quite naturally, connect their interest in the record with its disappearance, thus leading agents of Laban to search for them. So, without turning back to their estate, the sons hastened southward with Zoram to their father's tent. (1 Ne. 4.)

In the meantime, because her sons had been gone for several weeks—a round trip would have taken three weeks, assuming no difficulties—Sariah had begun to assume the worst and to grieve for them, believing that they had perished in the desert. Her grief was also saturated with complaints against her "visionary" husband, a term that she turned pejoratively on Lehi. Without much effect, he tried to console her about their sons, saying that the Lord would protect them. But it was only when they arrived back at camp, having been gone at least a month, that she found relief—nay, more than relief. She also received a testimony that her husband enjoyed divine guidance and that her sons had been protected by the Lord: "Now I know of a surety that the Lord hath commanded my husband to flee into the wilderness," an abiding assurance that she would need when the family finally moved farther south and east into the harshest parts of Arabia. In addition, she had come to "know of a surety that the Lord hath protected my sons." If ancient custom was as it is in modern Arabia, the woman in the family carried the main responsibility for the camp and the activities within it. She also took charge of the families of her sons and made the decisions about meals and the like.[13] In this light, Sariah was the key to the survival—physical and emotional—of the family as it made its way south into Arabia and then east. Having received a spiritual assurance that the Lord was guiding her family, Sariah was now ready to carry the arduous burdens that desert women carry, all to the good of the traveling party.[14] (See 1 Ne. 5.)

Now it was time to celebrate the safe return of the sons and the safe acquisition of the record. So Lehi offered the customary peace offering of thanksgiving for safety in travel. Then he added "burnt offerings." Why? Burnt offerings were for purging sin, for making atonement (see Lev. 1:2–4). The answer has to be that Lehi was in part purging the sins of his older sons—they had murmured about going and, after they were in Jerusalem, had beaten their younger brothers. In addition, he had to purge the sin of his wife. After all, she had complained bitterly against him and against his claim that the Lord had been leading him. But the darkest act that hung about their family was Nephi's killing of Laban. To be sure, the Lord had directed Nephi's act. Even so, taking the life of another person—except, for example, in the cases of self-defense, war, and justified vengeance[15]—would have placed Nephi's family on unfamiliar ground. On the chance that this deed might somehow bring a stain on the family, Lehi offered "burnt offerings," probably offering animals that he had acquired by bartering.[16] Once again, Lehi's devotion to the Lord apparently cost the family needed resources. (See 1 Ne. 5.)

Lehi's subsequent review of the scripture on the brass plates seems to be connected to his later vision of the tree of life, the coming Messiah, and the future of God's people (see 1 Ne. 8, 10). At first, Lehi's inventory of the plates told him that the record contained "the five books of Moses" and "a record of the Jews from the beginning . . . down to . . . the reign of Zedekiah," the puppet king whom the Babylonians had just put on the throne. Lehi then discovered a genealogy that linked him and his family to "Joseph . . . who was sold into Egypt." Finally, when the Spirit of the Lord came upon him as he read, Lehi prophesied. Under inspiration, he declared that, like ancient records inscribed on stone, "these plates of brass should never perish" nor "be dimmed any more by time." They were to be a part of a larger work of the Lord, including the Lord's efforts among future descendants. (See 1 Ne. 5.)

THE SECOND TRIP TO JERUSALEM

Another test now loomed. The Lord instructed Lehi to send his sons again to Jerusalem, this time to persuade the family of a man named Ishmael to join them in the desert. According to Erastus Snow, the Prophet Joseph Smith taught that Ishmael's two sons had married daughters of Lehi and Sariah.[17] If so, there was already a binding connection between the families. In any case, the sons returned more willingly than before because one of the objects in inviting Ishmael and his family to join them had to do with his daughters. As Lehi had learned, the Lord foresaw them married to Lehi's sons. (See 1 Ne. 7.)

The trip back to Jerusalem seems to have gone smoothly, including the successful effort to persuade Ishmael's family members—two married sons and five unmarried daughters—to join the band in the desert. Nephi does not indicate how long he and his brothers stayed in the area of Jerusalem or whether they had to keep out of sight because of the earlier incidents involving Laban. Ishmael would have needed a little time to put his affairs in order and to gather some of the provisions that Nephi referred to (see 1 Ne. 8:1; 16:11). Because Ishmael apparently brought provisions to Lehi's campsite, we may reasonably assume that he left his home soon after the grain harvests, possibly during the summer, after May or June.[18] (See 1 Ne. 7.)

On the way back to the camp, trouble arose. Lehi's older sons, conspiring with four of Ishmael's children, announced that they were returning to Jerusalem and that no one was going to stop them. Nephi, who occasionally pointed out his older brothers' faults, now scolded them, warning them that "if ye will return unto Jerusalem . . . ye will also perish; for thus the Spirit of the Lord constraineth me that I should speak." Angered, his brothers seized Nephi, tied him up tight, and intended to abandon him to the fate that comes to all who are helpless in the desert—death—when Nephi was rescued by divine assistance and by the pleadings of Ishmael's wife and a daughter, plus a son who had switched sides. Such pleadings would allow Nephi's brothers to change their minds without losing face. Of course, one is tempted to think that, months later, Nephi chose this daughter who pled on his behalf to be his bride. Finally, his brothers were so moved that they even sought Nephi's "forgiveness." In response, he says, "I did frankly forgive them . . . and I did exhort them that they would pray unto the Lord . . . for forgiveness." It is evident that Nephi understood the need of his brothers to obtain forgiveness from the Lord, besides from himself. This observation leads to the next scene. (See 1 Nephi 7.)

Naturally, when the travelers arrived safely at Lehi's tent, it was an occasion for rejoicing. To celebrate, "they did give thanks unto the Lord their God; and they did offer sacrifice," just as on the two previous occasions. Moreover, as Lehi had done when his sons arrived with the plates in hand, he also offered "burnt offerings." As we recall from the earlier scene, such sacrifices were to atone for sin. Where was the sin? One has only to look to the "rebellion" of the older sons of Lehi, along with the four children of Ishmael, to see the need for purging sin. Certainly, their effort to break up both families by returning to the city, as well as their effort to make Nephi a victim by abandoning him in the wilderness, required, in Nephi's words, the "forgiveness" of God. Again, Lehi's faithfulness to the Lord must have depleted the stores of the family. But he was determined to put the Lord first in all that he did. (See 1 Ne. 7.)

Lehi's sons and Ishmael's family had brought from Jerusalem "seeds of every kind, both of grain . . . and also of the seeds of fruit." Each little bit, of course, restored their larder. Unfortunately, because Nephi does not tell us how much Ishmael's family members brought with them, we have no way to judge how well stocked they were when the Lord ordered them farther into the desert, a topic that we take up in the next chapter. (See 1 Ne. 8, 16.)

LEHI'S DREAM

It is difficult to say exactly when Lehi received his dream, whether before Ishmael's family arrived or afterward. But it marked an important milestone in the Lord's education of his prophet. This dream taught Lehi much about the Messiah, including His atonement, thereby framing a view of the Messiah that would guide Nephite teachers for hundreds of years.[19] Lehi also learned about the house of Israel and his own family's future responses to blessings, symbolized by the tree of life, whose fruit "was most sweet, above all that I ever before tasted." In addition, the Lord gave him a glimpse of what lay ahead in his route through southern Arabia. For instance, Lehi's dream of the tree, highly symbolic on one level, was prophetically realistic in terms of the geography farther south, where his family was about to go. The scenes alternated between long, lonely stretches wherein Lehi traveled only with his guide (see 1 Ne. 8:4–8); deep wadis or canyons that were impossible to cross ("great and terrible gulf" [12:18; also 15:28]) and whose seasonal streams would fill with mud and debris ("filthiness" [15:26–27]); verdant areas graced not only by sources of water—there were already extensive irrigation works in south Arabia—but also by lush vegetation represented by the tree full of delicious fruit (8:9–13); heavily traveled paths or roads, which led to the green areas (8:20–21); "forbidden paths" and "strange roads" of the desert where the unwary would become "lost" (8:23, 28, 32); and the "spacious building" typical of the wealthy cities in southern Arabia—evidently several stories high as they were then[20]—wherein many prosperous, economically powerful people resided who were made wealthy by the highly developed commerce of the region (8:26–27, 33). In addition, the necessity of traveling into the night to avoid daytime heat appears in the dream when Lehi travels "for the space of many hours *in darkness*" (8:8; emphasis added; cf. 17:13: the Lord stands as "light in the wilderness"). Further, Lehi's mention of "a mist of darkness, yea, even an exceedingly great mist of darkness" (8:23) reminds one of the heavy mists and fogs of the monsoon season that blanket the southeast coast of Arabia, the place where the family emerged from the desert.[21]

"I have dreamed a dream," said Lehi, "or, in other words, I have seen a vision." Thus he introduced this vision of visions to his expanded family. The dream itself has several parts. In its own way, the section wherein Lehi expresses concern for his two older sons stands as the most poignantly personal notation: "I have reason to rejoice in the Lord because of Nephi and also of Sam; . . . But behold, Laman and Lemuel, I fear exceedingly because of you." For after seeing the white tree in his vision and after eating some of its fruit, which "filled my soul with exceedingly great joy," Lehi beckoned to family members, even shouting "with a loud voice." Some responded, others did not. Said he, "your mother Sariah, and Sam, and Nephi . . . did come . . . and partake of the fruit . . . [but] Laman and Lemuel . . . would not come unto me and partake." Thus began for Lehi—and for Sariah too—a deeper heartache than they had already experienced for their recalcitrant sons, a heartache made numbingly clear to them by the Lord's view of the future. (See 1 Ne. 8.)

At the center of the vision stood the tree. Without attempting to interpret what he saw, Lehi simply portrayed each scene as it came to him. The vision opened in "a dark and dreary wilderness" where Lehi met "a man . . . dressed in a white robe" who led Lehi for "many hours in darkness." When Lehi at last began to pray for the Lord's "tender mercies," an expression that occurs elsewhere (see 1 Ne. 1:20), he saw "a tree" in "a large and spacious field." As he soon discovered, "the fruit [on the tree] was most sweet [and] . . . was white, to exceed all the whiteness that I had ever seen." Alongside the tree ran "a river of water," not unlike the stream where he was camped. As we have remarked, some family members joined him in partaking of the fruit; others did not. The vision did not end here. (See 1 Ne. 8.)

Lehi's dream then filled with people as he beheld "numberless concourses of people"—a phrase that recalls his description in his second vision of the angelic host surrounding God (see 1 Ne. 1:8)—who were "pressing forward" to reach the tree, holding "a rod of iron" that ran along "a strait and narrow path." But only a small number of those who started on the path actually reached the tree, for "an exceedingly great mist of darkness" swept over them and, losing their grip on the rod (was it slippery? were they somehow enfeebled?), "they wandered off and were lost." Those who did not lose their grip had to face a mocking, taunting crowd of wealthy people gathered in "a great and spacious building," whose reproaches led many partakers of the tree to become "ashamed" and to fall "away into forbidden paths" where they "were lost." Naturally, there were those who "heeded . . . not" the jeering crowd. But that number did not include

Laman and Lemuel, who refused even to partake of the fruit, though it was freely offered to them, an action that led Lehi, with dread in his heart, to plead with them "with all the feeling of a tender parent, that they would hearken to his words." (See 1 Ne. 8.)

Although Lehi "did cease speaking unto" the members of the party for the time being (1 Ne. 8:38), possibly because of the onset of night, he continued presumably in the morning, this time drawing conclusions from his vision by commenting prophetically "concerning the Jews" who lived in Jerusalem. For, according to his words, after the prophesied destruction of the city, they would "return again . . . out of captivity" and would "possess again the land of their inheritance," something that Lehi's party would never do. The Lord had something else in mind for them. In fact, it would be to Jerusalem that the "Messiah . . . or this Redeemer of the world" would come "six hundred years from the time that [Lehi] . . . left Jerusalem." Lehi taught that "a number" of "the prophets" had not only spoken about "a Messiah, or, in other words, a Savior," but had also focused on "a prophet who should come before the Messiah, to prepare the way," even quoting words that this prophet would utter from the prophecies of Isaiah and picturing this prophet baptizing "the Lamb of God, who should take away the sins of the world."[22] Lehi was introducing his family to aspects of the Messiah's life that were new. (See 1 Ne. 10.)

The Messiah's ministry, Lehi continued, brought to an end by His execution, would go on after His triumphant resurrection "from the dead." Through the Holy Ghost, He would launch an effort to preach "among the Jews," also making "himself manifest . . . unto the Gentiles." While prophecies about the Gentiles formed a major part of Lehi's recollections from his vision, the part that specifically applied to his family had to do with the scattering and gathering of Israel. For he understood that his family "should be broken off" as it were from the main trunk of "an olive tree"—here is tree imagery again—and "should be scattered," as would others after the slaying of the Messiah. But "after the Gentiles had received the fulness of the gospel," then "the natural branches . . . or the remnants of the house of Israel," including descendants of Lehi's extended family, "should be grafted" into the main trunk of "the olive tree," that is, "come to the knowledge of the true Messiah." Thus Lehi found solace in his vision that his family would once again find a place among the main body of Israel, a place that for all appearances they were losing by their flight from Jerusalem. (See 1 Ne. 10.)

NEPHI'S VISION

Lehi's words kindled a flame in his fourth son: "I, Nephi, was desirous also that I might see, and hear, and know of these things." Assured through his "faith on the Son of God"—"the Son of God" was a new term that Nephi introduced to his readers—that the Lord would show him "the things which [Lehi] saw in a vision" as well as giving him a testimony of "the things which [Lehi] spake by the power of the Holy Ghost," Nephi pondered his father's words. (See 1 Ne. 10.)

As he "sat pondering" he "was caught away in the Spirit . . . into an exceedingly high mountain," evidently one in the nearby mountain range that runs along the entire west coast of Arabia, for he had to walk back to camp (see 1 Ne. 15:1). Here the Spirit asked, "[W]hat desirest thou?" Nephi's response was direct: "I desire to behold the things which my father saw." The Spirit then asked a question that reinforced the importance of belief: "Believest thou that thy father saw the tree?" Again, Nephi's answer was direct: "[T]hou knowest that I believe all the words of my father." It was the Spirit's turn to respond, this time with rejoicing. Reciting or singing lines from the biblical Psalms, which were sung on important occasions and would have been familiar to Nephi (this is sort of like a heavenly person singing a familiar hymn to reassure an earthly person that the coming message is inspired), and thus creating a climate of trust and reassurance, the Spirit uttered a beatitude: "[B]lessed art thou, Nephi, because thou believest in the Son of the most high God." Then, informing Nephi that he would behold "the tree which bore the fruit which thy father tasted," the Spirit promised "a sign" which would tie back to Lehi's earliest set of visions (1 Ne. 1:9; also 12:6): "[T]hou shalt also behold a man descending out of heaven" of whom Nephi was to "bear record that it is the Son of God." The circle of witnesses was thus complete. Both Lehi and Nephi beheld One "descending out of heaven," revealed by the words of the Spirit on this occasion to be the Messiah, "the Son of God." (See 1 Ne. 11.)

Nephi's vision, virtually a carbon copy of that of his father Lehi, is almost unparalleled in scripture for both its sweep and its detail. The first part focuses on the coming Messiah, his birth, ministry, and redeeming death. Nephi's record of the Messiah in this vision would become the standard for the doctrine of redemption among his people ever after.[23] It is the tree in both Lehi's and Nephi's vision that introduced the Messiah. As his father had claimed, "the beauty" of this tree "was far beyond . . . all beauty" and its "whiteness . . . did exceed the whiteness of the driven snow," a comparison that Nephi could make because winters in Jerusalem occasionally bring snow. (See 1 Ne. 11.)

At this point, one bumps into one of the most important insights about the Godhead recorded in scripture. The "Spirit of the Lord" had been Nephi's guide to this point in the vision. Such guides—usually angels—appear in all accounts of extended visions, whether recorded in scripture or in apocryphal literature. At the moment when the Spirit takes his leave from Nephi, to be replaced by an angel as the guide, Nephi records that "I spake unto him as a man speaketh; for I beheld that he was in the form of a man; yet nevertheless, I knew that it was the Spirit of the Lord." Every commentator who has discussed this passage, including modern prophets, has affirmed that Nephi was here speaking with the Holy Ghost. Hence, we learn that the Holy Ghost, while a spirit, is in human form.[24] (See 1 Ne. 11.)

When Nephi expressed his desire to know "the interpretation" of the tree, the Spirit "said unto me: Look!" Although the Spirit disappeared from view, Nephi next saw the Messiah, a clear linking of "the interpretation" or meaning of the tree to the Son of God. But the portrayal of the Messiah was not motionless, static, as in a photograph or painting. Nephi's view of the Messiah was in the form of a story, starting with His place of dwelling, "the city of Nazareth." Although it is not evident how Nephi recognized and thus could name this city, because it consisted of no more than a few buildings in his day, he saw that "in the city" lived "a virgin," the most important woman in the vision. Further, "she was exceedingly fair and white." At this point, Nephi needed a guide. Here enters "an angel" who "came down [from heaven] and stood before me." It was he who would teach Nephi the meaning of what he was seeing: "Behold, the virgin whom thou seest is the mother of the Son of God, after the manner of the flesh." In the next scene, "after she was carried away in the Spirit for the space of a time," Nephi "beheld the virgin again, bearing a child in her arms." Without waiting for Nephi's question, "the angel said unto [him]: Behold the Lamb of God, . . . the Son of the Eternal Father," immediately asking, "Knowest thou the meaning of the tree which thy father saw?" The answer was obvious. It had something to do with the child in the arms of the virgin, who personified "the love of God," which is "the most desirable above all things" and "the most joyous to the soul." (See 1 Ne. 11.)

At this point, Nephi began to witness events in the mortal ministry of the Savior, including "the prophet" who would baptize the Messiah and "prepare the way before him." From these events, Nephi learned the interpretation that "the rod of iron" of his father's vision "was the word of God" that brought one "to the fountain of living waters, or to the tree of life," which themselves represented "the love of God." For a brief moment, in a scene reminiscent of his father's early vision, Nephi "beheld twelve others following" the Messiah. (See 1 Ne. 11.)

But the vision soon brought him back to see "the Lamb of God going forth," healing the "sick" and those "afflicted with . . . diseases, and with devils." This happy part of the vision ground to a halt with the sobering scene of "the Lamb of God . . . judged of the world . . . [and] lifted up upon the cross and slain for the sins of the world." Omitting mention of the resurrection, Nephi painted a gray picture, portraying in dark hues "the multitudes of the earth"—evidently, both Jews and Gentiles—who "gathered together to fight against the apostles of the Lamb," again introducing a word new to himself and his readers. For Nephi has to explain the term apostles: "for thus were the twelve called by the angel." (See 1 Ne. 11.)

It was in this part of the vision that Nephi grasped the meaning of "the large and spacious building" of his father's account. It personified "the world and the wisdom thereof," more specifically "the pride of the world," which would come crashing down, "and the fall thereof was exceedingly great." In words, not scenes, the angel added, "Thus shall be the destruction of all . . . that shall fight against the twelve apostles of the Lamb." (See 1 Ne. 11.)

The scene then switched entirely to "the land of promise"—the Americas, although presumably Nephi would not yet have known this—where he "beheld multitudes of people." In a word, he saw the future story of his people played out before his eyes. In depressing tones, Nephi says sadly, "I beheld wars and . . . great slaughters with the sword among my people . . . and contentions in the land." The speed of the vision then seems to slow when he describes horrifying events connected with the appearance of "a mist of darkness on the face of the land," accompanied by "lightnings, and . . . thunderings, and earthquakes." The devastation was huge: "I saw mountains tumbling into pieces; . . . and I saw many cities . . . sunk; and . . . burned with fire; and I saw many that did tumble to the earth." But at the end, light shone forth in "the Lamb of God descending out of heaven." (See 1 Ne. 12.)

To the survivors of the devastation, "the Lamb of God . . . showed himself." He also organized the survivors by selecting "twelve disciples." Characterizing their chief earthly role, the angel declared that these "are chosen to minister unto thy seed," a ministry that was to continue into a second sphere beyond the grave. For, said he, "the twelve apostles" from the earlier part of the vision are to "judge the twelve tribes of Israel" as well as "the twelve ministers of thy seed." Curiously, the "twelve apostles" from the Old World have nothing to do with the rest of Nephi's people. In fact, it is "these twelve ministers whom thou beholdest [in the New World who] shall judge thy seed." Unlike the original twelve in the Old World, all twelve disciples in the New World would remain faithful, "righteous forever." (See 1 Ne. 12.)

After three generations, whose days passed "in righteousness," Nephi saw the rise of a new generation, which began to show cracks in its righteous resolve, followed hard by a view of "the multitudes of the earth gathered together . . . to battle." What then came to Nephi's eyes was an unrelenting scene of death and destruction until "the seed of my brethren did overpower the people of my seed." As Nephi would mourn later, this scene stabbed him with deep pain. He was still a teenager and there is a tender and poignant tone of sadness in his reaction. "I was overcome . . . for I considered that mine afflictions were great above all, because of the destruction of my people, for I had beheld their fall" (1 Ne. 15:5).

Not only was the view of the final end of his people wrenching for Nephi, but it also brought illumination. For he learned that "the mists of darkness" of his father's vision represented "the temptations of the devil, which blindeth the eyes, and hardeneth the hearts of the children of men." Further, the "terrible gulf" that divided the wicked from the righteous stood for "the word of the justice of the Eternal God, and the Messiah," forming a chasm that the wicked could not bridge. (See 1 Ne. 12.)

The scene completely switched again, this time evidently to Europe because "many waters" divided the "nations and kingdoms" of this part of the vision from "the seed of [Nephi's] brethren." Moreover, it was among these Gentile peoples that Nephi "beheld a man" upon whom "the Spirit of God" descended, inspiring him to go "forth upon the many waters, even unto the seed of my brethren . . . in the promised land." Further, "the Spirit of God . . . wrought upon other Gentiles" who "went forth out of captivity" to the Americas. These people, Nephi noted, "were white, and exceedingly fair and beautiful," and "did humble themselves before the Lord," becoming instruments in God's hands. For it was they who scattered and troubled "the seed of my brethren" in accord with "the wrath of God," and, aided "by the power of God," won their freedom from "their mother Gentiles [who] . . . came to battle against them." (See 1 Ne. 13.)

While this part of the vision had opened with the sighting of "a church which is most abominable [and] . . . which slayeth the saints of God," the chief focus featured "a book . . . carried forth among" the Gentiles. Employing unusual imagery, Nephi characterized the book as coming "out of the mouth of a Jew" and containing "the covenants of the Lord, which he hath made unto the house of Israel." In addition, "it is a record like unto . . . the plates of brass, save there are not so many" and would be "of great worth unto the Gentiles." But this book had suffered change. For "when it proceeded forth from the mouth of a Jew it contained the fulness of the gospel," going forth "in purity." But, in what seems to be a clear allusion to the Hellenizing influences in the early Christian church, "that great and abominable church" had "taken away from the gospel . . . many parts which are plain and most precious; and also many covenants of the Lord have they taken away."[25] (See 1 Ne. 13.)

Although partly crippled by the defective "book of the Lamb of God," the Gentiles would still receive blessings from the Lord, first by enjoying "the land which is choice above all . . . which the Lord God hath covenanted with thy father [Lehi] that his seed should have for . . . their inheritance" and, second, by receiving from "the Lamb . . . much of my gospel, which shall be plain and precious." This additional portion "of my gospel" would come to the Gentiles in the form of a book, which Nephi's descendants "shall write" after the Lamb "manifest[s] [him]self unto [Nephi's] seed." Because this second record "shall be hid up," the Lamb would bring it forth by His "gift and power" for blessing not only the Gentiles but also "the remnant of the seed of my brethren" and "the Jews . . . scattered upon all . . . the earth." All of these, "if they endure to the end," will "be saved in the everlasting kingdom of the Lamb." (See 1 Ne. 13.)

The vision then broadened to "other books," which, coming "from the Gentiles," and coupled with the second book, will convince all who receive them "that the records of the prophets and of the twelve apostles of the Lamb are true." In other words, the "last records" will "establish the truth of the first" and "shall make known the plain and precious things which have been taken away." Moreover, taken together, the records testify that "there is one God and one Shepherd over all the earth" and that "he shall manifest himself unto all nations." (See 1 Ne. 13.)

The scene changed again, this time to a highly symbolic portrayal of the "great and abominable church," which seems suspended from historical time. For, stepping away from the complexities of the earlier portions of Nephi's vision, in this view "there are . . . two churches only; . . . the church of the Lamb [and] . . . the church of the devil." Here reality is divided into two parts, rather than many. Hence, "whoso belongeth not to the church of the Lamb . . . belongeth to that great church, which is the mother of abominations." Drawing on the rich imagery of the alluring, corrupting female, who is the second important woman of the vision and stands opposite the virgin—"the Lamb of God," in contrast, is clearly male—the angel characterized the forces of evil as "the whore of all the earth" and as "the mother of harlots." In the angel's words, she holds "dominion . . . among all nations," gathering "multitudes upon the face of the all the earth . . .

to fight against the Lamb of God" and against his "covenant people" in order to preserve this dominion. To counteract the influences of evil, "the Lamb of God . . . will work a great and a marvelous work . . . which shall be everlasting." But because of the immense, sinister efforts to counteract the work of the Lamb, the Lord will pour out "the power of the Lamb . . . upon the saints of the church" so that they are "armed with righteousness and with the power of God." In addition, he will pour out "the wrath of God . . . upon that great and abominable church," undercutting its effectiveness by "wars and rumors of wars among all . . . which belonged to the mother of abominations," the Saints evidently escaping the devastation. When "that day" comes—the only reference to historic time in this section (see 1 Ne. 14:17)—"the work of the Father shall commence . . . for fulfilling his covenants, which he hath made to his people." (See 1 Ne. 14.)

The final scene recorded in Nephi's vision spotlights "a man . . . dressed in a white robe." The angel reveals a number of important features about this man. First, he is "one of the twelve apostles of the Lamb." Second, he "shall see and write the remainder" of what Nephi was yet to see, including "the end of the world." Third, his written work will be included "in the book which thou beheld proceeding out of the mouth of the Jew," which the Gentiles cherished. Fourth, the name of this man "was John." Nephi next learned that because this man would write the rest of the vision, he himself was forbidden to "write the remainder of the things which [he] saw and heard." Nephi closes by offering his testimony: "I bear record that I saw the things which my father saw." The vision was complete. (See 1 Ne. 14.)

THE LAST DAYS IN CAMP

We know that Nephi's vision followed soon after Lehi had rehearsed his own dream to the family. For, when Nephi stumbled back to camp, apparently having walked from the "high mountain" where the vision unfolded (see 1 Ne. 11:1), he found his brothers "disputing one with another concerning the things which my father had spoken unto them [from his dream]." It is at this point that we catch a glimpse of Nephi's character and remarkable staying powers. He must have been exhausted, both from the intensity of the experience of the vision and from the long walk back to his father's tent. He had also been sobered and emotionally devastated by the horrifying view of "the destruction of my people," a view that would haunt him for years to come (see 2 Ne. 26:7). And he must have longed for rest. But the inner need to offer help to his puzzled brothers overrode any craving for his own comforts. (See 1 Ne. 15.)

Nephi remarks that "after I had received strength"—both an admission of his weakened condition and an acknowledgment of the Lord's assistance to him—"I spake unto my brethren, desiring to know . . . the cause of their disputations." To their response that they could not understand their father's words about "the olive-tree" and "the Gentiles," Nephi asked, "Have ye inquired of the Lord?" In the context of Nephi's tremendous vision, this simple question brimmed with meaning. But the brothers boldly assured him that "the Lord maketh no such thing known unto us." Nephi's sharp reply betrays his fatigue: "How is it that ye do not keep the commandments of the Lord?" Evidently gaining control of himself, he then went on to explain—this time patiently—that the comparison of "an olive-tree" to "the house of Israel," also a feature of Isaiah's prophecies (see Isa. 5), pointed to a "remnant" of their posterity. After "dwindl[ing] in unbelief . . . for the space of many years," these descendants will receive "the fulness of the gospel of the Messiah . . . from the Gentiles." By this means "shall the remnant of our seed know that they are of the house of Israel, and . . . how to come unto [their Redeemer] and be saved." It will be as if they were "grafted in, being a natural branch of the olive-tree, into the true olive-tree." But, as Nephi noted, Lehi's words were more broad than this. Their father "hath not spoken of our seed alone, but also of all the house of Israel" in fulfillment of the "covenant [that] the Lord made to our father Abraham." Mention of Abraham's name, of course, offered assurance that their departure from Jerusalem fit within the umbrella of divine blessings promised ages before. (1 Ne. 15.)

Another point is worth making. Nephi's answers to his brothers illustrate that the dream of Lehi and the vision of Nephi are not interruptions of the narrative. They fit within it, even shaping it. Three aspects of the visions make this point. First, these experiences pointed to the desert environment of their camp and the area of Arabia farther south. When the brothers asked, "What meaneth the river of water which our father saw?" Nephi noted that it represented "filthiness." Lehi had been paying attention to "other things" in his dream so "that he beheld not the filthiness of the water," plainly a phenomenon of the rainy season in the desert when a stream suddenly comes to life, swollen by mud and debris, rushing forcefully from a deep valley or wadi, forming "an awful gulf." Second, Lehi's dream about some in his family accepting the fruit of the tree of life, and others not, frames the larger story of his descendants, who eventually separated from one another. Thus Lehi's dream ties closely with the rest of the Book of Mormon account. Third, the dream is symbolic for spiritual realities that the narrative will make clear. For instance, the "filthiness of the water" became a representation of "both temporal and spiritual" realities. Persons to whom "wickedness" clings "must be cast off" since "their works have been filthiness," disqualifying such individuals from entering "into the kingdom of God." For such, "a place of filthiness" has been "prepared" by "the justice of God" for "that which is filthy." (See 1 Ne. 15.)

After explaining these truths, all growing out of the vision, Nephi "had joy and great hopes . . . that [his brothers] would walk in the paths of righteousness." Perhaps his joy was heightened by the celebrations of at least five simultaneous weddings: those of himself, his three brothers, and Zoram, the former servant of Laban. One can only imagine the happy occasion. By custom, nothing was done for seven days while everyone was feasting and merrymaking.[26]

At some point after the wedding festivities, the Lord brought the group back to the tough reality of going on into the desert. For "the voice of the Lord spake unto my father by night, and commanded him that on the morrow he should take his journey into the wilderness." The energies of the extended family were now to be bent to their travels. As a gracious assist, when Lehi arose the next morning, inside his tent,[27] "to his great astonishment he beheld upon the ground a round ball of curious workmanship," equipped with "two spindles" to point "the way whither we should go into the wilderness." The family was being offered a divine aid to meet the extreme challenges that, as the presence of the ball indicated, obviously lay ahead of them. Taking all that they could carry, including "the remainder of our provisions which the Lord had given unto us," they loaded their heavy "tents" on their pack animals and departed "into the wilderness, across the river Laman." Jerusalem would now remain only a distant but vibrant memory kept alive in story and memory for generations to come. Jacob, Nephi's next younger brother who was born in Arabia and had never seen the city, reflected the general sentiment of losing one's place there: "[T]he time passed away with us, and also our lives passed away like as it were unto us a dream, we being a lonesome and a solemn people, wanderers, cast out from Jerusalem, born in tribulation, in a wilderness" (Jacob 7:26). The challenges ahead, far from home, were monumental and would shape the character of the family into that of a chosen people of God. (See 1 Ne. 16.)

NOTES TO CHAPTER ONE

1. Nephi records that his father's home lay "down" from Jerusalem and that one went "up" to the city where Laban's house was, strongly indicating that Lehi's estate was outside of the city (see 1 Ne. 3:15, 22–23). Consult also David R. and Jo Ann H. Seely, "Lehi and Jeremiah: Prophets, Priests, and Patriarchs," *Journal of Book of Mormon Studies* 8, no. 2 (Fall 1999): 24–35.
2. On the heavenly council of Jehovah, see E. Theodore Mullen Jr., "Divine Assembly," in *The Anchor Bible Dictionary,* David Noel Freedman et al., eds., 6 vols. (New York: Doubleday, 1992), 2:214–17.
3. The Lord called Jeremiah in 627 B.C., "the thirteenth year of [King Josiah's] reign" (Jer. 1:2). The first year of King Zedekiah's reign was 598 B.C. (see 1 Ne. 1:4).
4. On a dubious Yemenite Jewish tradition about a major migration in this era, consult Reuben Ahroni, *Yemenite Jewry: Origins, Culture and Literature* (Bloomington: Indiana University Press, 1986), 24–37; see also S. Kent Brown, "New Light from Arabia on Lehi's Trail," in *Echoes and Evidences of the Book of Mormon,* Donald W. Parry et al., eds. (Provo, Utah: FARMS, 2002), 55–125, especially 56 and 98.
5. For three of the routes, see M. Har-El, "Israelite and Roman Roads in the Jordan Desert," *Israel Exploration Journal* 17, no. 1 (1967): 18–25; "The Route of Salt, Sugar and Balsam Caravans in the Judean Desert," *GeoJournal* 2, no. 6 (1978): 549–56; for the easternmost route through the desert of Jordan, consult Nelson Glueck, *The Other Side of Jordan* (New Haven, Conn.: American Schools of Oriental Research, 1940), 128–34; for a summarizing description, see Brown, "New Light from Arabia on Lehi's Trail," 56–60.

6. Consult David R. Seely, "Lehi's Altar and Sacrifice in the Wilderness," *Journal of Book of Mormon Studies* 10, no. 1 (2001): 62–69.

7. See S. Kent Brown, *From Jerusalem to Zarahemla* (Provo, Utah: BYU Religious Studies Center, 1998), 1–8.

8. Consult Hugh Nibley, *Lehi in the Desert, The World of the Jaredites, There Were Jaredites,* The Collected Works of Hugh Nibley 5 (1959; reprint, Salt Lake City: Deseret Book and FARMS, 1988), 67–69.

9. See Lynn M. Hilton and Hope Hilton, *In Search of Lehi's Trail* (Salt Lake City: Deseret Book, 1976), 62–75.

10. George D. Potter's candidate lies north and west of Hiltons' choice ("A New Candidate in Arabia for the Valley of Lemuel," *Journal of Book of Mormon Studies* 8, no. 1 [Spring 1999]: 52–63). Years ago Hugh Nibley observed that Lehi had camped "not far above [north of] the Straits of Tiran" (*Lehi in the Desert,* 85). See also Paul Hedengren, *The Land of Lehi: A Book of Mormon Geography* (Provo, Utah: Bradford and Wilson, 1995), 3–6. Hedengren holds that Lehi made his first major camp in the Wadi Al-Nuwaybi, eighteen miles south of Aqaba. Consult the review of evidence in Brown, "New Light from Arabia on Lehi's Trail," 60–62.

11. Because Nephi entered Jerusalem "by night" and because there were no lights in the streets, the fact that he "beheld [Laban's] sword" and "the hilt [which,] . . . was of pure gold," as well as "the workmanship" of the sword, plainly points to a moonlit night (1 Ne. 4:5, 9).

12. The words that Nephi "heard" were, "Behold the Lord slayeth the wicked to bring forth his righteous purposes. It is better that one man should perish than that a nation should dwindle and perish in unbelief" (1 Ne. 4:13).

13. See Charles M. Doughty, *Travels in Arabia Deserta,* 2 vols. in one, with an introduction by T. E. Lawrence (New York: Random House, 1936), 1:281, 569.

14. On Sariah and the daunting tasks that she faced, consult Camille Fronk, "Desert Epiphany: Sariah and the Women in 1 Nephi," *Journal of Book of Mormon Studies* 9, no. 2 (2000): 4–15.

15. Consult Ex. 21:12–14; also John W. Welch, "Legal Perspectives on the Slaying of Laban," *Journal of Book of Mormon Studies* 1, no. 1 (1992): 119–41, especially 122–23.

16. On the types of Lehi's sacrifices, see Brown, *From Jerusalem to Zarahemla,* 1–8.

17. Brigham Young et al., *Journal of Discourses,* 26 vols. (Liverpool: F.D. and S.W. Richards, 1854–86), 23:184; Nephi mentions "my sisters" in 2 Ne. 5:6.

18. According to the Gezer calendar, all grains had been harvested by the time of Pentecost (late May); see David C. Braund, "Agriculture," *The Anchor Bible Dictionary,* 1:97.

19. Consult John L. Clark, "Painting Out the Messiah: The Theologies of Dissidents," *Journal of Book of Mormon Studies* 11 (2002): 16–27, especially 18.

20. On skyscraper architecture, see Jean-François Breton, "Architecture," in *Queen of Sheba: Treasures from Ancient Yemen,* St John Simpson, ed. (London: The British Museum Press, 2002), 142–48, especially 143; also consult "The Queen of Sheba, Skyscraper Architecture, and Lehi's Dream," *Journal of Book of Mormon Studies* 11 (2002): 102–3.

21. For travel at night, see the remarks of the ancient author Strabo, *Geography* 17.1.45; also, for the broad number of connections between Lehi's dream and Arabia, see Brown, "New Light from Arabia on Lehi's Trail," 64–69, 102–4.

22. Consult S. Kent Brown, *Mary and Elisabeth: Noble Daughters of God* (American Fork, Utah: Covenant, 2002), 20, 33, for the influence of Elisabeth on John the Baptist's testimony of the Messiah.

23. See Clark, "Painting Out the Messiah," 16–27.

24. Consult, for instance, Joseph Fielding McConkie and Robert L. Millet, *Doctrinal Commentary on the Book of Mormon,* 4 vols. (Salt Lake City: Bookcraft, 1987–92), 1:76–77.

25. On the allusions to Hellenism, see Stephen E. Robinson, "Nephi's 'Great and Abominable Church,'" *Journal of Book of Mormon Studies* 7, no. 1 (1998): 32–39.

26. On the week of celebration following a marriage, consult Gen. 29:27–28 and Ze'ev W. Falk, *Hebrew Law in Biblical Times* (Provo, Utah: BYU Press; Winona Lake, Indiana: Eisenbrauns, 2001), 149.

27. Had the compass not been *inside* the tent of Lehi and Sariah, its custody would have been in question, especially if someone had walked by before Lehi awoke.

Into Arabia and Across the Sea

CHAPTER TWO

. . . we did take our tents and depart into the wilderness, across the river Laman. (1 Ne. 16:12.)

It is a tale of heroic coping in the worst of climes. Out of the harsh, debilitating heat of Arabia's desert the party of Lehi and Sariah unexpectedly blossomed as heroes and heroines. They were refugees from the political and religious snarls in Jerusalem. In the desert, they were battered and bruised by braving the endlessly rolling sands and pitted craggy mountains. They suffered days and months from the shadowy, relentlessly stalking threat of "hunger, thirst and fatigue." After eight long years of bone-tiring affliction, they emerged from the desert as a people of divine destiny. In effect, the Lord had sculpted them internally by leading them into the superheated wilderness of Arabia. But tragically, their numbers hid the seeds of a terrible destruction a thousand years hence when a series of devastating wars between descendants of these people, growing out of the rivalry between the sons of Laman and Nephi, would utterly destroy one side of the family.

Even in the most stable of times, trudging off into the bowels of the Arabian desert invited a swarm of troubles, what with marauding bands and a lack of water, food, and fuel. The party of Lehi and Sariah had left behind their civilized Jerusalem, the one grand proof that they themselves were inheritors of the land promised to Abraham and his descendants. One senses the attraction of Jerusalem for Lehi's family by noting that he had pitched his camp on the Jerusalem side of the river Laman, something that Nephi—writing thirty years later (see 2 Ne. 5:28–30)—tells us indirectly. When the members of Lehi's party finally crossed the river Laman, they could only have suspected that they were forsaking Jerusalem forever. Striking out into the desert as they did, they were ultimately cutting themselves off from home.[1]

PREPARATIONS FOR THE JOURNEY

Measuring from beginning to end, the family traveled more than 2,100 miles through the desert, the distance from Los Angeles to Chicago or from Paris to Cairo. Up to that point, their desert trek had moved them only ten percent of the total land distance of their journey, although there is no indication from Nephi's account that anyone had a clear notion of their final destination.[2] To be sure, Lehi's dream billowed with allusions to what they would find farther south and east in Arabia.[3] But, other than the desert conditions pictured in the dream, some of which are unique to that area, it is not evident whether anyone even understood this fully as they set out, for Lehi had drawn the main attention of his family not to desert imagery but to the Messiah and to Israel's future. (See 1 Ne. 8, 10.)

The fact that the Lord provided a compass should have been warning enough of challenging difficulties ahead. But no one could have anticipated their enormity, including confrontation with "enemies," dealing with "famine and . . . sickness" (Alma 9:10, 22),[4] experiencing lack of "progress in their journey," even being "driven back" (Mosiah 1:17), and probably selling their services for protection or for food.[5] After the experience, Lehi termed the years in the desert "the days of my greatest sorrow" (2 Ne. 3:1). And decades later, Jacob, a son of Lehi, would mournfully recall that his family was "a lonesome and a solemn people" who had wandered as outcasts from Jerusalem (Jacob 7:26).

The compass itself—called Liahona by later generations (Alma 37:38)—appeared "upon the ground" at Lehi's "tent door." It probably lay inside the tent so that Lehi's custody of it was not in doubt when he "arose in the morning" to pack up belongings for the next,

BLACK SEA
ARMENIA
AZERBAIJAN
TURKMENISTAN
Ankara
Kizil Irmak
CASPIAN SEA
TURKEY
CYPRUS
MEDITERRANEAN SEA
SYRIA
Euphrates
Tigris
Tehran
LEBANON
Beirut
Damascus
Haifa
Baghdad
IRAN
IRAQ
Tel Aviv
Jerusalem
Amman
ISRAEL
JORDAN
Suez
Sinai
Gulf of Suez
First Camp
KUWAIT
Kuwait
The Persian Gulf
EGYPT
RED SEA
HIJAZ
Straits of Hormuz
BAHRAIN
QATAR
Gulf of Oma
Al Madinah
UNITED ARAB EMIRATES
Muscat
Sur
SAUDI ARABIA
OMAN
Jiddah
Mecca
Nubian Desert
Rub' al Khali (Empty Quarter)
ASIR
Tihamah
SUDAN
Najran
BOUNTIFUL
Salalah
Nihm Tribal Area
Wadi Sayq
Khor Rori
Atbara
ERITREA
San'a
Marib
Tarim
Shabwah
Hadhramaut
Al Hudaydah
Al Mukalla
YEMEN
Gulf of Aden
Qana (Bir Ali)
Blue Nile
Aden
N
DJIBOUTI
ETHIOPIA
SOMALIA
MAP COURTESY OF FOUNDATION FOR ANCIENT RESEARCH AND MORMON STUDIES
0
500
1000 Miles
0
500
1000
1500 Kilometres

and longest, stage of the trip. Nephi described it as "a round ball of curious workmanship; and . . . of fine brass." By any standard, it was no ordinary compass. The family soon learned that one of "two spindles . . . pointed the way whither we should go." Perhaps surprisingly, the account never specifies the purpose of the second spindle. Evidently, it was experience that taught family members that the compass, when accompanied by their "faith and diligence and heed," would miraculously lead them into "the more fertile parts of the wilderness" where they could find food for themselves and their pack animals. Once when Lehi was praying about where his son Nephi might look for food, the Lord evidently surprised him by telling Lehi to look "upon the ball" for written instructions. (See 1 Ne. 16.)

In what form the writing appeared, we do not know. But the appearance of writing on a metal surface should not have surprised members of the party; they carried a record written on brass plates, and it was a common practice farther south in Arabia to inscribe official records on brass.[6] In fact, the Lord even changed the writing "from time to time, according to the faith and diligence which we gave unto it." Hence, the compass became both guide and revelator, even scolding family members for ill behavior so that, at least on the first occasion, they came to "fear and tremble exceedingly." And because the compass came from the Lord—a genuine "extraterrestrial" product, so to speak—it worked only upon the principles of faith and obedience, ceasing to operate when any of the company decided to do otherwise. For much of the journey, disobedience and the consequent malfunctioning of the compass may not have brought the company into life-threatening situations. But in certain circumstances, of which Nephi recorded only a few examples, misconduct led to severe difficulties for everyone, especially after they turned "eastward" and headed across the harsh interior of southern Arabia. (See 1 Ne. 16, 17.)

There can be no doubt that pack animals carried the family's belongings. Each of the "tents"—and there were several, typically one for each married couple—would have weighed several hundred pounds, far too much for one person to cart.[7] Moreover, the "seed of every kind," which was destined to be planted in the promised land (1 Ne. 18:24), would have required a person to shoulder seed bags commonly weighing in excess of 150 pounds.[8] While donkeys may have been able to do the job, camels were the animal of choice for desert travel.[9] Probably domesticated before 1300 B.C., camels had proven their worth long before Lehi's day for transporting heavy loads through the deserts of the ancient Near East. To be sure, one has to guide camels around patches of stony ground because of their soft, padded feet, a type of surface that donkeys could travel through. But, noting the assistance of the divine compass, one presumes that the Lord would not lead the family into areas where Lehi's pack animals would struggle excessively because of difficult terrain. Of course, there were to be struggles. But according to the accounts, they had to do with water and forage, not terrain.[10] In this connection, it is worth noting that loaded camels can go two or possibly three days in the summer without water, traveling early and late in the day, if they can eat fresh greens. In the winter, they can survive for longer periods.[11] But donkeys cannot.[12] If the pack animals had been donkeys, or even mules or horses, the difficulties that arose because of lack of water and food would have multiplied. On their part, the people walked, as Nephi hinted when he spoke hopefully that his brothers might "walk in paths of righteousness." (See 1 Ne. 16.)

The route south from the base camp, which Lehi had set up "in the borders . . . nearer the Red Sea" (1 Ne. 2:5), has been a matter of discussion. All agree that the family followed generally the caravan route along which camel trains carried huge amounts of goods, especially frankincense and myrrh from southern Arabia. By Lehi's time, merchants and their agents were shipping these sorts of products out of Arabia, along with gold and precious gems, to Egypt and Babylonia. Of course, several centuries later, this caravan traffic would also bear these aromatics and jewelry, plus spices from India, to Gaza, where they would be shipped by boat to Rome and to other destinations in North Africa and Europe. In fact, in 25–24 B.C. the Roman governor of Egypt, Aelius Gallus, led an ill-fated expedition into western Arabia whose purpose was to find the source of these products so that Rome could gain control of the overland route. But many of the 10,000 soldiers under Gallus's command died in the desert of "hunger and fatigue and diseases." Some seventy-five years later, the Romans commissioned a fleet to sail around the western and southern coasts of Arabia to accomplish the same goal. By this time, Romans knew how Arabs imported goods from India and China by sea. They then set up commercial contacts that effectively cut out the Arabian middlemen and crimped the overland caravan trade, which had flourished for more than a thousand years, since before Lehi's day.[13]

There was one main trade route running inland in a direction southeast from the location of modern Aqaba.[14] (To reach the trade route, the party had to cross the Al-Sarāt range of mountains.) One should not think of a narrow roadway or single trail, for at points the inland trade route grew to be several miles wide, running between wells through long valleys or across wide stretches of desert. This route passed through the interior in a south-southeast direction from the Arabah Valley, paralleling the coast of the Red Sea, but a hundred miles inland, on the east side of the range of mountains that marches along the Red Sea coast. For his part, Lehi seems to have started along a different route, one that initially takes a person along the coastline itself. After the first stage of the trek, which lasted "the space of four days," Nephi records that the party next kept to "the most fertile parts of the wilderness, which were in the borders near the Red Sea." There is a reason to believe that "borders" refers to mountains in this passage. Moreover, the notable hunting success of the men during the days and weeks following their departure from the first camp also points to cover in mountainous terrain.[15] (See 1 Ne. 16.)

After Lehi's family had spent a long time at the base camp, perhaps as long as a year,[16] their trek began in a way that we have come to expect, with the Lord speaking "unto my father [Lehi] by night," commanding him that "on the morrow he . . . take his journey into the wilderness." Evidently, it had not been long since the marriages between the older children of Lehi and Ishmael. The extended family now consisted of Lehi and Sariah and their four sons, in addition to Ishmael, his wife, two sons (who were married) and five daughters, plus Zoram, former servant of Laban. Moreover, a later source hints that as many as two daughters of Lehi and Sariah may have been part of the company (see 2 Nephi 5:6).[17] Besides bonding everyone into one family unit, the marriages must have increased the baggage quotient because the newly married couples would have required their own tents, adding several hundred pounds to the total, unless, improbably, married members of the party decided to break with custom by doubling up in tents. (See 1 Ne. 7 and 16.)

That the family was able to pack up belongings within a few hours, including the new supplies brought by the sons and the family of Ishmael, indicates an acquaintance with desert ways. Naturally, a complicating factor that morning would have been the excitement at finding the compass. One must grasp that the act of folding up tents and their contents, including items as diverse as rugs, pillows, and cooking utensils, requires at least a couple of hours, even for skilled travelers. In this light, the time needed both to set up camp properly in the evening and then to strike camp in the morning would dictate that, as long as the party was on the march, they would not pitch tents and unpack all of their gear for a night.[18] Instead, family members would have wrapped themselves in blankets or rugs and slept on the ground. Nights tended to be short owing to the need to travel early in the morning and late into the evening because of the heat, and to rest during the midday hours. Only when party members "did pitch our tents" in order to "rest ourselves and to obtain food" did they unpack tents and other materials. (See 1 Ne. 16.)

THE JOURNEY SOUTH-SOUTHEAST

In a passage bearing the markings of a written itinerary, Nephi wrote that "we traveled for the space of four days, nearly a south-southeast direction."[19] When the party stopped, "we did call the name of the place Shazer," now in the midst of the Hijaz region of northwest Arabia. This naming of a spot was becoming a pattern with Lehi, who was acting according to desert custom.[20] Calculating a pace of twenty to twenty-five miles per day, one possible spot along the coast of the Red Sea for the family to rest would have been the oasis at Wadi Al-Azlan, possibly Lehi's Shazer, lying ninety or so miles south-southeast of their former camp.[21] Wherever the locale, we must assume that only local people hunted in the area since travelers would not have had the time. The area certainly provided good hunting for the sons who "did take our bows and our arrows" and obtain "food for our families." (See 1 Ne. 16.)

The family moved again, traveling "for the space of many days, slaying food by the way." By this point, they had learned to follow carefully "the directions of the ball" or compass, "which led us in the more fertile parts of the wilderness," a feature of the journey that was envisioned by no less a prophet than Isaiah. For Nephi affirmed that Isaiah spoke "concerning us" (1 Ne. 19:21), prophesying that "they shall feed in the ways, and their pastures shall be in all high places."[22] At the end of this arduous part of the trip, "we did pitch our tents for the space of a time, that we might rest ourselves and obtain food." They rested, but supplying food proved difficult. (See 1 Ne. 16.)

As we have noted, a subtle warning of intense challenges ahead lurked within the miraculous gift of the compass. But this warning seems not to have caught anyone's attention until, at this third camp site, Nephi broke his bow "of fine steel" and the bows of the others "lost their springs." For the first time, everyone stared into the frightening face of starvation. Evidently the campsite was remote enough that local food supplies were beyond reach, except possibly forage for the pack animals. Hence, hunting held the only possibility for reprovisioning, for they were saving the seeds and grains from Jerusalem for planting in the promised land (see 1 Ne. 18:24). When Nephi and the other young men returned empty-handed to camp, following the disasters with their bows, all fell to complaining—except Nephi. As he described the scene, predictably "they were all exceedingly sorrowful." But "they did murmur against the Lord" to such a pitch that Nephi felt "afflicted" with their complaints. In his typically understated way, Nephi informs us of the growing crisis which was grinding the family down: "[I]t began to be exceedingly difficult, yea, insomuch that we could obtain no food." (See 1 Ne. 16.)

Nephi dealt with the crisis as he had learned how—he first acted and then sought divine aid. He began by making "out of wood a bow, and out of a straight stick, an arrow," and then asked his father, "Whither shall I go to obtain food?" Lehi, who had known all along that the Lord was guiding the journey, "humbled [himself] because of [Nephi's] words" and brought himself to "inquire of the Lord" for help. The response was surprisingly sharp, even frightening. First the "voice of the Lord came unto my father" and "chastened [him] because of his murmuring against the Lord." Then "the voice" instructed him to "look upon the ball, and behold the things which are written." Because of "the things which were written . . . [Lehi] did fear and tremble exceedingly, and also my brethren and the sons of Ishmael and our wives." Evidently, even Nephi's wife was part of the complaining crowd. But the crisis had its intended effect—it led the party back to its proper dependence on the Lord, much as the crises over food and water had led the ancient Israelites to seek the aid of the Lord in the desert (see Exodus 16, 17). (See 1 Ne. 16.)

Thus the scolding worked. Not only did everyone learn more clearly that "the ball . . . did work according to [their] faith and diligence and heed" but the writing, which "changed from time to time," plainly taught them "concerning the ways of the Lord." Moreover, to meet the crisis the writing on the ball directed Nephi to "go forth up into the top of the mountain" where he "did slay wild beasts, insomuch that I did obtain food for our families." With Nephi's "return to our tents, bearing the beasts which I had slain," the crisis ended. Everyone was happy and, acknowledging the Lord's hand, they "did give thanks unto him," though Nephi does not mention the expected sacrifices. Perhaps at this point there were no clean animals traveling with the camp, or perhaps Nephi intended his mention of "thanks" to the Lord to point to proper sacrifices. (See 1 Ne. 16.)

THE WOMEN AND THEIR CHILDREN

Family members set up the fourth camp after "traveling nearly the same course . . . for the space of many days." Nephi says that they wished to "tarry for the space of a time" without specifying other reasons. One suspects that Ishmael had become seriously ill and, as a consequence, was suffering while traveling. Whatever the deeper causes for the stop, "Ishmael died, and was buried in the place which was called Nahom," an event that brought on both mourning—"exceedingly," says Nephi—and shrill complaints "against my father [Lehi]" from Ishmael's daughters. To this point, as we shall see, the family had apparently traveled more than eleven hundred miles "south-southeast" from the first base camp, sharpening the sense of the distance from home. Particularly Ishmael's daughters felt "the loss of their father." The unrelenting strains of dealing with the physical challenges of the desert, particularly for women who had grown up in an urban setting, with necessities and conveniences of the day at their fingertips, intensified their sadness at the loss of their father. For, while mourning the death of their father, they complained "because of their afflictions . . . and they did murmur against my father [Lehi], because he had brought them out of the land of Jerusalem." They desperately missed their deceased father and their Jerusalem home. (1 Ne. 16.)

There is another component in the emotional outburst from Ishmael's daughters who "did mourn exceedingly" at his death (1 Ne. 16:35). It was the births of the first children in this place, as Nephi tells us (1 Ne. 17:1–2). Hence, Ishmael's daughters not only lost their father in death but some were also about to give birth to their first babies. The emotional climate was poignant and thick.

Importantly, the mourning for Ishmael opens a window through which one can hear the voices of the women who were in the party. Nephi's purposeful placement of certain elements in his account offers a view of women who learned to cope in one of the most challenging environments on earth. For example, Nephi carefully balanced the mourning and complaints of Ishmael's daughters (1 Ne. 16:35), which occurred before embarking on what was apparently the most difficult part of the journey, across southern Arabia, with his record of the complaints of these same women—expressed by their husbands in this instance—after emerging from the desert (1 Ne. 17:20). Neatly wedged between these accounts lies Nephi's "tribute" to the heroism of the women in the party:

> Our women did bear children in the wilderness. And . . . while we did live upon raw meat in the wilderness, our women did give plenty of suck for their children, and were strong . . . and they began to bear their journeyings without murmuring. (1 Ne. 17:1–2)

By inserting this tribute between the shrill voices of complaining, Nephi literally puts at center stage the women's successes at coping in the most difficult of deserts.[23]

There is a further chronological piece of the story that comes clear at Nahom: the length of the journey thus far. The family cannot have spent a lot of time journeying between the base camp and the point where they began to "travel nearly eastward" (1 Ne. 17:1). To theorize that they stopped for a long season, whether to reprovision or for some other purpose, misses a key clue in Nephi's narrative about the passage of time. Explicitly, of course, Nephi informed his readers that the family spent "eight years in the wilderness" (17:4) before arriving at their Bountiful on the seashore. He also offers implicit information. While we do not know how long the family spent at the base camp—perhaps a year, probably less—Nephi tells readers indirectly that the journey from the base camp to Nahom, where the party turned "eastward," required less than a year. How so?

The five marriages performed at the base camp (see 1 Ne. 16:7) would naturally have led to the birth of two or three children less than a year afterward, for some of the new brides would likely have become pregnant within the first months of marriage. Since the extended family evidently departed the base camp soon after the marriage festivities and since Nephi does not mention the birth of any children until the party turned to "travel nearly eastward" (17:1), one concludes that the almost 1,200 mile trip to this locale took at most ten or eleven months. Moreover, taking account of the three prior stops to rest and to reprovision the party, their rate of travel across this segment must have been only moderately slower than that of the Roman army which, 575 years later, marched about the same distance and over the same terrain in six months. Under forced-march conditions, however, the army covered the same ground in reverse in only two months.[24] On the basis of Nephi's notes on the marriages and the births of the first children of the new brides, then, the family took a year or less to move from the northeast tip of the Red Sea to the turning point at Nahom, whereas they required perhaps as much as six years to travel the 700 miles across southern Arabia from the turning point to the sea.

NAHOM

Not surprisingly, the location of "the place . . . called Nahom" has generated discussion. From Nephi's language, it seems clear that "the place" already carried a local name. Its general locale is now known. It lies south of the Wadi Jawf, a place known variously as Nihm or Nehem.[25] Three votive altars, dated to the seventh or sixth centuries B.C., all attest to the antiquity of this tribal and regional name. In effect, these altars offer the first archaeological correlation to specific events noted in the Book of Mormon.[26] (See 1 Ne. 16.)

As a term, Nahom betrays an interesting set of possible meanings in Hebrew. In one of its forms, the root n-h-m in Hebrew—vowels do not appear in writing—has the basic verbal sense to growl or to groan, as in mourning. The other possible form of the verb, n-h-m, with a rasped h sound in the middle, means to comfort or to regret.[27] Each of these meanings, of course, generally matches the events that overtook the family at "the place . . . called Nahom," what with the need to comfort those who were groaning or mourning because of the loss of Ishmael and because of unrelenting hardships.[28] (See 1 Ne. 16.)

THROUGH THE INTERIOR OF ARABIA

As soon as party members entered the interior of Arabia, after crossing to the east side of the Al-Sarāt Mountains, they would have run into people, farms, and cities. Before reaching Nahom, the family most certainly passed through the region of Najran, if not the city itself—one of the important stops on the caravan trail. Here they would have caught an early glimpse of the splendid urban architecture of the Sabaeans. Najran's large buildings and magnificent temples remind one of the "large and spacious building" of Lehi's dream (1 Ne. 8:26). In fact, the skyscraper buildings farther south—erected up to six stories by the eighth century B.C.—may well have been what Lehi saw. For he described the building of his dream "as . . . in the air, high above the earth" (8:26).[29] In a different vein, here and elsewhere in the Arabian peninsula, people worshiped the moon god in temples. Arabians believed that this god assisted those who traveled at night in order to escape the heat of the day.[30] Interestingly, the Lord had already promised through Lehi that "I will . . . be your light in the wilderness," allowing the party to keep going when it was necessary, even "in darkness" (1 Ne. 17:13; 8:8).

At Najran, a settlement that would become an important city of the Minaean kingdom a century later, family members would also have begun to notice the prosperity of the south. Lehi's dream had foreseen this affluence among the inhabitants of the "large and spacious building" whose "manner of dress was exceedingly fine" (1 Ne. 8:26–27). It seems that everyone prospered because of the caravans. But profits were not limited merely to the personal wealth of individuals. The kingdoms through which the caravans passed also amassed wealth, allowing them to erect beautiful buildings, especially temples and palaces, an aspect that archaeology has begun to affirm.[31]

From Najran, the party would have continued south for another 170 miles to the Wadi Jawf into "the place which was called Nahom." From this area, it was another eighty or so miles to the city of Marib, the capital city of the Sabaean kingdom. It was during this stage of the journey that Ishmael died, at Nahom in the area of the Wadi Jawf.

Nephi writes that from "the place which was called Nahom . . . we did travel nearly eastward" (1 Ne. 16:34; 17:1). In fact, from the region of Nahom-Nihm, all roads turned east. Even the shortcuts across the Ramlat Al-Saba'tayn desert, which connected to the incense trail north of Nahom-Nihm, ran east-west, connecting to Shabwah, which lay more than 200 miles east of Nahom and was the main center for gathering incense harvested in south Arabia. The caravan traffic out of Shabwah traveled westward to the general area of Nahom and then turned north to Najran. The party of Lehi and Sariah were traveling the opposite direction from the loaded camels of the caravans, an observation that helps to explain why some members of the party thought that they could return to Jerusalem even though at Nahom they were about 1,400 miles away (see 1 Ne. 16:36). Indeed, it is Nephi's note about the tribal area of Nahom and its connection to the eastward turn that signals to readers that his party was traveling along the incense route.[32]

Marib, of course, would have been even more impressive than Najran. Its status as the seat of the Sabaean government insured that it was the commercial and cultural center of south Arabia. Perhaps its most impressive physical feature was the system of waterworks that ran out of the Marib dam and irrigated dozens of square miles of land.

The famous Marib dam, truly a wonder of the ancient world, lay some 1,200 miles south of Lehi's base camp. The dikes and channels that preceded the dam had evidently been built several centuries before Lehi's party came into the region. Already the Sabaeans—whose queen the Old Testament knows as the queen of Sheba, visitor to King Solomon about 950 B.C.—had developed a far-flung system of waterworks that used a sophisticated series of dikes and sluices, or channels, to guide runoff rainwater into cisterns and reservoirs as well as into fields kept verdant by such carefully planned public works. Of course, drinking water came from wells and a few springs in the mountains because water behind the dam was brackish. But the hydrological works watered large fields and orchards. The dam itself, begun in 685 B.C., would have been impressive to travelers, even though it was still under construction in the days of Lehi and Sariah. Most significantly, all of these waterworks were visible in Lehi's dream when he saw a stream running alongside the tree, a silt-laden stream that Nephi later described as "filthy water" in one place (1 Ne. 12:16) and "filthiness" in another (15:27). This is exactly as it would appear after a rainstorm in a desert area: the water, brimming with mud and debris, gushing out of mountain valleys or wadis and eventually caught behind dikes and the Marib dam, then running out with its silt in channels to farms 15 miles distant.[33]

In this area, Lehi also saw the greenery that he and his family had learned about from his dream. On that occasion, he had spoken of "a large and spacious field" (1 Ne. 8:9), obviously set off from the "wilderness" where little grew, calling the wilderness "dark and dreary" (8:4). In this light, Lehi's dream anticipated that party members would see Arabia's large cultivated fields—a result of irrigation—as well as its vast and dreary landscapes, particularly in the western, central, and southeastern sectors where the family was to travel. We note that in his dream Lehi had to walk "for the space of many hours" with his guide, the guide possibly being a metaphor for the compass. The distinction in the dream, then, between the "wilderness" and the cultivable "field" wherein the tree grew seems intentional. Large tracts of southwest Arabia were already under cultivation long before Lehi's day, supporting the huge caravans—a thousand animals at times—that required fodder and water.[34] In fact, modern hydrologists point out that southwest Arabia sustained life for many more people 2,000 years ago than it does today.

Perhaps strangely, under any and all conditions, the caravans kept moving, another detail that Lehi's dream picked up. Although the first serious threats to the dominance of the Sabaean kingdom—established possibly by 1000 B.C.—did not rear their heads for more than a hundred years after Lehi's party passed through the territory, inscriptions point to times of unrest. But all commentators agree that civil and political strife did not interfere seriously with the movement of goods north to Egypt and beyond. Because people all along the caravan route made a good living off the caravans—either through taxation or through providing goods and services—everyone with a stake in the profits generally cooperated in keeping the roads open for traffic, and marauders and bandits were largely kept in check.[35] This aspect of wealth, too, Lehi foresaw in the people who inhabited the "large and spacious building," wearing "exceedingly fine" apparel (1 Ne. 8:26–27), obviously very well off economically.

And what were the goods shipped through Arabia? In the earliest period, it was salt. But eventually the goods of choice were frankincense and myrrh, produced from trees that flourished chiefly near the southeast coast of Arabia where the monsoon winds off the Arabian Sea brought rain for three or four months of the year. Heavy clouds and fog blanketed the coastline for months, evidently the "mist of darkness" of Lehi's dream (1 Ne. 8:23). The trees that produced frankincense and myrrh grew mainly on the north slopes of the mountains, away from the heavy summer rains that drenched the seaward side of the mountain range. Records from Egypt as early as the Sixth Dynasty (2341–2181 B.C.) disclose the use of frankincense in religious and funerary celebrations.[36] Some must have come from the region that is now modern Somalia, on the horn of Africa. But the best grades of frankincense were harvested in southern Arabia. In time, spices, silks, and precious metals and stones brought by boat to Arabia from India and beyond became important trade items carried by caravans. But in Lehi's day, the bulk of transported goods consisted of frankincense and myrrh, some of which were destined for the temple in Jerusalem (see Ex. 30:34–38; 1 Kgs. 10:10; Isa. 60:6).

One is left to speculate, of course, about any influences that the traders and wealthy cities may have exercised on members of Lehi's extended family. It is possible that, of those who valued possessions—particularly the older sons, who complained the loudest at the loss of family property to Laban—some were drawn to the high life of southwest Arabia. In a revelation on marital fidelity received by Lehi and quoted by his son Jacob (see Jacob 2:23–33), the Lord addressed "this people" whom he had led "out of the land of Jerusalem." Clearly the context tells us that the Lord was not speaking of the inhabitants of Jerusalem, or of Arabia for that matter. Those to whom He was speaking sought "to excuse themselves . . . because of the things which were written concerning David, and Solomon his son." The Lord was referring to members of Lehi's family. On this basis, one might surmise acts of infidelity on the part of certain family members, actions possibly tied to enticements found in the rich lands and cities of southwest Arabia.

One of the unusual features of Nephi's narrative is his omission of other people. Did not the family run into traders, desert-dwellers, and settlements, even cities? The answer has to be yes. The family met others.[37] Most watering holes—wells or oases—would have seen constant traffic from those seeking to slake their thirsts. Even so, water resources were closely guarded, creating cause for conflict. Although many conclude, perhaps rightly, that western and southern Arabia were wetter in the first millennium B.C. than now,[38] the existence of sophisticated irrigation works before Lehi's time points to the fact that dry years were the norm, as they currently are. It is just that the ancient inhabitants were conscientious about providing abundant food and water resources for the huge caravans that had become a regular feature of life long before Lehi's arrival. Twelve hundred years later, after Mediterranean seafarers had learned how to skip around the Arabian middlemen, the caravans carrying precious commodities northward out of Arabia shrank in size and importance, bringing an economic malaise to the kingdoms that had grown rich and fat sitting astride the incense trail.

TURNING EASTWARD

The family began to "travel nearly eastward" from the tribal region of Nahom/Nihm, perhaps passing through the city of Marib itself. The opportunity to reprovision was certainly available there, although we do not know how the family did so, with little or no disposable wealth that they could trade for food or exchange for failing animals. It was possibly here, or farther east, that family members evidently sold themselves for a time—perhaps more than once—as servants in order to earn enough to acquire supplies needed for the most arduous part of the journey, across the southern edge of Arabia's Empty Quarter. This segment ran approximately 700 miles to the seacoast at Dhofar, Oman, Lehi's Bountiful. To theorize that the party may have farmed for a season in the Nahom or Marib regions misses the point that every square foot of cultivable ground was owned by someone whose own needs came before those of itinerant travelers. We do know that at Nahom the party was perilously low on supplies and that, after a family reconciliation, "the Lord did bless us again with food, that we did not perish" (1 Ne. 16:39). But by all odds, this last part of the journey across southern Arabia was the toughest segment of the trip. (See 1 Ne. 16, 17.)

In the region of Nahom, all roads turned east in that era, including both the shortcuts across the desert and the main caravan route that ran eastward to Marib and then bent southeast to the city of Timna before turning northeast to Shabwah, the main center for gathering incense before shipping it more than 1,500 miles to the Mediterranean. To be sure, a single track ran south over mountain passes to Aden. But by far the bulk of the traffic ran east and west. Only persons who had traveled this route would know that the incense road followed an eastward path from the territory of Nahom. In fact, Nephi's notation that his party turned "nearly eastward" in this region forms one of the strongest indicators that his group was following the incense road. Beyond Shabwah, however, there were no roads in that era that continued east to southern Oman, the party's Bountiful. In that territory between the high dunes of the Empty Quarter on the north and the elevated and fractured tableland to the south, the party would have found itself among hostile, warring tribes who jealously protected their territories and water and food resources.[39]

Evidently, it was during this stage of the journey that the family "did not prosper nor progress in their journey, but were driven back" (Mosiah 1:17). We must observe in this connection that later Nephite authors enjoyed access to the fuller account of this trek. They offer a few glimpses that Nephi's spare narrative does not. For instance, in the words of King Benjamin (died about 121 B.C.), "the ball or director" ceased to work, at least part of the time, because party members did not give "heed and diligence" to the Lord's commands. As a result, "they were smitten with famine and sore afflictions," incurring "the displeasure of God upon them" (1:17). In the words of Alma, because they "forgot to exercise their faith and diligence . . . they did not progress in their journey . . . or did not travel a direct course, and were afflicted with hunger and thirst" (Alma 37:41–42; also 18:37–38). Even so, as both Omni and Alma remind us, the Lord "delivered our fathers out of the hands of their enemies and preserved them from being destroyed" (Omni 1:6; Alma 9:10). In addition, the Lord "saved [them] from famine, and from sickness, and all manner of diseases," strengthening them "in battle" so that "they might not be destroyed" (Alma 9:22). Truly, it was a period of extreme adversity, entailing "many afflictions and much difficulty." In a word, circumstances could not have been more unkind.[40] (See 1 Ne. 17.)

Whether the party entered the city of Shabwah remains unknown. But this large settlement would have offered a final chance to family members to reprovision themselves before pushing farther eastward. For they evidently did not follow the path down the Wadi Hadramaut, the largest system of canyons and valleys in Arabia, which carried runoff and spring water toward the Arabian Sea in a long curving arc east and south beyond Shabwah for 290 miles. The party seemingly maintained their eastward journey along the southern edge of the Empty Quarter, traveling just to the north of the high plateaus of southern Yemen. These plateaus rise sharply from the dunes, their northern slopes carved anciently by ribbons of water into deep, boulder-filled valleys.

Some have suggested that an overland caravan route connected Shabwah to the Dhofar area of modern Oman, the area with the best frankincense in antiquity. If so, then Lehi's party might have been generally following or paralleling this trade route. But no real evidence exists that caravans of any size traveled through this region during Lehi's era, for water was unavailable in the quantities needed by caravans. From the last major water hole north of Dhofar, the well at Shisur, one had to travel west eight days by camel toward Shabwah to reach the next one on the southern edge of the Empty Quarter.[41] Such were the severe conditions that a traveler would meet when crossing the southern edge of the Empty Quarter, whose current inhabitants have been called "thin, half-starved."[42]

There is also another aspect of danger and hardship. The Empty Quarter—Ar-Rub Al-Khali in Arabic—remains the harshest desert clime on earth, with summer daytime temperatures exceeding 125 degrees Fahrenheit. Except in the brief rainy season, there would have been little water and no feed for pack animals on the edge of the desert. Moreover, to cross any part of the Empty Quarter from west to east would have entailed endless effort and constant peril. The winds, which blow across Ar-Rub Al-Khali from the southwest in summer and from the northeast in winter, have shaped the dunes and valleys of sand basically in a north-northeast and south-southwest direction. Most ridges rise 600 feet and some as high as 800 feet. It was owing to this feature that the first modern explorer to cross the Empty Quarter, Bertram Thomas, traveled from south to north so that he could generally follow the contour of the dunes and wind-shaped valleys rather than having to cross their dangerously precipitous slopes, if he had traversed from east to west or vice versa.[43]

Anciently, merchants carried goods from the Dhofar region of Oman, particularly frankincense, either by boat or on barges built atop inflated animal skins, arriving at a port city south of Shabwah known anciently as Qana but today as Bīr Ali. From here, after inventory, camels carried them northward to the warehouses at Shabwah.[44] Because of this pattern of moving goods by sea rather than by land, Lehi's party evidently traveled across southern Arabia beyond Shabwah without regular contact with traders, unlike the earlier stages of the trip. (See 1 Ne. 17.)

It was in this region, one supposes, that the Lord instructed the party not to "make much fire." Although to this point family members had rarely been out of danger from marauding raiding parties, it was during the crossing of the south desert that they would have been most at risk to unfriendly tribesmen and to long-standing tribal conflicts.[45] As long as they were traveling or camping in the general area of a caravan trail, they would have enjoyed a measure of security. And a journey from the area of modern Aqaba to the region of Shabwah, approximately 1,600 miles, would normally have brought some sort of protection, even if irregular. But stepping away from areas where even occasional caravan contact occurred left Lehi's party without a protective presence, so to speak. (See 1 Ne. 17.)

Because the party would have become most dependent on the compass in this region for safety, water, and food, the need for strict obedience to the Lord became paramount, with no wiggle room.

When even one person failed—"every one" had to obey (Mosiah 1:16)—the whole group was affected by the result: a malfunctioning compass. When recalling this episode generations later, King Benjamin reminded his son Mosiah that "the ball or director . . . led our fathers . . . [and] as they were unfaithful they did not prosper nor progress in their journey, but were driven back, and incurred the displeasure of God . . . and . . . were smitten with famine and sore afflictions" (Mosiah 1:16–17). Naturally, the reference to famine conjures up a dark scene of lack of food and water, twin terrors of the desert. (See 1 Ne. 17.)

Of course, the family probably faced starvation or dehydration a number of times. The desert is a treacherous place even for the experienced. And Nephi specifically drew attention to one incident of threatened starvation early in his narrative, perhaps as a representative sample (see 1 Ne. 16:17–32). This early experience must surely have taught the extended family that they were to look to the Lord to survive: "[T]he Lord did bless us *again* with food" (16:39; emphasis added). What is indeed remarkable is the apparent fact that everyone except Ishmael came through the journey alive and in good health, including infants born in the desert, demonstrating the Lord's "great . . . blessings." So even if the actions of individual family members interrupted the proper functioning of the compass, the resulting setback was only temporary. The fact that everyone came through the journey alive and well is a more accurate measure of the loving care of the Lord than is any catalogue of deliverances from misfortunes (see Ps. 105:37). (See 1 Ne. 16, 17.)

BOUNTIFUL

The ultimate destination, whether known to the family or not, was the Dhofar region in the south of modern Oman. It constitutes a botanical anomaly in Arabia, a virtual Garden of Eden during the rainy season. No other region, north or south, matches even remotely the Bountiful described by Nephi, a place of "much fruit and also wild honey." Here he found "timbers" sturdy enough for constructing an oceangoing vessel, although the kinds of trees currently growing in this area might not have qualified. Moreover, the territory supported abundant game so that the family was able to load onto the ship "meat from the wilderness," along with "much fruits . . . and honey in abundance, and provisions" (1 Ne. 18:6).[46] Clearly, the Lord had led the family to a gardenlike spot where, compared to the desert that began just a few miles to the north and west of their Bountiful, they could meet their needs with some ease. (See 1 Ne. 17.)

Little is known of the ancient history of Dhofar. Archaeologists have uncovered remains from peoples that predate Lehi's arrival by several centuries, remains that document the activities of harvesting and shipping frankincense as well as trade. It is also apparent that the zenith of the abundant life there, and thus the era of most archaeological remains, occurred in the early centuries A.D.[47] One has to assume, of course, that from early times, desert tribes had learned of the verdant growing seasons and had moved in and out of the area. Moreover, centuries before Lehi's time, inhabitants had begun to harvest frankincense from the trees that used to grow in abundance throughout the *najd,* the drier, northern slopes of the mountains. These mountains rise precipitously out of the Arabian Sea, some to heights over 5,000 feet, and then run gradually downward and northward toward the sand desert.

Some of the small inlet bays along the Dhofar coast became staging points where harvested frankincense was loaded aboard westward-bound vessels headed for ancient Qana, and would have offered to Nephi a choice of places to construct his ship. Such shipping activities stopped during the summer months. The strong, southwest monsoon winds that kicked up in May would bring water-laden clouds from the Arabian Sea, which would lose most of their rain before crossing the tops of the mountains that ran along the coast. As a result of the four-month wet season, which extended into September, there was year-round fresh water and plenty of fodder for animals, essentials for Lehi's family as they began to prepare for their long voyage to the Americas.

Again, it is odd that Nephi mentions no other people in the vicinity of his Bountiful. Surely, because of its natural abundance, there were people living in the region. It is possible, of course, that he and his family found themselves on a part of the coast that was not inhabited by others, even seasonally, leaving them essentially alone. It is more likely, however, that one or more neighboring tribes lived in the vicinity but that the family of Lehi did not seek connections with them, keeping to themselves as much as they could. Whatever the case, the family seems to have been self-sufficient, not relying on others for their needs. (See 1 Ne. 17.)

One of the vexing issues, until recently, concerns Nephi's making of tools with which he worked the timbers for his ship. The matter becomes even more puzzling when one realizes that the nearest known copper mines lay in what is now known as northern Oman, some 600 miles distant across forbidding terrain. From the way that Nephi writes his recollections, it seems improbable that he traveled so far to find ore to smelt for making tools. And even if he had traveled that far, it also seems unlikely that local miners would have allowed him to work a vein of ore for his own needs. And Nephi certainly hints at no such experience. (See 1 Ne. 17.)

The question of ore for tools has largely been solved by recent geological studies of the Dhofar area. The person who conducted the first field study in 1995, Eugene Clark, found a number of small deposits of specular hematite, the easiest source to smelt in order to make iron. Then, in 2000, a small group of geologists from Brigham Young University, under the leadership of W. Revell Phillips, surveyed locales along the Oman coast and found other deposits of iron ore that are readily accessible. Although none of the deposits is large enough for economic development, an aspect that the Oman government asked the geologists to report on, the surveys prove conclusively that iron ore was available within a few days' walk of any place along the shore in the Dhofar region.[48] Whether Nephi made nails for fastening the ship as well as his tools for shaping the timbers is not known. (See 1 Ne. 17, 18.)

Concerning shipbuilding, it is evident that Nephi knew something about this skill, for he speaks of working "timbers after the manner which was learned by men," though he did not pursue this approach (1 Ne. 18:2). Instead, "the Lord did show me from time to time after what manner I should work the timbers," with the result that "I did [not] build the ship after the manner of men; but . . . after the manner which the Lord had shown unto me" (18:1–2). And where did Nephi learn the skill of shipbuilding? One answer has to be that he learned at least some techniques through the Lord's tutoring.

Another answer is that he may have acquired at least some skills before reaching the southern coast of Arabia. Although there is a long tradition of boat building and repairing in the Dhofar area, there is no firm evidence that these skills were plied among inhabitants as early as Lehi, though it would be surprising if people living along the seashore had not developed skills at least for repairing boats. The firmest evidence of early shipbuilding in Arabia comes from Bahrain in the Persian Gulf, on the north, whence vessels sailed to the southern shores.[49] (See 1 Ne. 17, 18.)

At first, Nephi's project to build a ship did not enjoy wholehearted support among family members—quite the contrary. As soon as it became known that he was about to construct such a vessel, he became the object of scorn and ridicule: "Our brother is a fool . . . lacking in judgment" his brothers cackled, thinking "that he can build a ship; yea, and . . . cross these great waters" (1 Nephi 17:17, 19). Nephi laid their complaints squarely at the feet of laziness: "[M]y brethren . . . were desirous that they might not labor" (17:18). Certainly, even though the family had been led to a virtual paradise, life must still have been full of challenges, what with the needs of providing food both from fishing and from hunting, and of rebuilding their lives in a strange setting. Hence, there was much work to do without the energies of the family being siphoned off for other purposes, including efforts to construct a ship. In addition, because Nephi's intent to build a ship apparently came as a surprise to everyone—the Lord had initiated the contact directly with him in requiring that he construct a ship (17:7)—there is reason to believe that some family members may have thought that in arriving at Bountiful they had already reached the land of promise.

The ensuing scene highlights again one of the painful elements of the narrative, that of rivalry among the sons of Lehi and Sariah. Throughout the story, it becomes evident that Nephi had been the most responsive of the sons to instructions from the Lord, whether through his father or, in a more direct manner, because of his own sensitive spirit. In fact, Laman and Lemuel were surprisingly obtuse in such matters, an aspect that Nephi comments on from time to time (e.g., 1 Ne. 3:31; 4:3–4; 15:10–11; 16:1–3). On the occasion of their jeering at him for starting work on a ship, Nephi appeared to lose heart. In fact, he says that he was merely "sorrowful" owing to "the hardness of their hearts," for "they [did not] believe that I was instructed of the Lord" to build a ship (1 Ne. 17:18–19).

The jeering quickly turned to vindictive complaining. The older brothers sneered, "[T]hou art like unto our father, led away by the foolish imaginations of his heart." While we do not know whether Lehi was present when his sons spoke these words, he must have been deeply disheartened by his sons' protests when he learned of them, knowing that they knew of the Lord's guidance throughout the journey. But once they had begun to complain, they pressed their spiteful remarks, declaring that their father "hath led us out of the land of Jerusalem, and we have wandered . . . for these many years; and our women have toiled, . . . and suffered all things, save it were death; and it would have been better that they had died . . . than to have suffered these afflictions." Their thoughts then raced back to their Jerusalem home: "[W]e might have enjoyed our possessions and the land of our inheritance; yea, and we might have been happy" rather than crossing the desert and thereafter facing the daunting prospect of building a new life in a distant land. (See 1 Ne. 17.)

Even though he was younger, Nephi was not one to shrink from a good fight. In fact, his brothers' murmurings seem to have energized him. He took on the complaints of his brothers when they were clearly wrong. For they believed that their father, Lehi, had acted on his own, had unfairly judged the "righteous people" of Jerusalem to be unrighteous, and thus had "led us away because we would hearken unto his words" (1 Ne. 17:22). Not so, declared Nephi. In his response, he turned attention to the rescue of the Israelite slaves from Egypt as his example, comparing the exodus of their family from Jerusalem to the divinely orchestrated exodus of the Hebrew slaves. For him, the Lord had been involved in both events.

Nephi's speech reviewing the Israelite exodus and comparing it to the exodus of his own family is a classic and reinforces the main theme of his book, that of deliverance (see 1 Ne. 1:20). His chief points were two. First, the Lord had played a major role in both sets of experiences. Second, the resistance by certain family members to the Lord's direction exactly mirrored that of the former slaves, who had "hardened their hearts and blinded their minds, and reviled against . . . the true and living God . . . even as ye have" (17:30, 41). In his presentation, Nephi compared his own father, Lehi, to Moses.[50]

Although other comparisons are possible between Moses and Lehi, five that have to do with the journey in the desert will suffice. First, for each, a revelation from God began the entire chain of events that resulted in the exodus events to which their names are tied. Second, each faced and had to overcome the endangerment of losing the promises from the Lord because of rebellion among their respective people. Third, Moses became the *pater familias* of all Israel, not just of his own family. Likewise, Lehi filled this role both for the members of Ishmael's family and for Zoram, former servant of Laban. Fourth, Moses crossed the physical boundaries of many tribes and nations of people, including Midianites, Egyptians, and Canaanites, as well as other metaphorical boundaries. So did Lehi, crossing the physical barriers of the Arabian desert and the ocean, and hostile tribal territories, as well as metaphorical and spiritual frontiers. Fifth, Moses named his son Gershon, meaning "sojourner," a name that points to alienation. Similarly, Lehi gave the name Jacob to his first-born child in the wilderness, recalling the ancestor who spent much of his adult life living in a foreign land away from family and home.

In the aftermath of Nephi's impassioned speech, we learn of two important dimensions of their Bountiful. The first is a topographical feature. When Nephi had finished his address, his brothers were "angry" with him and came forward to seize him and "throw [him] into the depths of the sea," indicating that near "our tents," which were set up "by the seashore," there was a precipice of considerable height that overlooked the sea (1 Ne. 17:48, 6). The second involves a characteristic of the Lord's purposes. The Lord granted Nephi power to "shock" his brothers by extending his hand toward them, "that they may know that I am the Lord their God" (17:53). The experiences that the Lord had led the family through were not simply for window dressing in their lives. They had purpose, the chief of which was to teach family members that the Lord was their keeper and corrector. The brothers' reaction was almost predictable. They not only confessed that the "shock" came from the Lord but, in the face of raw power—and it is evident that they respected such power—they "were about to worship" Nephi, an honor that he saw as misplaced.

Subsequent mention that family members "did worship the Lord" raises the question of whether they built a more or less permanent structure in Bountiful where they could worship; that is, a building whose remains might be recovered by archaeology even today. The answer is that we do not know. In addition, it was apparently unnecessary. We know that Lehi led the family in worship at the base camp on at least three occasions, worship that consisted partially of offering sacrifices (see 1 Ne. 2:7; 5:9; 7:22). For such acts of devotion, Lehi constructed "an altar of stones" that he found in and around the camp, an altar that stood outside of any structure, whether permanent or temporary (2:7). Hence, there is no need to postulate that the family erected a permanent structure for worship, though it is not impossible. (See 1 Ne. 17, 18.)

As a result of the roller-coaster scene in Bountiful, which began as a shouting match and ended with the older brothers docilely acknowledging the Lord's hand, the whole family joined in the effort to build the ship—"*we* did work timbers" (1 Ne. 18:1; emphasis added). What had started as the project of one became the enterprise of all. When the project was finished, even the most skeptical had to admit that the boat was wonderfully built. Nephi recorded that "my brethren beheld that it was good," that is, "the workmanship thereof was exceedingly fine." The result was that "they did humble themselves again before the Lord." With everyone in a proper frame of mind, the Lord could give the order for them to depart. (See 1 Ne. 18.)

Of course, one has to ask what type of timber Nephi used in constructing the ship. Of the trees that currently grow in the Dhofar region, several species grow to a height that would provide timbers long enough for a ship, but it is not clear whether they could withstand the strains of a long voyage. After all, the stresses on an ocean-going vessel are more severe than those on a smaller boat that weighs less and carries far less cargo. In fact, there is reason to believe that before the Roman period the shipwrights of northern Arabia imported lumber from India—teak and coconut—presumably because trees that grew natively were not sturdy enough for ships that carried large cargoes year after year.[51] In the case of Nephi's ship, it was needed for only one very long voyage, beginning in Arabia and ending in the land of promise, the New World. (See 1 Ne. 18.)

The ancient techniques for shipbuilding were essentially two: sewing and nailing. The technique of choice in the Arabian peninsula was sewing timbers of the hull together. Nails were known, for the remnants of ancient iron nails, predating Lehi, have been recovered near the modern Jordanian seacoast town of Aqaba. But knowledge of this sort of construction technique seems not to have altered how ancient Arabians plied their skills. Basically, one went about the job by drilling holes at specific intervals through the edges of the planks that formed the hull. Then one sewed the planks together using coconut-fiber ropes, and sealed both the holes and rope strands with caulking made of a resin or oil. The advantages of sewn ships were two: lower costs in building, and a vessel that could withstand mishaps with less damage. The disadvantages included constant leaking between planks and the endless need for maintaining the fiber ropes and caulking.[52] (See 1 Ne. 18.)

The matter of sails is important. For it is evident that Nephi's ship was not powered by oars. If it had been, it would have been foolish for the older brothers, during their onboard rebellion, to "bind [Nephi] with cords"—possibly the same kind of cords used to sew ships—because Nephi would have been very helpful in providing muscle power for rowing. After all, he had said of himself that he was "a man large in stature" (1 Ne. 4:31). Rather, the ship must have depended on sails. Although it is not possible to tell whether they were square or rectangular, as were those of antiquity, or whether the Lord's instructions had modified the design, it is certain that the ship responded to winds and thus was rigged with sails: "we . . . were driven forth before the wind towards the promised land" (1 Ne. 18:8) and "we sailed again towards the promised land" (18:22).[53]

VOYAGE AT SEA

Finally, after perhaps two or three years in Bountiful, the day came to board the ship. Naturally, there must have been sufficient storage space for foods and seed-grains. One has to assume that the family must have prepared animal skins and possibly ceramic ware as storage units in order to keep dry goods from mildew and seawater. Why animal skins? Because they were available after family members killed the animals that supplied the "meat from the wilderness" that was taken aboard. And from experience, family members would have known of their utility for storage. In addition, they may have observed, firsthand, animal skins serving as air pods under rafts for shipping incense by sea from the region.[54] (See 1 Ne. 18.)

We do not know how the family disposed of their pack animals. We have to assume that they still owned such animals because of the need to transport the local timbers from where they grew to the place where Nephi and his brothers were building the ship, even if the distance were short. When one inspects Nephi's list of items taken aboard, one finds no mention of animals. Instead, one reads of "fruits and meat from the wilderness," as well as "honey in abundance," this latter note leading one to conclude that honey may have formed the chief ingredient of their diet at sea. Other grains and seeds "which we had brought from the land of Jerusalem" also receive notice. But Nephi mentions living animals only after arriving in the land of promise, animals which the family found "in the wilderness" and "in the forests." (See 1 Ne. 18.)

Going aboard ship also meant trouble. How so? As background, one of the sores that continually festered within the family concerned its future leadership, dramatized in the seemingly endless tugs-of-war between Laman and Nephi. One of the complaints of Laman's descendants about losing the leadership of the clan, a complaint recorded generations later, was that Laman and his family "were . . . wronged while crossing the sea" (Mosiah 10:12). One naturally asks whether there is any clue in Nephi's narrative that would help us to understand this accusation. The answer is yes.

Nephi described the boarding scene in the following way. First, "the voice of the Lord came unto my father, that we should . . . go down into the ship." Clearly, the Lord orchestrated even the act of boarding. Next, "after we had prepared all things . . . according to that which the Lord had commanded us, we did go down into the ship, with all our loading." Again, the Lord's hand is evident, this time in the types and amounts of goods that the family was to take aboard ship. But people did not swarm onto the ship. When it was time to board, they went in a particular order, "every one according to his age." Hence, of the children of Lehi, Laman with his wife and children would have boarded first. While this may seem like a small thing, in effect it pointed to Laman as the heir apparent to the leadership of the clan. In fact, this order of boarding recalls the scene in which Joseph of Egypt, before he revealed his identity to his brothers, hosted a meal and seated them in his presence, "the firstborn according to his birthright, and the youngest according to his youth" (Gen. 43:33). (See 1 Ne. 18.)

Perhaps it was Laman's exuberance at finally finding himself properly honored as the oldest son that led him to behave badly aboard ship. The time in the desert and the experiences in Bountiful had pushed Nephi to the front of family leadership. Perhaps the physical separation from these land areas brought a certain sense of relief to Laman. Whatever the case, his ill behavior, along with that of others in the party, brought Nephi to "fear exceedingly lest the Lord should be angry with us." For, like the Israelites at the building of the golden calf (see Ex. 32:6), Nephi's "brethren and the sons of Ishmael and also their wives began . . . to dance and to sing, and to speak with much rudeness." In response, Nephi demanded that these activities cease. But his brothers "Laman and Lemuel," in order to show that they were in charge, "did take me and bind me with cords." As Nephi had feared, "the compass . . . did cease to work" and "there arose a great storm." For "three days" a "great and terrible tempest" drove the ship out of control so that everyone, including the brothers, "began to be frightened exceedingly lest they should be drowned in the sea." Even so, "they did not loose" Nephi. And even though "Lehi . . . said many things unto them, and also unto the sons of Ishmael," and even though Nephi's "wife with her tears and prayers, and also [Nephi's] children" pled with the brothers, "they would [not] loose me." Plainly, it was a contest of power. (See 1 Ne. 18.)

The oldest son, Laman, had much to lose. He had decided to take dramatic action by binding Nephi. He compounded the situation by not allowing others to intercede in the dispute, as was customary, in order not to lose face. Further, if he were to release Nephi, Laman would be admitting that he had been wrong and accordingly that his leadership of the family was flawed. But the Lord had his own agenda—and it did not include Laman as leader of the clan. Finally, on the fourth day of the storm, "when they saw that they were about to be swallowed up in the depths of the sea," the brothers "repented" and "they loosed" Nephi. As we have seen, Laman and Lemuel respected raw power. For Laman, any hopes of leading the family were dashed. From that time on, "I, Nephi, did guide the ship . . . towards the promised land." It was a staggering miscalculation by the brothers, especially Laman. The Lord had employed His power over the elements to elevate Nephi above Laman, the one whose right it had been to lead as the oldest son. (See 1 Ne. 18.)

Is it possible that the ship docked at various points along the way in order to take on fresh water? The answer has to be yes. Water was one commodity that they could have acquired from others with little or no expense. Thus they would not have needed to dip into their precious cargo for items to trade. Certainly the use of skins for storage of fresh water has to be affirmed. Presumably, ceramic ware would have served to store honey and certain other goods. As all who are acquainted with sea voyages will know, however, fresh water is a minimum requirement. The family may have stored hundreds of gallons on board the ship. But with forty or so people drawing on the supply,[55] it would not take many weeks to consume the entire amount, creating the need to go ashore to replenish the stores of water. (See 1 Ne. 18.)

THE LAND OF PROMISE

Which way did the ship sail? Two possibilities exist, and they depend on the direction of the monsoon winds. During the winter months, the winds blow from the northeast. If the family had set out, say, between November and April, they would have been carried southward along the east coast of Africa. In this view, they would have rounded the Cape of Good Hope and landed on the eastern shore of the Americas, presumably at a spot somewhere north of South America.[56] The other view ties to the monsoon winds that blow from the southwest during the summer months. If the family had departed Bountiful, say, between May and September, they would have been pushed eastward toward India, eventually finding themselves in the Pacific Ocean. On this view, the party would have landed on the west coast of the Americas, anywhere from Chile northwards.[57] (See 1 Ne. 18.)

The latter view, that of sailing east from Arabia and landing on the west coast of the Americas, is more attractive for several reasons.

The first has to do with terrain, the second with a glaring omission, and the third with the book of Isaiah. In setting the stage for a discussion, one notes that at the landing site in the promised land there were "wilderness" and "forests" as well as "all manner of ore, both of gold, and of silver, and of copper." We assume that the animals that family members found there could have been found on or near either coastline. Hence, the animals are not decisive for any discussion. (See 1 Ne. 18.)

The matter of terrain arises in Nephi's description of the initial separation of the family into two parts some years after their arrival in the promised land. Again, the issue concerned leadership. The quarrels had reached such a dangerous pitch that the Lord instructed Nephi to take as many as would follow him and depart. He did so, journeying "in the wilderness for the space of many days" to a place where they finally "did pitch [their] tents," calling "the name of the place Nephi" (2 Ne. 5:2–8). From later sources we learn that the area of Nephi, both what is termed the "land of Nephi" and the city in its midst, were located in an upland, because generations later, a group led by the first King Mosiah fled this area and "*came down* into . . . the land of Zarahemla" (Omni 1:13; emphasis added). Less than twenty years later, a number of the people who had fled with Mosiah to Zarahemla sought to return, "to *go up*" to take possession of their old homesteads (Mosiah 9:3; emphasis added). In this light, it becomes clear that the area to which Nephi and his followers originally fled was a highland, evidently not a long distance from those who stayed by the seashore because the two groups maintained at least a casual contact (see Enos 1:20), and the lowlanders eventually mounted a number of invasions of the upland (see Jarom 1:7). Knowing that the highland was within reasonable distance of the lowland where the family had landed their ship and begun to establish themselves, we can rule out virtually the entire east coast of the Americas, from southern Argentina to the Maritime Provinces of Canada, as a landing site for the family of Lehi. Because of their mountains, only the east coast of southern Brazil and Central America might qualify as the place of landing. In contrast, along the entire west coast of the Americas runs a mountain chain which can be reached from the shoreline merely by walking. (See 1 Ne. 18.)

The glaring omission, the least compelling reason for proposing a landing on the western shore, comes in a brief notice of the arrival of the people of Zarahemla. Their origins reach back to a younger son of Zedekiah, the last king of Judah. It is widely and reasonably assumed that those who traveled with this younger son to the Americas came from the east, landing at a spot on the east coast of the Americas. In fact, it was while discussing the territories held by Lamanites and Nephites at the time of the mission of the sons of the younger King Mosiah that Mormon noted that "the place of [the] first landing" of the ancestors of the people of Zarahemla was "the land . . . northward" which "was called Desolation" (Alma 22:30–31). What Mormon did not say, and could have said if it were true, was that his own Nephite ancestors had landed on the same shoreline.

The selection from Isaiah, chapters 48 and 49, which Nephi added to his first book, may offer a clue about the direction that the family of Lehi sailed to reach the land of promise. In introducing these chapters from Isaiah, Nephi declared that the Lord had shown "unto many [prophets] *concerning us*" (1 Ne. 19:21; emphasis added). Nephi had just cited prophecies of Zenock, Neum, and Zenos, prophets from the Old Testament era whose works are lost. Then he turned to Isaiah. As the context demonstrates, Nephi plainly understood that Isaiah was among those whom the Lord had shown "concerning us." And what does Isaiah say? In speaking of the scattering and gathering of the "house of Israel," he points to those traveling "from the north and from the west," the very directions of travel that Nephi's family members had followed from Jerusalem through Arabia to Bountiful. Isaiah then commands, "Sing, O heavens; and be joyful, O earth; for the feet of those who are in the east shall be established; and break forth into singing, O mountains; for they shall be smitten no more." Who are "those who are in the east" and "shall be smitten no more"? For Nephi, they were his family members. Of course, Isaiah's mention of "those who are in the east" could geographically point to Nephi's family in Bountiful. But "the east" could also refer to the direction that Nephi's ship sailed (1 Ne. 21:12–13; Isa. 49:12–13).

In looking back on the entire journey from Jerusalem—the eight-year trip through the desert, the long stay in Bountiful, the arduous voyage—Nephi could rejoice that, having departed Jerusalem with divine help, his people had arrived in the New World and, as the Psalmist sings about the Israelite exodus, "there was not one feeble person among [them]" (Ps. 105:37). Yet he sensed that the spirits of his people needed lifting. They had endured much. They were far from their ancestral home in Jerusalem. They could not return even if they wanted to do so. So he tried to lift their spirits in the way that he knew best, by appealing to scriptures that spoke of the scattering and gathering of Israel, as well as the Messiah who was to come "six hundred years" from the time that his father left Jerusalem. He turned to the writings of prophets recorded on the brass plates, some of which are in the Bible. From these, he tried to center the hope of his people on the Messiah, who would bring redemption. In sum, he had written "these things unto my people, that perhaps I might persuade them that they would remember the Lord their Redeemer." In an attempt to beam a light on their blessings, he declared that without the aid of the Lord, his people would have been like "those who are at Jerusalem" who "have perished." Hence, the trip had been worth it because they had preserved their lives and had obtained a new land of promise. (See 1 Ne. 19.)

As he concluded his record of the amazing trip of his family, Nephi bore his testimony of the Lord's work among those Israelites who were to be scattered, as his own people had been. With the aid of "the Gentiles," the Lord "will bring them again out of captivity, and they shall be gathered together to the lands of their inheritance." At the same time, "they shall be brought . . . out of darkness; and they shall know that the Lord is their Savior and their Redeemer." (See 1 Ne. 22.)

NOTES TO CHAPTER TWO

1. That the desert formed a watershed for the family appears in how Lehi addressed his son Jacob at the time of his blessing—"my first-born in the wilderness" (2 Ne. 2:2, 11)—clearly distinguishing this child from his brothers born in Jerusalem.
2. Nephi, and presumably Lehi, had seen in vision "the land of promise" (1 Ne. 12:1), which was separated from the "man among the Gentiles" by "the many

waters" (13:12). But we cannot suppose a sophisticated view of world geography on Nephi's part, even after his vision, that would give him an understanding of where the land of promise was located in relationship to the region of Jerusalem.

3. Nibley, *Lehi in the Desert,* 43–46; S. Kent Brown, "New Light from Arabia on Lehi's Trail," 64–69.
4. Illness is known to have plagued others in Arabia. The ancient geographer Strabo wrote about a failed Roman military expedition to western Arabia (25–24 B.C.), saying that large numbers of soldiers died from "hunger and fatigue and diseases" (*Geography* 16.4.24).
5. See S. Kent Brown, "A Case for Lehi's Bondage in Arabia," *Journal of Book of Mormon Studies* 6, no. 2 (1997): 205–17; also *From Jerusalem to Zarahemla,* 55–59.
6. For mention of records on brass and stone, see Brian Doe, *Southern Arabia,* 21–22; see also the summary in Brown, "New Light from Arabia on Lehi's Trail," 87–88.
7. Not all of the tents were full sized because the four sons "took . . . tents" when they went back to Jerusalem for the plates of brass (1 Ne. 3:9).
8. See Nibley, *Lehi in the Desert,* 61.
9. Nibley argues that Lehi owned camels (*Lehi in the Desert,* 54–56). The Hiltons theorize that the family started with donkeys and then used camels (*In Search of Lehi's Trail,* 49, 91–92).
10. See 1 Ne. 16:18, 21; Mosiah 1:17; cf. Alma 9:22.
11. Nigel Groom, *Frankincense and Myrrh: A Study of the Arabian Incense Trade* (London: Longman Group, 1981), 174.
12. Doe notes that the earliest attempts to move goods north from southern Arabia, specifically salt, went by donkey and mule. But their inability to travel far without water eventually led to the use of camels (*Southern Arabia,* 50).
13. On the discovery of the summer monsoon winds as a vehicle for shipping, consult George F. Hourani, *Arab Seafaring* (Princeton, N. J.: Princeton University Press, 1951), 21–28.
14. See the map in Groom, *Frankincense and Myrrh,* 192.
15. Concerning mountains, consult Brown, "New Light from Arabia on Lehi's Trail," 77–79; George D. Potter and Richard Wellington, *Lehi in the Wilderness* (Springville, Utah: Cedar Fort, 2003), 25.
16. Estimates vary. Nibley suggests one to three years at the first camp (*Lehi in the Desert,* 60), while the Hiltons believe that the family spent between two and three years (*In Search of Lehi's Trail,* 50). In my view, the two return trips of the sons to Jerusalem would have taken between four and six weeks each, maximum. Whether the family spent a season or two growing crops seems

doubtful (see Hilton, *In Search of Lehi's Trail,* 70–71) because (1) a family consumes what it grows, (2) there was probably no arable land that was not already claimed (see Nibley, *Lehi in the Desert,* 66), and (3) Lehi's family was evidently reprovisioned with the return of the sons with the family of Ishmael (see 1 Ne. 16:11). That Nephi speaks of "provisions which the Lord had given unto us" is likely an expression pointing to God's gifts, especially that of food by hunting ("slaying food by the way" [1 Ne. 16:15]), rather than an indicator of farming (Nibley, *Lehi in the Desert,* 59).

17. For the makeup of the party, see John L. Sorenson, "The Composition of Lehi's Family," in *By Study and Also by Faith: Essays in Honor of Hugh W. Nibley,* John M. Lundquist and Stephen D. Ricks, eds. (Salt Lake City: Deseret Book, and FARMS, 1990), 174–96.

18. The flight undertaken by Nephi and his followers only a few years after arriving in the promised land illustrates that people did not "pitch [their] tents" while on the move (2 Ne. 5:7).

19. A discussion of this written itinerary, apparently kept by Lehi, appears in Brown, *From Jerusalem to Zarahemla,* 30–32.

20. See Nibley, Lehi in the Desert, 74–79, 86; also Doughty, *Travels in Arabia Deserta,* 1:88.

21. See the Hiltons, *In Search of Lehi's Trail,* 77–80. The suggested place seems possible, although the hint that the family may have raised a crop here does not. Potter and Wellington favor Wadi Agharr (*Lehi in the Wilderness,* 73–78).

22. 1 Ne. 21:9; Isa. 49:9). Isaiah also prophesied of divine aid to travelers, promising that "they shall not hunger nor thirst . . . for he that hath mercy on them shall lead them, even by the springs of water shall he guide them. And I will make all my mountains a way" (1 Ne. 21:10–11 [= Isa. 49:10–11]). See Brown, *From Jerusalem to Zarahemla,* 17–19, 25–27.

23. See Camille Fronk, "Desert Epiphany: Sariah and the Women in 1 Nephi," *Journal of Book of Mormon Studies* 9, no. 2 (2002), 14.

24. Strabo, *Geography* 17.1.45.

25. Warren P. Aston and Michaela J. Aston, "The Search for Nahom and the End of Lehi's Trail in Southern Arabia, Preliminary Report" (Provo, Utah: FARMS 1989); *In the Footsteps of Lehi,* 3-25. The Astons' identification was inspired by a note published by Ross T. Christensen entitled "The Place Called Nahom" (*Ensign,* August 1978, 73).

26. See S. Kent Brown, "The Place That Was Called Nahom," *Journal of Book of Mormon Studies* 8, no. 1 (1999): 66–68; Warren P. Aston, "Newly Found Altars from Nahom," *Journal of Book of Mormon Studies* 10, no. 2 (2001): 56–61; Terry L. Givens, *By the Hand of Mormon: The American Scripture That Launched a New World Religion* (New York: Oxford University Press, 2002), 120.

27. See Ludwig Koehler and Walter Baumgartner, *The Hebrew and Aramaic Lexicon of the Old Testament* (Leiden: E. J. Brill, 1995), 676, 688–89; Hans Wehr, *A Dictionary of Modern Written Arabic* (Wiesbaden, Germany: Otto Harrassowitz, 1961), 948, 950. According to Ernst Jenni and Claus Westermann (*Theological Lexicon of the Old Testament* [Peabody, Mass.: Hendrickson, 1997], 735), the earliest occurrences of *nhm* appear on occasions of death.

28. In Old South Arabian, the root *nhm* had to do with chipped or dressed stones. See Joan Copeland Biella, *Dictionary of Old South Arabic: Sabaean Dialect, Harvard Semitic Studies,* 25 (Chico, Calif.: Scholars Press, 1982), 296.

29. Consult "The Queen of Sheba, Skyscraper Architecture, and Lehi's Dream," 102–3.

30. Strabo, *Geography* 17.1.45; Doe, *Southern Arabia,* 25–26.

31. Consult the summary in Pierre Robert Baduel, ed., *L'Arabie antique de Karib'îl ā Mahomet: Nouvelles données sur l'histoire des Arabs grâce aux inscriptions, La Revue du Monde Musulman et de la Méditerranée* 61 (1991–93): 45–53.

32. See Brown, "New Light from Arabia on Lehi's Trail," 88–89.

33. On the Marib dam, consult Werner Daum, ed., Yemen: *3000 Years of Art and Civilization in Arabia Felix* (Innsbruck: Pinguin Verlag, 1987), 49–61; Jürgen Schmidt, "Baugeschichtliche Untersuchungen an den Bauanlagen des grossen Dammes von Mārib," *Archäologische Berichte aus dem Yemen,* Band I (Mainz am Rhein: Verlag Philipp von Zabern, 1982), 17–25.

34. On the size of caravans before Lehi's day, see Israel Eph'al, *The Ancient Arabs: Nomads on the Borders of the Fertile Crescent 9th–5th Centuries B.C.* (Jerusalem: Magnes Press, Hebrew University; Leiden: E. J. Brill, 1982), 95.

35. See Eph'al, *The Ancient Arabs,* 4, 12, 98–99.

36. Doe, *Southern Arabia,* 30; Hourani says that by the Sixth Dynasty "journeys were made quite frequently [from Egypt] by land or by sea to the country of Punt" for trade (*Arab Seafaring,* 7).

37. George Reynolds and Janne M. Sjodahl say that the compass minimized such contact (*Commentary on the Book of Mormon,* vol. 1 [Salt Lake City: Deseret News Press, 1955], 167). Hiltons say yes, but then the party avoided contact in the far south (*In Search of Lehi's Trail,* 28, 101). Astons say yes ("The Search for Nahom," 15; *In the Footsteps of Lehi,* 10). Nibley says little because he believes that they avoided contact (*Lehi in the Desert*, 63–67).

38. For an illustrated review of waterworks in ancient Qataban, for example, with comparisons to other similar works of ancient Arabia, see Richard LeBaron Bowen and Frank P. Albright, eds., *Archaeological Discoveries in South Arabia* (Baltimore: Johns Hopkins Press, 1958), 43–131.

39. Consult Wilfred Thesiger, *Arabian Sands* (New York: E. P. Dutton, 1959), 155–56, 180; Brown, "New Light from Arabia on Lehi's Trail," 88–92.
40. Consult Brown, "A Case for Lehi's Bondage in Arabia," 207–13.
41. Phillips, *Unknown Oman,* 220; Juris Zarins, *Dhofar—Land of Incense: Archaeological Work in the Sultanate of Oman 1990–1995* (Muscat, Sultanate of Oman, unpublished manuscript), 48–49.
42. Phillips, *Unknown Oman,* 211.
43. Phillips, *Unknown Oman,* 214–31.
44. See Groom, *Frankincense and Myrrh,* 165–68.
45. On tribal conflicts, consult Thesiger, *Arabian Sands,* 155–56, 180.
46. On the general needs for an oceangoing ship, see Potter and Wellington, *Lehi in the Wilderness,* 143–46.
47. Juris Zarins, *Dhofar—Land of Incense,* 48–49; Brown, "New Light from Arabia on Lehi's Trail," 120.
48. Eugene E. Clark, "A Preliminary Study of the Geology and Mineral Resources of Dhofar, Sultanate of Oman, Preliminary Report" (Provo, Utah: FARMS, 1995); W. Revell Phillips, "Metals of the Book of Mormon," *Journal of Book of Mormon Studies* 9, no. 2 (2000): 36–43.
49. Hourani, *Arab Seafaring,* 3–11.
50. On Lehi as Moses, consult Noel B. Reynolds, "Lehi and Moses," *Journal of Book of Mormon Studies* 9, no. 2 (2000): 26–35. On Nephi's skills in composing his speech, see Robert A. Rees, "Irony in the Book of Mormon," *Journal of Book of Mormon Studies* 12, no. 2 (2003), 20–29.
51. Hourani, *Arab Seafaring,* 89–91; also Potter and Wellington, *Lehi in the Wilderness,* 147.
52. Hourani, *Arab Seafaring,* 92–98.
53. On sails and rigging, see Potter and Wellington, *Lehi in the Wilderness,* 147–48.
54. On skins as floating devices, see George W. B. Huntingford, trans., *The Periplus of the Erythraean Sea* (London: Hakluyt Society, 1980), 35.
55. On the number of people on the ship, consult Sorenson, "The Composition of Lehi's Family," 194–95.
56. One of the most recent to espouse this view is Paul Hedengren, *The Land of Lehi,* 16–18.
57. Latter-day Saints who hold to this view are the Hiltons, *In Search of Lehi's Trail,* 22–23 (map), 114–15; the Astons, *In the Footsteps of Lehi,* 56–57; Sorenson, *An Ancient American Setting for the Book of Mormon* (Salt Lake City: Deseret Book and FARMS, 1985), 25–26.

Coronation

CHAPTER THREE

Whether Mormon found the book of Mosiah arranged more or less as it now exists we cannot know. But we can be confident that the unifying, underlying concepts of its parts—deliverance by God and salvation through Christ—would have captured his attention.[1] After all, in his day, Mormon had been seeking desperately to deliver his own people, both physically and spiritually, from a looming, certain destruction. And he knew that he could do this only if they would turn to the Savior. Because the book of Mosiah chronicled one divinely assisted deliverance after another, all because people had exercised faith, it gleamed brightly as a shining proof that God would intervene in human affairs on the side of those who earnestly sought His aid. The widely acclaimed speech of King Benjamin, which immediately preceded the coronation of his son Mosiah as the new king, is positioned near the beginning of Mosiah's record and brims with assurances of temporal and celestial deliverance—chiefly personal—from a person's lowly status as dust of the earth to becoming a servant of God, from being an enemy to God to becoming His child, from being a beggar to becoming an heir of Christ who "stands at the right hand of God" (Mosiah 5:9). On a community level, God possesses power to deliver an entire people from threatening, crippling danger. And He does it through His Son.

CHANGING KINGS

It was perhaps King Benjamin's most pressing challenge to hold the nation together. Changes of government, of course, require both a delicate balance between competing interests, a reassuring voice to calm the public, and a promise that good times will continue. Frozen in the memory of some in his audience was the scene of the Nephites' first arrival in Zarahemla a few dozen years before. The people of Zarahemla already possessed a deep and rich tradition. God had led their ancestors "from Jerusalem at the time that Zedekiah, king of Judah, was carried away captive into Babylon," arriving in their New World home after crossing "the great waters" (Omni 1:15–16; see 2 Kgs. 25:1–7). Their forebears had settled the land and flourished for more than 400 years. Moreover, one of King Zedekiah's sons, Mulek, was among that first generation that reached the New World. This fact meant that "the seed of Zedekiah," a monarch who was a descendant of Israel's King David, were among the people of Zarahemla and thereby possessed inherited rights to rule (Hel. 8:21). One suspects that rancorous quarrels over royal succession had erupted among the New World descendants of King David and shaped the petty excuses that dragged the people of Zarahemla down into "many wars and serious contentions . . . from time to time" (Omni 1:17). Then suddenly the Nephites came into their land, unlooked for and unbidden.

The Nephites, under Mosiah their king, father of Benjamin, were themselves fleeing "out of the land of Nephi," their homeland, after "being warned of the Lord" (Omni 1:12). This flight, which included "as many as would hearken unto the voice of the Lord" (1:12–13), took place under God's nursing care. For Mosiah's refugees "were led by many preachings and prophesyings . . . and by the power of [God's] arm" (1:13). Nevertheless, the flight must have been emotionally and psychologically difficult. The refugees were abandoning their homes, their towns, their capital city. Moreover, one surmises that many in Mosiah's fleeing throng had gone through the heart-tearing experience of leaving behind family members who refused to abandon homes and lands. For not all of the Nephite people had joined in the exodus. Hence, feelings would have been tender, no matter the circumstances of each individual who had fled.

In this condition, the people of Nephi "discovered a people, who were called the people of Zarahemla" (Omni 1:14). Naturally, "there was great rejoicing" as each group learned about the other, discovering to their delight strands of common Israelite heritage (1:14–16). Then the hard part began. The Nephites had to find places to live. The people of Zarahemla, in effect, had to move over to accommodate the crowds of newcomers. Despite the initial good will, frictions would have surfaced. To compound matters, the economy of the people of Zarahemla would have suffered terribly because of the sudden increase in demand for goods and services. Prices would have soared. The costs—economic, human, social—for settling the Nephites into the society would have been gnawingly high. Perhaps the rawest point of friction came about because of the change of government. The Nephites took control, evidently without military conflict. To be sure, the people of Zarahemla outnumbered the Nephites, a situation that persisted long after Benjamin's death (see Mosiah 25:2). But the Nephites arrived with a king, with records, with the sword of Laban, and with the Liahona. Such tokens conferred an aura of legitimacy on Mosiah's right to rulership. The people of Zarahemla seem to have possessed no such sacred artifacts. They certainly possessed "no records" (Omni 1:17). Their only claim to leadership seems to have been the tie of lineal descent of some of their number to the family of King David. It was not enough. The leading families therefore moved aside, graciously permitting the Nephite Mosiah to don the robes of kingship.

Plainly, not all of the people of Zarahemla were happy with the new arrangement. But difficulties did not push immediately to the surface. Mormon writes about "contentions" bursting into the open only after King Mosiah's death, contentions that dogged Benjamin's early years (W of M 1:12). Even though Benjamin and his supporters, who included "the holy prophets who were among his people" (1:16), were able to "establish peace in the land" (1:18)—aided by a need for military unity when fending off their common enemies in a pitched war (see 1:13–14)—the smoldering embers of resentment broke out darkly in civil conflict a generation after Benjamin. On that occasion, five years after the Nephite monarchy had been dismantled in favor of a representative form of government, a man named Amlici persuaded a significant number of people to install him "to be a king over the people" (Alma 2:2). Even though a majority of the populace rejected his claim to kingship, his supporters "did consecrate Amlici to be their king," leading to civil war (Alma 2:9). While the record does not specify whether Amlici was a descendant of Mulek and therefore King David, the fact that a charismatic leader could rally support for kingship outside the Nephite royal family illustrates the potentially explosive situation that Benjamin had to address when he was about to turn over royal power to his son.

THE KINGDOM

It is difficult to establish how far people traveled from towns and villages to reach Zarahemla for the coronation festivities. In King Benjamin's era, the kingdom seems to have been rather compact.[2] Evidence for organized, sustained expansion comes only in the next generation, late in Mosiah's reign.[3] To be sure, the combined population of the peoples of Zarahemla and Nephi had reached a size that it could sustain itself even after the loss of several thousand lives in military actions.[4] But the pressures of population expansion had evidently not yet reached the pitch that later coaxed people to cross the River Sidon and establish settlements on the east bank (see Alma 6:7). That would occur only after the welcome immigrations of the peoples of Limhi and Alma the Elder, peoples who arrived suddenly and almost together in the seventh year of Mosiah's reign.[5]

In this light, distances across Benjamin's kingdom cannot have been great. It may be telling that people traveled to and from the festivities in Zarahemla largely by families, as on this occasion (see Mosiah 2:1, 5; 6:3). This observation leads us to surmise that colonization away from the central city, such as it was, occurred chiefly among families who sought land and opportunity away from the crowded metropolis. Years later, authorities in Zarahemla would build military outposts in distant, strategic spots, and encourage people to move into unsettled territory in an evident attempt to thwart any Lamanite designs to establish military colonies beyond them, in the land northward.[6]

AT THE TEMPLE

It was the last time that King Benjamin—soldier, protector of his people, saint—called his people together. Because it was his last chance, he had planned well. The details of the record bear this out. Anticipating a large crowd for the king's speech and for the coronation of his son, workers had constructed a tall tower on the edge of the temple grounds so that the aged, beloved monarch could speak to as many of the expected gathering as possible. When people began to arrive in large numbers, it became clear that scribes would have to write his words so that copies could be read in the distant corners of the makeshift camp. The days preceding the king's address had been filled with worship and thanksgiving, singing and offering sacrifice. Now it was time to listen.

King Benjamin stepped to the front of the tower. The moment was electric, especially for the prince Mosiah. Stretched before the king's gaze lay a sea of tents and temporary huts, each open doorway facing the tower, each opening filled with a family waiting expectantly to hear the elderly monarch's most important address. Behind the king stood the Zarahemla temple, a familiar, reassuring sight that reminded the crowd of the sacred character of this gathering wherein—with the heavens as witness—the old king would solemnly crown his successor.

The chief purpose for the gathering, of course, was the formal transfer of royal authority from king to crown prince. Borrowing an expression that recalled ancient covenant making, Benjamin also intended to "give . . . a name" to the assembled crowd[7] whereby "they may be distinguished above all the people which the Lord God hath brought out of the land of Jerusalem" (Mosiah 1:11). As we soon learn, the giving of this name—that of Christ—formed the climax in a day of renewing covenants with the Lord, thus tying Benjamin's people by covenant to their Savior Jesus Christ and supplanting in part their loyalties to tribes and clans (see Mosiah 5:2–12). It was to be a grand, unifying event, staged at the temple and witnessed by most everyone in the kingdom. Naturally, preparations had gone on for months, even years if one counts the training of the youthful Mosiah.

FIRST STEPS

In his earlier years as a parent, King Benjamin had properly seen to the education of his three known children, all sons: Mosiah, Helorum, and Helaman, a point that Mormon purposely stresses in his narrative—"so fulfilling the commandments of God." Probably through experienced tutors, Benjamin "caused that [his sons] should be taught in all the language of his fathers." Besides language studies, which included "the language of the Egyptians," their reading must have covered the literatures that had been composed among their people as well as law and religion (see Mosiah 1:2–4). As proof of the latter, years later Mosiah would show a firm acquaintance with matters of law when he reformed the legal system of the country (see Alma 1:1; 11:1–4).[8] In addition, the literary compositions that the sons studied encompassed religious records, for they were introduced both to "the prophecies which had been spoken by the mouths of their fathers" as well as to "the [sacred] records which were engraven on the plates of brass" (Mosiah 1:2–8).

The formal transfer of royal power from Benjamin to his son Mosiah actually began before the coronation. It took place in a series of preliminary acts carried out by the old monarch. First, Mormon reported, Benjamin had summoned his son Mosiah and required that he "should make a proclamation throughout all this land." As one might expect, Mosiah obeyed (Mosiah 1:10, 18; 2:1). He must have been as keenly anxious as Benjamin to bring about a seamless transition of power. As a point of emphasis, by such an act, Benjamin conveyed a clear message to his subjects that the prince had already begun to shoulder responsibility for the affairs of state with the full blessing of his father. Second, Mormon noted that on the same occasion, Benjamin "gave [his son Mosiah] charge concerning all the affairs of the kingdom," an essentially private yet ceremonial act that evidently endowed Mosiah with the authority to succeed his father in the event of the latter's sudden demise (Mosiah 1:15). The transfer of regal authority had begun.[9]

Third, in the same meeting the king gave the prince "charge concerning the records . . . and also the sword of Laban, and the ball or director." This last, "the ball or director," had been "prepared by the hand of the Lord" to lead the founding generation "through the wilderness" as they made their arduous way from Jerusalem to the promised land. Its value as a sacred memento of God's direct intervention in the lives of "our fathers" was beyond price. In fact, except for the ongoing official record of the realm on "the plates of Nephi," a chronicle that the first family began to keep only after it had arrived in the Americas, each item that Benjamin entrusted to Mosiah tied their era to the founders' departure from Jerusalem almost 500 years earlier. Such items included "the plates of brass," which had been retrieved from Jerusalem by Lehi's sons, and the sword of Laban, which had belonged to Lehi's distant cousin (see 1 Ne. 3–5). In this transfer of stewardship between king and son we are privileged to see the tokens of Nephite civilization, each with a link to heaven, including the sword (see 1 Ne. 4:9–18). Custody of these items singled out the possessors as the inheritors of a civilization and heritage established in an earlier age under the direction of the Almighty (see Mosiah 1:15–17).

HOLY ACTS

An essential action of the king during these days of celebration and remembrance took the form of public sacrifices. Actually, Mormon does not record that the king himself participated in offering "sacrifice and burnt offerings," although we may reasonably guess that he did. Instead, Mormon writes that beforehand "the people gathered together" in groups, in proper pilgrimage fashion, to travel to the capital city Zarahemla "to hear the words which king Benjamin should speak unto them." One wonders, of course, whether traveling in groups was a customary part of the celebration; it probably was, though one cannot rule out the evident safety of traveling in large numbers. While at the sanctuary, in accord with known worship practices, participants offered "the firstlings of their flocks" as sacrifices, as well as "burnt offerings."[10] The mood was definitely festive, for they gave "thanks to the Lord their God, who had brought them out of the land of Jerusalem" (Mosiah 2:1–4). Most likely, these sacrifices of thanksgiving included those known in the law of Moses as "peace offerings" (Lev. 3:1–4; 7:11–13) and were customarily offered in the morning at the temple with the "burnt offering" or "burnt sacrifice" (Lev. 3:5; Ex. 29:38–39).

Mormon's narrative sheds further light on the sacred character of the occasion by repeating small details. For example, on the model of pilgrims traveling "up" to Jerusalem and its temple, from whatever direction (see Ps. 24:3; Isa. 2:2–3; Acts 21:4), he wrote that Nephite worshipers also went "up to the temple" in Zarahemla, even though the city lay in a river valley. Plainly, people thought of themselves as symbolically ascending "the hill of the Lord" (Ps. 24:3). In addition, although custom seems to have required it, officials "did not number" the "great" multitude of people because "they had multiplied exceedingly . . . in the land." By noting the omission, Mormon hinted that officials knew the law from the Lord about numbering, but were seemingly unable to carry out its requirement because of the huge size of the crowd (see Mosiah 2:1–2; also Num. 1:2, 47–49; 26:2). This scene, however, contrasts with the later diligent effort at the end of the king's address to record "the names of all those who had entered into a covenant" (Mosiah 6:1). By the end of the day, so to speak, officials had done their duty after all.

Regrettably, reference to "the firstlings of [the] flocks" does not help in determining the time of year for the festivities, whether spring or fall (Mosiah 2:3). It was during these periods that the major holidays occurred, except the Feast of Weeks or Pentecost, which fell in the early summer exactly fifty days after Passover. Lambs typically were born in the spring. And from the time of the Exodus the law of the Lord had required that all firstborn animals, "all that openeth the matrix," were to be His (Ex. 13:12; Num. 3:12). That is, owners were to offer them as sacrifices to the Lord. But Mosaic law did not specify the occasion for sacrificing such firstlings, whether during the spring or autumn festivals. Of course, it would seem easier to shepherd six-month old lambs from one's home to the temple in the fall than to essentially carry newborns all the way to the sanctuary in the spring. Hence, the fall season, when everyone was to come to the temple for mandated holidays, may have been the time of year when most sacrifices of this sort were carried out.

Mormon also lists the items for which the crowd expressed their thanks to the Lord in prayer and sacrifice. For example, they offered "thanks to the Lord . . . who had brought them out of the land of Jerusalem," an expression that pointed backward to the safe arrival of the first family in the promised land (Mosiah 2:4). The rather formal way that Mormon summarizes the thanksgiving service raises the possibility that celebrating this earliest arrival had become part of a regularized ceremony now associated with the sacrifices, specifically peace offerings. The multitude had offered sacrifices, Mormon assures us, so "that they might rejoice," one of the purposes of peace offerings (2:4).[11] As an additional tie to the first family, worshipers typically sacrificed such offerings after experiencing safe travel, whether by land or sea (see Ps. 107:4–8, 19–32).

The other prayers of thanksgiving recited that day would also have fit with sacrificial worship. For the Lord "had delivered them out of the hands of their enemies," a phrase that mirrors the divine rescue in the Exodus of those under "the shadow of death" who were "bound in affliction" (Mosiah 2:4; Ps. 107:10, 14). For such divine aid, the redeemed were to "sacrifice the sacrifices of thanksgiving, and declare [the Lord's] works with rejoicing" (Ps. 107:22). Indeed, it was an occasion for thanksgiving.

CONNECTIONS TO ISRAELITE FESTIVALS

A number of studies by Latter-day Saints have sought links between certain dimensions of the coronation of Mosiah and one or another of the festivals known from the Old Testament.[12] The Bible, of course, mandated that Israelites celebrate three such feasts annually, as well as one fast. They were the feasts of Unleavened Bread, Weeks, and Booths, and the fast of the Day of Atonement. The festival of Unleavened Bread was tied to Passover, and Israelites celebrated them together. Following the exile of the people of Judah in Babylonia in the sixth century B.C., these occasions have kept their place in the religious calendar of Jews. The combined feast of Unleavened Bread and Passover occurs in the spring of the year, the festival of Weeks or Pentecost comes fifty days later, and the commemorations of Booths and Day of Atonement occur in the autumn. One problem facing researchers is the fact that no one knows whether these festivals occurred at the same time of year before the exile, that is, when Lehi and Sariah were still living in Jerusalem.[13] Thus, a person cannot be certain about the time of year when Lehi's descendants celebrated these festivals.

Even so, in events associated with Mosiah's coronation, a number of details point to a regular celebration.[14] We draw attention to only a few. As we have noticed, people traveled together in pilgrim fashion (see Mosiah 2:1), and camped in tents that were oriented to the temple (see 2:6). These activities recall the Israelite festival of Booths. In addition, the celebration included "sacrifice and burnt offerings according to the law of Moses" (2:3). Such sacrifices, of course, were part of ancient Israelite sacred occasions. Moreover, the activities took place at the sanctuary, as did all important Mosaic festivals, and involved the renewal of sacred covenants. In Lehi's day, the major Israelite festivals centered at Solomon's temple and also involved covenant renewal.[15]

In this connection, we must also be open to the possibility that the Nephites had shaped their celebrations to fit their obviously different circumstances. This possibility arises most directly when we ask the question as to how these people remembered the Lord's deliverance of their forebears from Jerusalem. From the record, as we have noticed, we sense that the Nephites may well have formalized this recollection as a part of the celebration that we are reviewing, whatever it was. As added proof, in writing of the days leading up to the coronation, Mormon records that King Benjamin, when handing over the brass plates and other tokens to his son, made pointed reference to the journey of their forebears through Arabia (see Mosiah 1:16–17). Afterward, when the crowd had gathered, they gave "thanks to the Lord their God, who had brought them out of the land of Jerusalem" (Mosiah 2:4). Finally, in his culminating speech, King Benjamin drew specific attention to Lehi by touching on "the prophecies which have been spoken by the holy prophets, even down to the time our father, Lehi, left Jerusalem" (2:34). It is these multiple references to the founding generation that lead to the real possibility that the Nephites had added to this festival a formal remembrance of their forebears' deliverance.

It is difficult, in contrast, to get a firm grasp on many dimensions of religious life outside the temple.[16] Before the unexpected arrival of Alma the Elder and his fellow colonists some seven years later, religion apparently consisted chiefly of worship practices established under the law of Moses, most of which took place at the temple (see

Jacob 1:17; 2:2). Events just prior to Benjamin's speech underscore this observation (see Mosiah 2:3). Although leaders had encouraged people to keep their focus on the coming Messiah and had taught them that the law of Moses pointed to Him (see Jacob 4:4–5), there seems to have been no religious organization like a church among the Nephites and people of Zarahemla in the days of Benjamin. To be sure, we learn that synagogues existed in certain eras, including the age of the founding generation (see 2 Ne. 26:26). But how synagogues functioned within Nephite society remains somewhat problematic, except to say that people gathered in them for worship. Perhaps we should understand that synagogues and then churches functioned in essentially the same way among Nephites. Not incidentally, in Lamanite society, synagogues became a feature of religious practice among Nephite dissidents who erected buildings for worship and, apparently, scripture study (see Alma 21:4–11; 22:7).[17] Hence, it may be safe to conclude that these dissidents had brought synagogue practices from their original Nephite homeland.

There is one final point. When one reads the words of King Benjamin to the effect that he had taught his people not to "commit any manner of wickedness" (Mosiah 2:13), we may be correct in seeing him measuring his doctrine by standards set out in the law of Moses against spiritual wickedness.[18] Although it is a full generation later that we read of the encroachment of idolatry and sorcery,[19] we may presume that such religious expressions existed in Benjamin's day, probably out of public view because of the moderate size of the society and because of Benjamin's forceful efforts to eliminate such.[20]

BENJAMIN'S ADDRESS

Recent studies have shown that the king's speech is a marvel.[21] It has survived in its entirety because scribes copied it and rehearsed it to those in the multitude who were too far away from the tower to hear (see Mosiah 2:8). Moreover, we know that Benjamin's words remained deeply influential in the society because later generations show a thorough acquaintance with them and thought them important enough to pass on to others (see Mosiah 8:3; Hel. 5:9). One might compare the American public's general acquaintance with, and esteem for, the Gettysburg Address of Abraham Lincoln.

The heart of the king's speech that day raised to view the majesty and goodness of God, who, in Benjamin's words, is a benevolent King. This view contrasts to the "nothingness" of humans (Mosiah 2:19; 4:11). Thus, for a person even to become a servant constituted a step upward. (This role of servant forms another major theme of Benjamin's remarks.) Further, the king, who placed himself between God and His people (e.g., 2:11, 19, 30, 31; 6:3), had modeled for his society the role of the benevolent king who is also servant, as is "the Lord Omnipotent" who comes down from His celestial throne to serve His people (3:5).

Hence, one focus of the message of Benjamin rested on *God the king, God the servant,* a focus that he tied to Jesus Christ. In Benjamin's case, being both king and servant, he had diligently carried out his duties in accord with his evident conception that he was merely imitating God. In fact, soon after beginning his speech, King Benjamin readily acknowledged his utter dependence on the Lord. "I have been . . . suffered by the hand of the Lord that I should be a ruler and a king over this people," he intoned, in order "to serve you with all the might, mind and strength which the Lord hath granted unto me" (Mosiah 2:11). Besides possibly repeating here some of the stipulations of his pledge of office,[22] the king recalls in his words the tri-partite relationship that had always existed in the terrestrial economy of God when He has called someone on earth to represent Him to His people: God – king – people. In addition, the king properly recognized the sources of his authority in that society: "this people . . . my father, and . . . the hand of the Lord" (Mosiah 2:11).

The opening of Benjamin's speech, verses 9–28, consists of a tidy accounting of his actions to his people, much as the prophet Samuel did shortly after selecting Saul to be king of Israel (see 1 Sam. 12). Indeed, it is possible that Benjamin modeled his own remarks on those of Samuel.[23] Benjamin's purpose in accounting for his actions was so "that I might rid my garments of your blood . . . that I might go down [to the grave] in peace" (Mosiah 2:28). Plainly, he had been a responsive, good king. In fact, his long discussion of his untiring efforts to rule in righteousness, underlining the duties of a monarch, seems to carry a subtle but clear message to Mosiah, his son and successor, about what he should do when he came to the throne (see

2:11–17). In the long run, we can easily see that Benjamin's actions did indeed influence those of his son when we consult the listing of Mosiah's virtues at the end of his own reign (see Mosiah 29:40).

Out of his lifelong service, Benjamin was able to coin important lessons for his hearers. One of the famous lines from his speech is, "when ye are in the service of your fellow beings ye are only in the service of your God." Then taking the notion of imitating God a step further, the king brought home to ordinary people a key principle that had characterized his own life: "[I]f I, whom ye call your king, do labor to serve you, then ought not ye to labor to serve one another?" Further, employing almost identical terms, "if I, whom ye call your king . . . do merit any thanks from you, O how you ought to thank your heavenly King!" (Mosiah 2:17–19). What was good for the king was also good for his fellow citizens. And as his life drew to a close, he hoped to "answer a clear conscience before God" (2:15).

. . . MADE KNOWN UNTO ME BY AN ANGEL

In a moment that must have caused a stir about midway through his address, the king unveiled his unexpected experience with an angel (see Mosiah 3:2–3). It had probably happened at night, for the angel woke him from sleep. This appearance to the king had evidently come well in advance of the assembly, for the angel speaks as if it is in the future: "when thou shalt have taught thy people" (3:22; see 5:5). In this connection, it should not surprise us that the angel's message came to offer a framework of sorts for Benjamin's address. While this observation may seem self evident—after all, who would not want to follow the lead of an angel?—it does allow us to suggest how the angel's message influenced that of the king. First, the king cites the angel as a source for some of his remarks. For example, in a summarizing declaration about those who "have come to the knowledge of the glory of God," he notes that his summary arises from that "which was spoken by the mouth of the angel" (4:11). Second, phrases and terminology of the angel enliven the language of Benjamin. We highlight three examples.

First, anticipating the act of conferring the name of Christ on the multitude, Benjamin must have happily quoted the angel as saying, "there shall be no other name given . . . [for] salvation . . . [except]

the name of Christ, the Lord Omnipotent" (Mosiah 3:17). As previously mentioned, in the preparation stages of his address, when directing his son Mosiah to summon citizens for the coronation, the king had divulged that he would confer a name on his hearers: "I shall give this people a name" that "never shall be blotted out, except it be through transgression." This name, he affirmed, would make his people "distinguished above all the people which the Lord God hath brought out of the land of Jerusalem" (Mosiah 1:11–12). One of his intents, of course, was to unify the two people in his domain, the people of Nephi and those of Zarahemla, who had each come "out of the land of Jerusalem" by a different route, under a national covenant (2:4). In fact, the Lord had guided each group (see 2 Ne. 1:6; Omni 1:16). More than this, however, Benjamin sought to put his people under "covenant with God" that they "be called by the name of Christ" (Mosiah 5:8–9). "This is the name," he announced, that they should "retain . . . always in [their] hearts" (5:11–12). This name is most significant because by it the Lord "shall call" his own people so that they "may be brought to heaven," presumably by an escort, and thereafter enjoy "everlasting salvation" (5:12, 15).

Second, one thinks of expressions reminiscent of temple sacrifice. For example, one looks for and finds reference to fire and smoke associated with an altar. In fact, it is the angel who first brought forward language that recalls sacrifice. He declares that the torment of the wicked "is as a lake of *fire* . . . whose *flames* . . . and whose *smoke ascendeth up*" (Mosiah 3:27; emphasis added). Similarly, in a passage that reinforces the observation that Benjamin borrowed language from the angel, the king speaks of a wicked person's "lively sense of . . . guilt" which fills the soul with "guilt, and pain" that are "like an unquenchable fire, whose flame ascendeth up" (2:38). This passage may be doubly tied to sacrificial imagery by the king's accompanying reference to "the presence of the Lord," which could also point to the altar itself, a consecrated structure that aided a person in gaining access to the presence of God (2:38).

Third, references to blood present a natural link to sacrifice. Again, it is the angel who raises the subject in connection with the future suffering of Jesus Christ: "behold, blood cometh from every pore, so great shall be his anguish for the wickedness . . . of his people" (Mosiah 3:9). Then, in reviewing the place of the law of Moses in the scheme of salvation, the angel declares "that the law of Moses availeth nothing except it were through . . . [Jesus'] blood" (3:15). He further points out that "the blood of Christ atoneth for [the] sins" of "little children" (3:16). The king follows the angel's lead in his remarks, altering the context of the term blood, but keeping temple allusions intact. He intones, "I had served you . . . that I might be found blameless, and that your blood should not come upon me, when I shall stand to be judged" (2:27; also 2:28). Benjamin's words recall vividly the ceremonial cleansing both of people making covenant as well as of the garments of priests at the time of their ordination, in each case by sprinkling sacrificial blood on the clothing (see Ex. 24:8; 29:21; also Mosiah 4:2).[24]

The angel also bequeathed to us one of the most sublime declarations in all of scripture about the coming Christ and His Atonement. Hymnic in its character, it bears distant similarities to the hymn embedded in Paul's letter to the Philippians, which speaks of the Savior's descent from heavenly realms to participate in this world before His sacrificial death and return to His exalted station (see Phil. 2:6–11). The angel's masterful language, which also ties to the theme of deliverance, falls out in balancing lines whose emphatic center features the Savior's redeeming blood.

For behold,
    the time cometh,
    and is not far distant,
        that with power,
the Lord Omnipotent
        who reigneth,
        who was,
        and is
                from all eternity to all eternity,
    shall come down from heaven among the children of men,
    and shall dwell in a tabernacle of clay,
    and shall go forth amongst men,
        working mighty miracles,
                such as healing the sick,

raising the dead,
causing the lame to walk,
the blind to receive their sight,
and the deaf to hear,
and curing all manner of diseases.
And he shall cast out devils,
or the evil spirits which dwell in the hearts of the children of men.
And lo, he shall suffer temptations,
and pain of body,
hunger,
thirst,
and fatigue,
even more than man can suffer, except it be unto death;
for behold, blood cometh from every pore,
so great shall be his anguish for
the wickedness
and the abominations of his people.
And he shall be called Jesus Christ,
the Son of God,
the Father of heaven and earth,
the Creator of all things from the beginning;
and his mother shall be called Mary.
And lo, he cometh unto his own,
that salvation might come unto the children of men
even through faith on his name;
and even after all this
they shall consider him a man,
and say that he hath a devil,
and shall scourge him,
and shall crucify him.
And he shall rise the third day from the dead;
and behold, he standeth to judge the world;
and behold, all these things are done
that a righteous judgment might come upon the children of men. (Mosiah 3:5–10)

INDIVIDUAL COVENANTS

One of the king's prime purposes for gathering his people was to guide them into making a covenant with their God. To borrow his words, it meant that they clothe themselves as if with a name (see Mosiah 5:8). As we have seen, the king had announced to Mosiah, "I shall give this people a name, that thereby they may be distinguished above all the people which the Lord God hath brought out of the land of Jerusalem" (1:11). Benjamin knew of two such peoples led from Jerusalem: his own and the people of Zarahemla. And they both sat before him. He was right to suppose that there were others, though not in the New World.[25] Later, near the end of his speech, his now inspired hearers declared that "we are willing to enter into a covenant with our God" (5:5). To this declaration the king replied, repeating terms that recall donning a robe or garment, an act that carries overtones for temple worship: "I would that ye should *take upon you* the name of Christ, all you that have entered into the covenant with God" (5:8; emphasis added). By doing so, they then became "the children of Christ, his sons and his daughters; for behold, this day he hath spiritually begotten you" (5:7).

In ancient cultures, covenants were frequently communal rather than individual. But because Benjamin used expressions such as "this is the man" (Mosiah 4:7) and "O man" (4:18), he evidently thought of the covenant process on one level as singling out individuals. It was within the embrace of this covenant, wherein individuals had pledged "to be obedient to [God's] commandments in all things that he shall command" (Mosiah 5:5), that one was "made free" (5:8) and thereafter became an heir of Christ, "spiritually begotten" by Him (5:7). Thus the covenant became the lifting agent that elevated a person from the status of a "beggar" to that of an heir (4:16, 19–20; 5:7–8).[26]

NATIONAL COVENANT

Benjamin was not content to allow his people to take up only one dimension of covenant-making. He knew the long-term value of unifying his people who were made up of large families and clans. On the model of the covenant at Sinai between God and the former Hebrew slaves, the king sought to weld his people, as a unified whole, to their God. In effect, it was to be a national covenant founded on heavenly principles of obedience to divine law. To be sure, the law of Moses already conferred a certain level of cultural and religious unity onto Benjamin's fellow citizens. But centering individual covenants onto Christ meant that the king could also ask his people as a group to reach for a higher plane. It was worth a try, and he succeeded marvelously.

Viewed in legal terms, the king's accounting of his actions before his people mirror in part the laws given by God to the Israelites at Sinai (see Mosiah 2:9–28). Called by some "the holiness code," these laws appear in the Old Testament soon after the Ten Commandments, in some cases adding detail to them (see Ex. 21–23). Among other matters, they deal with personal interactions, personal property, penalties or fines, and slavery. Benjamin addressed each of these topics in his speech, in some cases lining up with the biblical law and in others departing from it. The most notable departure involved forbidding any institution whereby one person could become the slave or servant of another, a sometimes necessary but demeaning aspect of economic life permitted under the Mosaic law (see Mosiah 2:13; Ex. 21:2–6).[27] In contrast, an affirmation of biblical law comes in the king's rhetorical question, "[D]oth a man take an ass which belongeth to his neighbor, and keep him? I say unto you, Nay" (Mosiah 5:14). Such a sentiment also links back to law found in the "holiness code" (see Ex. 22:1).

In addition to remarks that remind one of the "holiness code" pronounced by God at Sinai, one finds allusions early in Benjamin's speech to the Ten Commandments themselves. For example, he affirms that he did not allow his subjects to "murder, or plunder, or steal, or commit adultery," a list that ties comfortably to the commandments received by Moses (Mosiah 2:13).

In the end, of course, the people responded with oneness as Benjamin wanted, each person repeating "the words which king Benjamin desired of them" (Mosiah 5:6). In response to his message, they acknowledged that they "believe[d] all the words which [the king had] spoken" (5:2). Further, they affirmed unitedly, "we are willing to enter into a covenant with our God to do his will . . . all the remainder of our days" (5:5). In a final scene, we learn that "there was not one soul, except it were little children, but who had entered into a covenant and had taken upon them the name of Christ" (6:2). Clearly, Benjamin had succeeded in establishing a unifying covenant under the Savior among all his citizens.

Even so, there is evidence that the national unity we see at the end of Benjamin's speech was rather fragile. We know, for example, that many children grew up without feeling loyalty to the principles that Benjamin espoused (see Mosiah 26:1–5). Further, people of the realm stood essentially and visibly divided along ethnic lines seven years later when Mosiah called his people together in order to welcome the two groups of colonists who had recently returned and to hear the reports of their experiences (see 25:1–6). People plainly felt more comfortable with those of their own kind. The fact that Benjamin and, in his turn, Mosiah were able to maintain a firm unity among their people during their reigns—they were all Israelites, of course—may be attributed in part to their governing skills and personal charisma rather than to any naturally cohesive force between the clans whom they ruled.

CORONATION

The public coronation of Mosiah apparently occurred after Benjamin finished his speech. But first a numbering took place, a census of sorts. As mentioned before, this act had not been carried out earlier as biblical law required, an omission that Mormon had noted (see Mosiah 2:2). At the end of the sermon, the purpose of numbering was to keep track of people by taking "the names of all those who had entered into a covenant with God to keep his commandments" (Mosiah 6:1). We then read that "when king Benjamin had made an end of all these things . . . [he] consecrated his son Mosiah to be a ruler and a king over his people" (6:3). Presumably, the consecration involved an anointing at a specific place in the temple, evidently in the presence of witnesses. The witnesses probably included the men who at the time were "appointed priests to teach the people" (6:3). How the new king made the decision about those whom he appointed to be priests we do not learn. But his action of choosing his own counselors and priests on this day seems to follow ancient precedent among Israelites which Benjamin himself had apparently followed (see 1 Kgs. 2:26–27, 35; 12:8; W of M 1:16–18). In a notable change, years later Mosiah transferred this responsibility of choosing priests to the spiritual leader of the church, Alma the Elder (see Mosiah 25:19).

The coronation also involved other activities. There may have been a public acclamation for Mosiah as there evidently had been for Benjamin: "I have been chosen by this people," he had recalled (Mosiah 2:11). Further, Benjamin gave Mosiah "all the charges concerning the kingdom" (6:3). This possibly involved the new king in some sort of oath making, perhaps including words that Benjamin may have highlighted earlier from his own coronation (see 2:11).[28]

Mormon's narrative tells us that, as his last official act, King Benjamin "dismissed the multitude," now a unified covenant nation under his son, "and they returned . . . to their own houses" (Mosiah 6:3). Even in retreat, the crowd was orderly, an aspect that must have impressed Mormon. For people "returned, every one, according to their families" (6:3). One remembers, of course, the orderly march of the children of Israel through the deserts after their flight from Egypt. It seems apparent that, even in returning home, Benjamin's fellow citizens observed an order that recalled this earlier era when their ancestors enjoyed the presence of God among them. Perhaps their actions also represented an attempt to hold on to the joy that they had felt when the Divine Spirit had descended on them while they listened to their beloved king (see 4:1–3; 5:2). For "the Spirit of the Lord came upon them, and they were filled with joy" (4:3). Thus, not only had Benjamin effected covenants among his people, but their receptiveness to the "Spirit of the Lord" had brought joy and order among them, aspects of life that would continue into the newly inaugurated reign of Mosiah.

THE DAY ENDS

It had been a long day. Remarkably, there seems to have been no rain or bad weather. And the children seem to have behaved rather well. By this point, we may imagine that the slanting sun was silently stretching the shadows of buildings and trees across the field where the tents and huts had shaded listeners from the warmth of the day. But even as the shadows grew longer, it was as if a new day had dawned, fresh and crisp and clean. It was as if the old king had escorted his people into a valley. Before them gleamed a celestial land that was green and bathed in the full light of a golden sun. Looking back on the extraordinary experiences of that day, one wonders quietly whether at any time the people had burst into spontaneous singing.

NOTES TO CHAPTER 3

1. On the book of Mosiah, see Alan Goff, "The Book of Mormon: The Book of Mosiah," *Encyclopedia of Mormonism,* Daniel H. Ludlow et al., eds. (New York: Macmillan, 1992), 149–50; S. Kent Brown, "Mosiah, book of," *Book of Mormon Reference Companion,* Dennis L. Largey et al., eds. (Salt Lake City: Deseret Book, 2003), 570–73.
2. Phrases such as "the land round about," which describe Zarahemla, the capital city, point to a rather compactly settled population (Mosiah 27:2). Consult John L. Sorenson, *Mormon's Map* (Provo, Utah: FARMS, 2000), 61–62.
3. The first note of wide expansion occurs at Mosiah 27:6, more than twenty-five years after Mosiah's coronation. We read that "the people . . . began to scatter abroad . . . building large cities and villages in all quarters of the land." It is this situation that required Alma the Younger to travel far in his missionary labors (see Alma 7–15).
4. See Omni 1:24; W of M 1:13–14; compare also Omni 1:17, which notes heavy losses among the people of Zarahemla in civil war, and Alma 44:21, which refers to heavy casualties in a series of battles almost fifty years after Benjamin's death.
5. Mosiah was a co-regent with his father Benjamin for three years (see Mosiah 6:5). Then after another three years, evidently in the seventh year of his reign, Mosiah sent a squad of soldiers to find those in the colony, now led by King Limhi (6:7; 7:1–2). The soldiers returned with the colonists in the same year (22:11–14). Apparently Alma's colony arrived within weeks or months of Limhi's arrival (see 24:18–25:6).
6. These settlements, military or otherwise, were evidently not in place when King Limhi's squad of soldiers went in search of Zarahemla and instead found their way into the land northward and back without meeting anyone (see Mosiah 8:7–11; 21:25–27). The soldiers returned to Limhi "not many days before" the coming of Mosiah's squad of soldiers that he had sent in the seventh year of his reign to find Limhi's colony (21:26). On keeping Lamanites out of the land northward, see Alma 22:29, 33; 50:7–15; etc. Consult Sorenson, *Mormon's Map,* 26–28.

7. The key term here for covenant making is to give or to grant (Hebrew *ntn*); see Gen. 9:12 and 17:2 where this term occurs.

8. See John W. Welch, "The Law of Mosiah," in *Reexploring the Book of Mormon,* John W. Welch, ed. (Salt Lake City: Deseret Book, and FARMS, 1992), 158–61.

9. Consult Stephen D. Ricks, "The Coronation of Kings," in *Reexploring the Book of Mormon,* 124–26.

10. The law on "firstlings" is set out in Deut. 15:19–29; for "burnt offerings," see Lev. 1. Consult also John A. Tvedtnes and Matthew Roper, *Animals in the Book of Mormon,* chap. 12 (unpublished manuscript).

11. See Jacob Milgrom, *Leviticus 1–16, The Anchor Bible* (New York: Doubleday, 1991), 204, 217–219.

12. Terrence L. Szink and John W. Welch have gathered the references in their study, "King Benjamin's Speech in the Context of Ancient Israelite Festivals," in *King Benjamin's Speech,* John W. Welch and Stephen D. Ricks, eds. (Provo, Utah: FARMS, 1998), 203.

13. See the very helpful discussion by James C. Vanderkam, "Calendars: Ancient Israelite and Early Jewish," in *The Anchor Bible Dictionary,* 6 vols., David Noel Freedman et al., eds. (New York: Doubleday, 1992), 1:814–20.

14. Szink and Welch have suggested a series of possible ties in their article, "King Benjamin's Speech in the Context of Ancient Israelite Festivals," in *King Benjamin's Speech,* 147–223.

15. See Stephen D. Ricks' study on these issues, "Kingship, Coronation and Covenant in Mosiah 1–6," in *King Benjamin's Speech,* 233–75.

16. For a brief treatment, consult John W. Welch, "Book of Mormon Religious Teachings and Practices," *Encyclopedia of Mormonism,* 201–5.

17. On synagogues, consult William J. Adams Jr., "Synagogues in the Book of Mormon," *Journal of Book of Mormon Studies* 9, no. 1 (2000): 4–13.

18. Lev. 19:31; 20:6, 27; Deut. 18:9–14.

19. Mosiah 27:8 speaks of Alma the Younger as "an idolatrous man" and another source speaks of the presence of "priestcraft" and those who engaged "in sorceries, and in idolatry or idleness, and in babblings" (Alma 1:12, 32).

20. On popular religion, see John L. Sorenson, "Religious Groups and Movements among the Nephites, 200–1 B.C.," in *The Disciple as Scholar: Essays on Scripture and the Ancient World in Honor of Richard Lloyd Anderson,* Stephen D. Ricks, Donald W. Parry, and Andrew H. Hedges, eds. (Provo, Utah: FARMS, 2000), 163–208.

21. The most recent assessments include the collected studies in *King Benjamin's Speech,* edited by Welch and Ricks.

22. The passage (Mosiah 2:11) exhibits formal traits that Benjamin may have drawn from his pledge of office, including the verb "granted" (Hebrew *ntn,* "to give, to grant"), which may point to covenant making (the same verb connects to covenants in Gen. 9:12; 17:2). Benjamin's reference to such a pledge may have offered reassurance to his hearers that he had fulfilled his obligation. Expressions such as "might, mind and strength" may rest on passages such as Deut. 6:5; 11:1; 30:6, 16. These terms, which Benjamin drew on, were framed earlier by Nephi (see 2 Ne. 25:29).
23. The similarities are impressive between the early part of Benjamin's speech and that of Samuel. Further, one can see similarities with Moses (Num. 16:15; Deut. 26:13–14) and Job (Job 31). John Tvedtnes has noted the possible links to Samuel's address (1 Samuel 12) as well as to those of Joshua (Josh. 23–24) and David (1 Chron. 28–29) near the end of their lives ("King Benjamin and the Feast of Tabernacles," in *By Study and Also by Faith,* 2 vols., John M. Lundquist and Stephen D. Ricks, eds. [Salt Lake City: Deseret Book and FARMS, 1990], 2:210–213, 219). Such ties are reviewed by John W. Welch and Daryl R. Hague, "Benjamin's Sermon as a Traditional Ancient Farewell Address," in *King Benjamin's Speech,* 89–145, especially 90 and 104.
24. There are other temple connections in the words of the angel that Benjamin latched onto. I note two. One lies in allusions to the creation. From the biblical Psalms we learn that worshipers coming to the temple sang about God's creative acts of old (e.g., Ps. 24:1–2). Following the lead of the angel, who speaks of Jesus as "the Creator of all things from the beginning," (Mosiah 3:8), the king also affirms that God has "created you from the beginning" (2:20–21). More to the point, the people acclaim that it was "Jesus Christ . . . who created heaven and earth" (4:2; also 4:9; 5:15). According to Benjamin, the Atonement itself was "prepared from the foundation of the world" (4:6–7), a reference to God's organizing acts before the creation.

    The second has to do with drinking, which recalls actions in sacred places. For instance, Moses and Aaron and a select group of priesthood holders ratified the covenant between the Lord and the Israelites by ascending the holy mount where they "did eat and drink" in God's presence (Ex. 24:9–11). One also recalls drink offerings mandated by the law of Moses that were to be brought to the altar (Ex. 29:40; Lev. 23:13; etc.). In the scene under review, the angel raises the act of drinking. In this case, drink has to do with damnation that results when one breaks a covenant: "men drink damnation to their own souls except they humble themselves and become as little children" (Mosiah 3:18; also 3:25). A second passage tightens the imagery and ties the drinking to the smoke and fire of the altar. Speaking of those who are not "blameless in the sight of God," the angel warns that "they have drunk out of the cup of the wrath of God" (3:22, 26). It is these, he affirms, whose "torment is as a lake of fire . . . whose smoke ascendeth up" (3:27). In his turn, the king sketches a similar picture. For the unrepentant person who "remaineth and dieth in his sins, the same drinketh damnation to his own soul" (2:33). Likewise, Benjamin's hearers pray for a way that they might "not drink out of the cup of the wrath of God" (5:5).

25. There are a number of important references to those whom the Lord led away from Jerusalem, including 1 Ne. 22:4; 2 Ne. 10:22; Jacob 5:3–14.

26. On the whole question of covenants in this scene, see Ricks, "Kingship, Coronation and Covenant in Mosiah 1–6," *King Benjamin's Speech,* 254–60.

27. Welch touches on this issue in "A Masterful Oration," *King Benjamin's Speech,* 40, 58.

28. Ricks offers a description of such a scene for the coronation of Israelite kings in "Kingship, Coronation, and Covenant in Mosiah 1–6," *King Benjamin's Speech,* 244–54.

Royal Missionaries

CHAPTER FOUR

Breathing hard from the climb, Aaron turned and gazed back at the five other men[1] *who were following him up the canyon. Although he was agile and strong from the years of physical training that he had received as a Nephite prince, the climb was taxing and his efforts to push through the brush were draining his strength. He then let his eyes rise slightly higher. Miles behind them he could see the last Nephite outpost on the southern frontier. The town was framed by the V-shaped canyon. Surrounding the settlement lay cultivated fields of corn and grain just coming to maturity. It would be the last time he would see a Nephite town for fourteen years.*

Aaron and the others had committed themselves to preaching the gospel message to people who were their enemies. Though there were no roads that connected the two peoples, the six companions knew from the accounts of earlier travelers that they had to travel southward and upward to reach the lands of the Lamanites. Aaron turned and began climbing again with a determination that would sustain him and the other five through reversals and reprisals. Eventually, tens of thousands would come to Christ through their ministry. But their success would come at a high cost both to themselves and to the Lamanite hegemony, for most of the missionaries would endure painful personal privation and public rejection. And the Lamanite kingdom would fall into a debilitating civil war which would force the missionaries' converts, including the royal house, to flee their homes and lands, throwing themselves on the mercy of the Nephite nation with whom they had fought a long series of devastating wars.

PROLOGUE

The missionaries had certainly not intended to disrupt political and social life among the Lamanites. But that is exactly what they did. As their successes rose, opponents stiffened their resolve to rid their society of the missionaries, no matter the cost. Because the Lamanite royal family embraced the new message, and even decreed protections for the Nephite preachers, the effect of the schism was blindingly clear: civil war. The object of those who refused to accept the gospel was not simply to bring down the long-lived and secure monarchy, which had evidently survived more than 400 years. They also wanted to eliminate Lamanite adherents to the new church as well as Lamanite preachers who were traveling among their own people seeking to spread the missionary message (see Alma 23:4). Such aims underscore both the astonishing strength of the opposition to the new religion and the enormously persuasive power of the opposition leaders to organize a resistance, which could—and did—bring down the oldest political institution in Lamanite society.

THE BROTHERS' PAST

Only a few years back, Aaron and his three brothers had been in no position to preach to others. They and a friend named Alma had led an effort to undo the good that their fathers had been trying to accomplish (see Mosiah 27:8–10). And it wasn't as though their fathers did not hold high positions in the society: Aaron's father was the king and Alma's was the head of the church. In the words of Mormon, the sons had been "the very vilest of sinners" (Mosiah 28:4). Aaron's father, Mosiah, would be the last monarch to rule the Nephite people. Aaron's great-grandfather, also named Mosiah, had fled the land of Lehi-Nephi when God had warned him that he and his people should depart (see Omni 1:12). Now Aaron, his three brothers and two companions were trudging toward the land of Lehi-Nephi to preach to Lamanites who had taken over the territory.

We know very little about the youth of the four princes. And all we know about their two companions is that the four brothers selected them to accompany the princes on their mission to the Lamanites (see Mosiah 28:1; Alma 17:8). There are clear indicators, of course, that these two companions shared in the vicissitudes and rewards of the missionary labor (see Alma 20:2; 21:11, 13; 23:1; 25:17). But we hear no more of them after their mission ended.

Concerning these four princes, we can safely assume that they had received the best education that was available to youths of their day. As in the case of their father, such an education included literary, religious, and physical or military training (see Mosiah 1:2–3; Alma 17:34–37). But at some point they had agreed with Alma the younger to attempt to destroy the struggling church that Alma's father had established only a few years earlier (see Mosiah 27:8–10; Alma 26:18). Mormon calls the younger Alma "a very wicked and an idolatrous man," presumably meaning that he—and very possibly his friends—had embraced the worship of idols (Mosiah 27:8). In the light of Mormon's statement that these five friends had been "the very vilest of sinners" (Mosiah 28:4), it would not be out of order to say that these men had much to repent of, which they eventually did (see Mosiah 28:3–4; Alma 26:17; 36:24).

But their repentance came about in a highly unusual way. In effect, they received a heavenly push from an angel. As a result of the prayers of their parents and others, an angel appeared to the five friends, shouting at them in "a voice of thunder" and causing a minor earthquake in the process (Mosiah 27:11, 14–5). We know that the five of them fell to the earth at least twice during the angel's deafening speech wherein he called on them to repent (see 27:12, 18). Although Alma needed three days to recover, the four brothers seem to have regained their senses rather quickly; for they were able to carry Alma to his father and recount their experience to him (see 27:19–20). The appearance of the angel began to turn these five young men to the Lord. In Alma's words, they had been "born again"; they had been "born of God" (Mosiah 27:25).

The conversion experience of the four brothers carried almost immediate consequences for the future of the Nephite kingdom. First, each of them set aside any aspiration to succeed Mosiah as king. Instead, to a person, they wanted to go on a mission to teach their enemies, the Lamanites (see Mosiah 28:1–3, 5). And Mormon offers no clue why they came to this decision. Second, when their father interviewed each of them, he found himself unable to persuade any of the brothers to accept the crown (see Mosiah 29:3).

We can readily understand Mosiah's reluctance to let his sons step away from their obligations to the kingdom and then travel among his enemies as missionaries. In fact, the biggest challenge for the brothers, after refusing "the kingdom which their father was desirous to confer upon them" (Alma 17:6), was to convince their father to allow them to go. They did not want to undertake the mission without his blessing. Mormon writes that the brothers pestered Mosiah, pleading "with their father many days that they might go up to the land of Nephi" to preach (Mosiah 28:5). It was only after the Lord had promised divine protection that the king granted his permission: "Let them go up," said the Lord with a pledge, "for many shall believe on their words . . . and I will deliver thy sons out of the hands of the Lamanites" (Mosiah 28:7). So with the Lord's assurances ringing in his mind, Mosiah permitted his sons to go as missionaries to his enemies, never to see them again in his mortal life (see Mosiah 28:6–9).

Because his sons refused to rule the kingdom, Mosiah initiated a change of government among his people. He abolished the monarchy that had persisted for almost 500 years and introduced a system of popularly elected officials who were called judges (see Mosiah 29:37–41). The younger Alma, who did not join his four friends on their mission, was elected "to be the first chief judge," the first non-king to serve as head of state among the Nephites since the days of Lehi. In addition, Alma also bore the responsibility of head of the church, "the high priest." Alma's father "conferred [this] office upon him" and gave "him the charge concerning all the affairs of the church" (Mosiah 29:42). Although Alma resigned his political post eight years later in order to tend the affairs of the church full time (see Alma 4:11–17), the era of government by judges persisted for the next 120 years.

THE MISSION BEGINS

Rather than staying to celebrate the change of affairs in the kingdom, the four missionary brothers took "leave of their father" in the year of governmental transition and "departed out of the land of Zarahemla . . . to go up . . . to preach the word of God unto the Lamanites" with their two companions. In a way, it was fortuitous that the brothers, the most visible reminders of the permanency of the monarchy, were not around during the transition. Their presence may have complicated the transition even more for Alma and the other elected officials. For within five years there was a serious movement to restore the monarchy, first by referendum and then by civil war (see Alma 2).

On their journey, the brothers naturally carried weapons to "provide food for themselves." It was a long way to travel, and they spent "many days in the wilderness." While traveling, "they fasted much and prayed much that the Lord would grant unto them a portion of his Spirit." In response, the Lord honored their request and "did visit them with his Spirit." Subtly warning the six men of future difficulties, the Lord commanded, "Go forth among . . . thy brethren, and . . . ye shall be patient in long-suffering and afflictions, that ye may show forth good examples unto them in me." Further, the Lord intoned, "I will make an instrument of thee in my hands unto the salvation of many souls" (Alma 17:6–11; also 26:27). The six missionaries each now had a divine commission and warning. It was time to go to work. So they split up, each person going in a different direction to share the gospel with the Lamanites.

THE LAMANITES

The ethnic makeup of the Lamanite people must have been rather diverse during this era. For example, Mormon makes us aware of two distinct groups whose origins were tied to the Nephites and possibly to the people of Zarahemla, although it is not obvious whether they came chiefly from one or the other of these peoples. They were the Amalekites and the Amulonites (see Alma 21:3). In addition, three generations earlier a certain segment of the original Nephite population had remained behind in the land of Nephi when Lamanites had forced their way into the region. For, when Mosiah, the great-grandfather of the four brothers, had fled that area because of Lamanite encroachment, some Nephites had remained behind, namely, those who would not "hearken unto the voice of the Lord" (Omni

1:12–13). Mormon also speaks of others who were unhappy after the initial uniting of the Nephites and people of Zarahemla. They were dissenters who withdrew "unto the Lamanites" (W of M 1:16; also Jarom 1:13). Further, there were the "Lamanitish servants" whom Ammon, one of the four brothers, would meet (Alma 17:26). They may have been from a people enslaved by the Lamanites and thus been of separate origin. It is also possible that the Lamanites had absorbed other peoples into their population over the years, although there is no other record of such. Even so, we can see that the Lamanite people embraced a number of different groups in this era.[2]

The six Nephite missionaries, of course, were taking huge risks. Lamanites did not feel obliged to extend hospitality to strangers who wandered into their midst. In fact, over the years Lamanite rulers had adopted the policy of arresting and binding "all the Nephites who fell into their hands." Such individuals were then taken "before the king" who, depending on his mood, might "slay them, or . . . retain them in captivity, or . . . cast them into prison, or . . . cast them out of his land" (Alma 17:20). There were no guarantees what one's fate might be in this situation.

AMMON IN THE LAND OF ISHMAEL

Most of the events highlighted in Alma, chapters 17–22, featuring the spectacular conversion of two royal households, could have taken place within a few weeks or months. The bulk of the fourteen years, it seems, rolled out after the official proclamation that protected the missionaries (see Alma 23:1). In chapters 23 and 24, Mormon chronicles the conversion of entire cities and towns, a process that must have required a lot of time, as well as sketching out the darkening opposition moving against the missionaries and their converts. This latter development would also have taken considerable time because its growing intensity eventually led to civil war in a kingdom that apparently had enjoyed a long period of peace.

Mormon's narrative first follows the brother Ammon whose initial success was the most impressive and spectacular. It became so because the Lord used Ammon as His instrument in converting virtually an entire segment of the population. It all happened after Ammon was able to meet and influence the regent king, a man named Lamoni.

For whatever reason, when "Ammon was carried before the king"—it is almost as if the king's subordinates had lifted and carried Ammon in some way (Alma 17:21)—the two men seemed to hit it off. We also suspect that before their meeting, Lamoni had learned Ammon's identity as a Nephite prince.

Mormon hints that the two went quickly to the heart of the matter before them, that is, what Ammon's status would be in Lamoni's realm. During the process, King Lamoni offered to the newcomer one of his daughters as a wife. It would have been a political coup, of course, for Lamoni to marry his daughter to a Nephite prince. But the issue is more complex than we might appreciate at first. Both men seemed to understand that Ammon's new status in the Lamanite realm could be linked to Ammon's former status back home, that of a prince. But Ammon refused to allow his royal standing to enter the discussion. Instead, Ammon evidently appealed to the well-known Israelite law that allowed him to become a servant for a limited period (up to six years) or, after seeing whether he liked his situation, forever (see Alma 17:23; Deut. 15:12–18). In the end, of course, they agreed that Ammon "will be [Lamoni's] servant," presumably for a limited period (Alma 17:25).[3]

The event that shaped the future of missionary work in Lamoni's realm occurred three days later when Ammon was in the company of other "Lamanitish servants going forth with [the king's] flocks to the place of water" (Alma 17:26). Although, as we have noted, we do not know whether Mormon's expression "Lamanitish servants" refers to servants of Lamanite origin or to individuals from another people who had been enslaved by the Lamanites, we do know that Ammon saved both the king's flocks from rustlers and his fellow servants from execution. Significantly, this incident proved Ammon's loyalty to Lamoni, his master. Ammon, who had started out to impress his fellow servants, ended up impressing the king and his court.

We must bear in mind that Ammon was a skilled warrior, largely because of his training in the house of his father, the Nephite king. So when he and the other servants went "forth with their flocks to the place of water, which was called the water of Sebus," and "a certain number of Lamanites . . . scattered [their] flocks," Ammon was by training almost a match for those who sought to steal any stray animals (Alma 17:26–27). But because he carried the power of the Lord so that, in the words of his fellow servants, "he cannot be slain," he was more than a match (Alma 18:3).

The day began normally with Ammon working with the other servants to tend the king's flocks. But it all changed about midday when they took the flocks to water. At the "water of Sebus" other shepherds purposely frightened the king's flocks so that they would scatter. These shepherds intended to round them up later for themselves (see Alma 17:27; 18:7). When the king's servants "began to weep exceedingly" because they feared that the king would execute them for losing some of the animals, Ammon saw his chance to "win the hearts of these my fellow-servants" by leading them to recover the flocks and bring them back to water (17:28–29). At that moment, he likely had no idea that his actions would also make a dramatic impact on the king and thus on his hopes to bring the gospel message to the Lamanites.

A trained leader, Ammon organized his fellow servants and led them in a swift recovery of the flocks. But when they later returned with the flocks to the watering place, they found the same thieving shepherds lurking menacingly. What to do? Ammon, knowing of "the [Lord's] power which is in me" (Alma 17:29), "went forth . . . to contend with those who stood by the waters of Sebus" (17:34). It did not take long for him to disrupt the plans of the smug shepherds. He first "began to cast stones at them with his sling," slinging rocks "with mighty power" such that he slew "six of them" with stones (Alma 17:36, 38). He then killed a seventh, "their leader[,] with his sword" (17:38). The remaining thieves, at first "astonished at his power" and then "seeing that they could not hit him with their stones," became enraged "because of the slain of their brethren" (17:36). They foolishly decided to rush Ammon in an effort to overwhelm him. But their attack failed. Instead, he "smote off their arms" when any of them "lifted his club to smite Ammon" (17:37). Cowed, the remaining shepherds fled. It had not been a good day for them.

On their part, Ammon's fellow servants were ecstatic. Hastily they gathered up the arms which Ammon had hacked off, possibly also taking an arm from each of the other seven bodies, so that they could show everyone the proof of Ammon's heroic efforts. (This practice of removing the hands of dead soldiers for the sake of an accurate body count is attested from other parts of the ancient world.[4]) Although Mormon says merely that the servants "returned [the flocks] to the pasture of the king" after watering them, they must have spent the balance of the afternoon in excited conversation. When the flocks were safely in their place for the night, the servants breathlessly "went in unto the king, bearing the arms . . . of those who sought to slay" Ammon. The detached arms, of course, lay limply as "a testimony" of Ammon's bold actions (Alma 17:39).

After the king had heard his servants stirringly "testify to all the things which they had seen" during that day, he "was astonished exceedingly" and then "began to fear exceedingly" (Alma 18:1–2, 5). Quite naturally, he concluded that Ammon was "the Great Spirit" who had "come down . . . to preserve" the lives of the servants, protecting them from execution (18:2, 4). But what stunned him even more was the information that, after returning the flocks "to the pasture of the king" (17:39), Ammon had gone dutifully to the royal stables to feed the king's horses and to "prepare his horses and chariots" for a trip "to the land of Nephi" for "a great feast appointed . . . by the father of Lamoni, who was king over all the land" (18:9). Lamoni had been impressed initially by "the faithfulness of Ammon in preserving his flocks" (18:2). But now he "was more astonished, because of the faithfulness of Ammon" in carrying out all his assigned tasks (18:10). Ammon's loyal service led Lamoni to declare with feeling, "Surely there has not been any servant among all my servants that has been so faithful as this man" (18:10). Then the king's fear overwhelmed him: "I would desire him that he come in unto me, but I durst not" (18:11).

Not long after this moment, Ammon finished his chores and approached the throne. Although we have no idea how one passed from the corrals to the place of public gatherings, Ammon knew the way and now stepped among those gathered there. We could imagine that a hush descended on the group. The most impressive man in their world had just come among them. Noting the unusual reception—the king did not speak to him—Ammon began to withdraw when "one of the king's servants" spoke up: "Rabbanah, the king desireth thee to stay" (Alma 18:12–13).[5] It was now time for Ammon subtly to assert himself. Perhaps breaking protocol, he spoke first, addressing the king. "What wilt thou that I should do for thee, O king?" Lamoni was silent for a long time. Possibly drawing on his courage as a prince, Ammon again broke the silence, "What desirest thou of me?" (18:14–15). At this point, we might imagine, a tense anticipation filled the hearts of all present.

But the king was taking his time. Experience had probably taught him not to say anything when he was unsure. And "he knew not what he should say" to Ammon. A third time Ammon broke the silence, this time hinting that he was now taking charge of the situation. He had "perceived the thoughts of the king" because he was "filled with the Spirit of God" (Alma 18:14–16). So, after briefly rehearsing the events of the day, he said, "whatsoever thou desirest *which is right,* that will I do" (18:16–17; emphasis added).

Do servants set bounds on what they will or will not do for their masters? Never. But Ammon did. He had sensed the fear and awe that were careening around inside Lamoni. The king was ready for a spiritual discussion. At last the king opened his mouth and, marveling that Ammon had known his thoughts, shaped the question of questions: "Who art thou?" (Alma 18:18).

AMMON AS GOD'S MESSENGER

Lamoni's pent-up thoughts now came pouring out. How had Ammon known "the thoughts of my heart?" How had the Nephite prince vanquished those who had "scattered my flocks?" (Alma 18:20). Sensing that Ammon was a special treasure, the king affirmed that, "if it were needed, I would guard thee with my armies; but I know that thou art more powerful than all they," (18:21). What could Lamoni offer to such a person? A few days before, he had offered the hand of his daughter. But that seemed paltry now. Raising the stakes, Lamoni declared that "whatsoever thou desirest of me I will grant it unto thee" (18:21). But Ammon's response was unexpected.

Ammon merely asked, "Wilt thou hearken unto my words?" A question asked in honesty invited a candid response from the king: "Yea, I will believe all thy words" (Alma 18:22–23). So Ammon began by asking Lamoni whether he believed in God. Lamoni did. Not quibbling over terminology that Lamanites used for God—the "Great Spirit"—Ammon plunged into a lengthy review of scripture and of the history of the Nephite and Lamanite peoples. Ammon addressed his remarks not only to the king but also "to his servants." He concluded by expounding "unto them the plan of redemption" and by speaking of "the coming of Christ." Significantly, as he had promised, "the king believed all his words" (18:24–40).

Sensing that the blessings of the Lord had rested forgivingly on the Nephites, Lamoni "began to cry unto the Lord," pleading for divine "mercy [to come] . . . upon me, and my people." He prayed earnestly that the Lord grant such blessings "according to thy abundant mercy [manifested] . . . upon the people of Nephi." He had not prayed long before "he fell to the earth, as if he were dead" (Alma 18:41–42). When the king fell, Ammon did not panic as most of us would. He had seen this sort of occurrence when his friend Alma had gone into a three-day swoon. The Lord had prepared Ammon for this moment (see Mosiah 27:18–23; Alma 36:10; 19:6).

THE QUEENS

Because the next set of scenes involved Lamoni's queen, it seems important to review what we can learn about her and, additionally, about Lamoni's mother, also a queen. Admittedly, the Book of Mormon offers few opportunities to view the character of a woman. Little is said, for example, about Sariah, Lehi's wife. But we can guess intelligently much about her character because we know something about the daunting challenges that she faced—personal and otherwise. In the case of Lamoni's queen, we do not know her name (it may not have been recorded in Mormon's source). But we can learn a good deal about her by reading carefully the little that Mormon has preserved. The second queen who comes into this section of Mormon's narrative is presumably the mother of Lamoni, although we cannot be certain. In her case, it is also possible to determine a fair amount about her character based on the brief account of how she responded to a crisis in her home.

We first turn to Lamoni's queen. Her immediate response to her husband's situation—he appeared to be dead—was to gather her children and begin to mourn "over him, after the manner of the Lamanites, greatly lamenting his loss" (Alma 18:43). Here we detect not only her deep love for her husband but also her sense of responsibility in bringing her family together in this crisis. Further, during the "two days and two nights" that the king "lay as if he were dead" (18:43), she kept her head about her and did not unjustly accuse Ammon of foul play. She could have, of course, because her husband was apparently dead after his dealings with Ammon and there was pressure on her to bury him (19:5). But she may have feared Ammon as those servants evidently did who had carried her husband to his chambers (see 18:43–19:1, 4).

She also was a woman of intelligence. After calling Ammon to the royal chambers—he responded obediently because he was still a servant—and after receiving assurances from him, both that her husband was not dead and that he would rise the next day, Ammon asked her, "Believest thou this?" Her reply is revealing: "I have had no witness save thy word, and the word of our servants" (Alma 19:2–3, 8–9). For her, and apparently for her culture, witnesses were important, for they provided the guarantees of information that one could act on. Moreover, even in the presence of Ammon, the most feared person in her realm at the time, she was careful when making a judgment. She then continued, showing that she distinguished between the word of witnesses and her own beliefs: "nevertheless I believe that it shall be according as thou [Ammon] hast said" (Alma 19:9).

The words of the queen led Ammon to declare that she was a woman of faith. In fact, he said, "there has not been such great faith among all the people of the Nephites" (Alma 19:10). How so? Evidently, she had believed the king's servants who had claimed that Ammon was "a prophet of a holy God" and that he possessed "power to do many mighty works" (19:4). Her lofty sensitivity made her inwardly susceptible to spiritual stimuli. For when her husband woke up and bore his testimony that he had "seen [his] Redeemer . . . the queen also sunk down, being overpowered by the Spirit" (19:12–13). When she was finally aroused by the touch of a faithful servant woman, Abish by name, the queen stood to offer praise, "O blessed Jesus, who has saved me from an awful hell!" She then evidently spoke in tongues, "speaking many words which were not understood" (19:29–30). This woman truly trusted her spiritual instincts.

The other queen exhibited a very different side to her personality, perhaps because she found herself in a somewhat dissimilar situation.

We do not know her name but clearly she was a woman who was accustomed to power and acted swiftly and decisively. These traits appear in a scene that is reminiscent of King Lamoni's swoon. Lamoni's father had received both Ammon's brother, Aaron, and his two companions. He had then allowed Aaron to explain his beliefs (see Alma 22:1–16). As a response to Aaron's invitation to pray, the old king "did prostrate himself upon the earth, and cried mightily" to God. In the midst of his prayer, "the king . . . was struck as if he were dead" (22:17–18). Like Ammon, Aaron had seen this sort of effect when his friend Alma had gone through his conversion experience years before. But no one else in the old king's presence was expecting him to collapse. When he did, confusion reigned.

Immediately, the king's "servants ran and told the queen all that had happened unto the king." When she rushed to the scene, "she saw . . . Aaron and his brethren standing as though they had been the cause of [the king's] fall." Her anger flared and, responding decisively, she "commanded that . . . the servants of the king, should take [the Nephites] and slay them." When those servants expressed fear, and she could see it in their eyes, "she also began to fear exceedingly." Even so, she was not to be denied. For she then "commanded her servants that they should . . . call the people, that they might slay Aaron and his brethren." (See Alma 22:19–21.)

As a prince, Aaron had grown up in the halls of power. It did not take him long to recognize "the determination of the queen" and that she would stop at nothing to inflict injury on those who she thought had attacked her husband, even if it meant assembling "a multitude" and causing "a great contention . . . among them" (Alma 22:22). Through mob action, she would gain her end. Indeed, some servant must have run from the scene to raise the cry because a crowd gathered quickly. To calm her and to defuse a dangerous situation, Aaron "put forth his hand and raised the king from the earth . . . in the presence of the queen" (22:22). We sense that this woman was mollified only after she saw her husband standing on his feet. In the end, of course, she was not only calmed but was brought within the circle of God's redeeming power (see Alma 22: 23). As Aaron and his companions had learned, she was a formidable opponent. But when she became "pacified towards Aaron and those who were with him," she became a staunch ally because she doubtless would have had a say in the proclamation issued by her husband that permitted the Nephite missionaries to continue their work unimpeded (see Alma 22:24–27; 23:1–3).

LAMANITE ROYAL HOUSEHOLD

Quite incidentally, the above scene offers a brief glimpse inside the organization of the Lamanite royal household. In a word, there were his servants and her servants. How do we know this? Because Mormon drew attention to it when he inadvertently slipped as he re-created the scene. After rehearsing the old king's collapse during his prayer, Mormon noted that the king's "servants ran and told the queen all that had happened" (Alma 22:19). In response, "she came in" and, seeing her husband lying "as if he were dead," she "commanded that her servants, or the servants of the king," take the Nephite missionaries into custody "and slay them" (22:19). Because Mormon began by writing "her servants" and then corrected himself, it becomes plain that there were two sets of servants on the scene. Mormon's continuing narrative affirms this point. For he writes that "the servants [who] had seen the cause of the king's fall" refused to obey the queen's orders because they feared the Nephites (22:20). These individuals were servants of the king. When the queen "saw the fear of [these] servants," she turned to her own servants who had not been present and barked out a different order: "she commanded *her servants* that they . . . call the people, that they might slay Aaron and his brethren" (22:21; emphasis added; cf. 19:17). Can we say more? Perhaps not. But we can observe that the queen did not ask her own servants to arrest the Nephite missionaries. Was it because they were women? Possibly. Perhaps it was because they were eunuchs whose strength might not have matched that of the Nephite men. Mormon does not offer enough detail to make a determination. But he does clarify that there was an entourage of servants attached to the king and one attached to the queen.

GOD RESCUES AMMON

Ammon's father, Mosiah, had received God's assurance that He would "deliver thy sons out of the hands of the Lamanites" (Mosiah 28:7). More specifically, God had said about Ammon: "I will spare him" (Alma 19:23). Trusting the Lord, Mosiah had permitted his sons to depart. To the sons themselves the Lord had implored that they "be patient in long-suffering and afflictions" (Alma 17:11; 26:27). The message? Afflictions would come. But through their father they had assurance that they would be spared. One of the occasions that required God's intervention occurred at Lamoni's residence.

The setting is the following. After two days and two nights in a swoon, Lamoni had aroused himself and had borne testimony that he had "seen my Redeemer; . . . and he shall redeem all mankind" (Alma 19:13). Lamoni then "sunk again with joy." But as we have seen, he was not alone. The "queen also sunk down, being overpowered by the spirit." At the moment, Ammon too "was also overpowered with joy; and . . . sunk to the earth." In addition, "the servants of the king," when they began to pray, all fell down. The only person left standing was a servant of the queen, "one of the Lamanitish women, whose name was Abish." She had "been converted unto the Lord for many years" because of "a remarkable vision of her father." When she gazed on those who had fallen, "she knew that it was the power of God" that had intervened (19:12–17). As events turned out, it was a good thing that she was still fully conscious.

In her excitement, the woman Abish quickly spread the news about God's astonishing work. A crowd gathered. But the crowd included some of the men who had suffered at the hands of Ammon a few days before when they had tried to scatter "the flocks which belonged to the king." In anger, "one of them, whose brother had been slain . . . drew his sword and went forth . . . to slay" Ammon. But when "he lifted the sword to smite him, behold, he fell dead" (Alma 19:17–22). (From this, Mormon drew the conclusion that "Ammon could not be slain" for God was protecting him because of his word to Ammon's father Mosiah.) As one might expect, "fear came upon them all." But before long the people in the crowd began arguing about the meaning of what they had seen (Alma 19:23–28). Now came the decisive moment that led to the conversion of virtually a whole people.

Feeling worried about the drift and tone of the argument, the woman Abish "took the queen by the hand." Immediately, the queen "arose and stood upon her feet." Her shouted words then held the crowd spellbound: "O blessed Jesus, who has saved me from an awful hell! O blessed God, have mercy on this people!" (Alma 19:28–29). No one standing within the sound of her voice would ever be the same. They would either accept or reject the words of the queen. For, after the king and Ammon and the servants were aroused from their reveries, they too began to bear witness to those in the crowd "that their hearts had been changed [and] . . . that they had seen angels and had conversed with them." Even though "there were many among them who would not hear" these testimonies, others "did believe in their words . . . and were baptized" (19:30–35). The work of Ammon had begun to bear abundant fruit. In Mormon's words, "the Lord did begin to pour out his Spirit upon" a whole people, the Lamanites (19:36).

RESCUING THOSE ENSLAVED ABROAD

As David Daube reminds us, the legal convention that governed how a person sought the release of another individual enslaved abroad is extremely old in the ancient Near East. It is this process, in fact, that God was following when He sent Moses as His envoy into Egypt seeking the release of the Hebrew slaves.[6] Actions that conform to this ancient Near Eastern convention appear twice in the Book of Mormon: once in the efforts of the Resurrected Savior to rescue his hearers from their sins,[7] and once in the efforts of Ammon and Lamoni to seek the release of Ammon's brother and companions.

According to the account that features Ammon, "the voice of the Lord came to" him soon after Lamoni's conversion, warning Ammon not to accompany Lamoni on a planned trip to visit Lamoni's father. Instead, Ammon was to "go to the land of Middoni" where his "brother Aaron" and two companions were "in prison" (Alma 20:2). Ammon, still technically a servant, then made the surprise announcement to Lamoni that his "brother and [other] brethren are in prison . . . and I go that I may deliver them." Sensing the difficulties in Ammon's plan, the king responded that he would "go with [Ammon] to the land of Middoni . . . that I may flatter the king . . . and he will cast thy brethren out of prison" (20:3–4). Thus the roles of the two became reversed. Lamoni, the king, now became the envoy of Ammon the servant. The king, effectively working at Ammon's bidding, would seek the release of Ammon's brother and friends. But as they traveled together, their intents were almost dashed in a chance encounter with Lamoni's enraged father. (See Alma 20:8.)

Actually, when we recognize the hand of the Lord orchestrating events, we see that the meeting with Lamoni's father did not really happen by chance. Tangible results flowed from that encounter, including the conversion of the old king and his important aid in the release of Ammon's brother and companions.

The old king had been offended and shamed when his son Lamoni had not attended a special feast in the capital city. Of course, he did not know that Lamoni's absence was because he had lain "two days and two nights" in spiritual reverie (Alma 18:43). As Lamoni and Ammon were traveling together to the land of Middoni, they chanced to meet the old king, who was consumed with rage. Naturally, he demanded to know, first, why his son "did not come to the feast" and, second, why he was "with this Nephite [Ammon], who is one of the children of a liar" (Alma 20:9–10). Here the king's words betray his awareness that the sons of his rival—the Nephite king—were in the land. Perhaps not surprisingly, the old king ordered his son not only to "slay Ammon with the sword" but also to "return with him to the land of Ishmael" where Lamoni ruled as regent king (20:13–14). To the astonishment of his father, Lamoni refused both orders. Enraged, the old king drew his sword to slay his son (20:16).

Ammon intervened. Of course, we do not know whether Lamoni would have allowed his father to execute him. But at the critical moment, "Ammon stood forth" and warned the old king that he was not to "slay thy son," a warning that Ammon backed up with force. Remarkably, in the heat of this confrontation, Ammon took the opportunity to declare eternal truths, perhaps in a loud voice. To the old king Ammon boomed the dire warning that, if he were to take the life of his son, "his [son's] blood would cry from the ground to the Lord his God, for vengeance to come upon" the king (Alma 20:17–18). But the old king took no heed of Ammon's words. In his blind fury, he physically attacked Ammon. With his skill, "Ammon withstood [the king's] blows, and also smote his arm that he could not use it." Disarmed and stunned, the king was now at the mercy of the Nephite prince and evidently beyond the help of a bodyguard (Alma 20:20–21). Would Ammon take the life of Lamoni's father?

Ammon did not. Instead, he sought two pledges. First, he wanted freedom for his brother Aaron and his companions who were languishing in a prison. Second, while he had the king at his mercy, he demanded that "Lamoni . . . retain his kingdom . . . according to his own desires" (Alma 20:22–24). Possibly Ammon understood that the old king had determined to depose his son, maybe even execute him, as Lamanite law may have required. Ammon wanted to turn the king's intent upside down, allowing Lamoni to rule freely, without interference. These requests surprised the old king. But he was even more astonished at "the great love [Ammon] had for his son Lamoni." Perhaps reluctantly, he agreed. Said he, "I will grant[8] unto you that my son [Lamoni] may retain his kingdom from this time and forever; and I will govern him no more—And I will also grant unto thee that thy brethren may be cast out of prison." Then came the words that must have thrilled Ammon. The old king spoke solemnly: "thou and thy brethren may come unto me, in my kingdom; for I shall greatly desire to see thee." In an unexpected turnabout, he "was desirous to learn" their message (20:26–27).

The end of this story sees Ammon and Lamoni continuing "on their journey towards the land of Middoni." There "Lamoni found favor in the eyes of the king of the land" (Alma 20:28). We note again that here king Lamoni acted as ambassador for Ammon, his servant, seeking the release of Ammon's brother and his companions. As a result, "the brethren of Ammon were brought forth out of prison." Although the sight of them brought both sorrow and joy to Ammon—the prisoners "had suffered hunger, thirst, and all kinds of afflictions"—at least they had been delivered (20:28–29). In the end, "they were fed and clothed," presumably receiving again their own clothing, and "were delivered for the first time out of prison" (Alma 21:13–15).

THE EARLY EXPERIENCES OF AARON

Mormon offers only a brief recitation of Aaron's early missionary experiences. Unlike his brother Ammon who brought almost an entire people to Christ seemingly within a few short weeks, Aaron bounced from the city of Jerusalem to Ani-Anti and then finally to Middoni where he was thrown into prison. We do not know why he went first to the city of Jerusalem (see Alma 21:4). Was it because the name carried an allure?[9] Was it because Aaron was aware that a significant part of the population consisted of dissident Nephites? Or was it because he believed that, since many people there followed the teachings of Nehor, the infamous contemporary Nephite teacher, he might find common ground for discussion? We don't know; we just know he tried to teach the gospel there. And even though some people in Jerusalem gave him an audience—Mormon reported one such reception in a synagogue, and it may have been typical of Aaron's experiences there (see Alma 21:5–10)—he was unable to persuade people to listen seriously.

Because his presence stirred anger among citizens in Jerusalem, he withdrew "to a village which was called Ani-Anti" where he found two companions, Nephite men named Muloki and Ammah. Their combined efforts yielded nothing. When they retreated to Middoni, they saw no further success. Eventually, "Aaron and a certain number of his brethren were taken and cast into prison" while "the remainder of them fled" (Alma 21:11–13). (This passage, incidentally, is one of the few that hints at a number higher than the six original missionaries. But the case is not certain.) It was from this imprisonment that Lamoni and Ammon rescued Aaron and the others with him. Aaron and his companions then traveled "whithersoever they were led by the Spirit of the Lord" (21:16). At last, they were "led by the Spirit to the land of Nephi, even to the house of the king . . . over all the land" (22:1).

LAMONI'S FATHER

We wish that we knew more about Lamoni's father. The few details that have been preserved reveal him clearly as a person of education, high principle, and noble qualities. We have already seen him in action against Lamoni and Ammon. In that situation he showed himself to be rather disagreeable and quick tempered. But he was also an experienced ruler, which meant that he was probably something of a pragmatist. Because of the favorable impression that Ammon had made—and here we can see the king's open heart—he was willing to listen to what Aaron, Ammon's brother, and his companions might say. Significantly, the king's willingness to hear their message would open an even larger door to the missionaries than they enjoyed in Lamoni's part of the kingdom, leading to many thousands joining the church.

The scene now turns to the old king's residence where Aaron and "his brethren" came to visit him (Alma 22:1). Aaron must have learned of the king's invitation to Ammon after Ammon and Lamoni had freed him from prison. Led by the Spirit, Aaron had evidently decided to accept the invitation on Ammon's behalf. After being granted an audience with the aged monarch and prostrating himself, Aaron adopted the strategy of Ammon. He offered himself and his companions as servants. But the king refused even to consider the gesture. Instead, referring to the custom that allowed him to execute foreigners who came into the midst of his people (see Alma 17:20), he cleared the air on this issue by formally declaring that "I will grant unto you your lives" (Alma 22:1–3). There was more.

Rejecting the wish of the Nephite missionaries to be placed in the king's household as servants, the old king spoke of his own request, announcing it almost as a command: "I will insist that ye shall administer unto me." Now addressing Aaron directly, he confessed that he was "troubled in mind because of the generosity and the greatness of the words of thy brother Ammon" and because Ammon had "not come up out of Middoni with thee" (Alma 22:3). It was while excusing his brother that Aaron struck a note that caught the old king's ear. Aaron had mentioned that "the Spirit of the Lord has called him another way." Facing the group of missionaries, the king asked, "What is this that ye have said concerning the Spirit of the Lord? Behold, this is the thing which doth trouble me. And also, what is this that Ammon said—If ye will repent ye shall be saved, and if ye will not repent, ye shall be cast off at the last day" (22:4–6).

In the next part of the exchange Aaron addresses the concerns of the old King. Their discussion reveals that the Lamanite royal house controlled religious activities within the realm, for, when Aaron asked the king whether he believed "that there is a God," the king responded that he himself had "granted unto" the Amalekites—Nephite dissenters—"that they should build sanctuaries, that they may assemble themselves together to worship" (Alma 22:7).[10] Knowing more about the Lamanites than we do, Aaron probably knew that, but what must have startled Aaron were the words that next came from the king's mouth: "if now thou sayest there is a God, behold I will believe." Rejoicing inwardly, Aaron bore testimony that "there is a God." Then identifying God with "that Great Spirit that brought our fathers out of the land of Jerusalem,"[11] Aaron affirmed that He had "created all things both in heaven and in earth." As a good missionary, Aaron next asked the king, "Believest thou this?" "Yea," the king said, "I will believe [all] thy words" (Alma 22:7–11).

As Ammon had done with Lamoni and his household, so Aaron began to rehearse "the scriptures unto the king," reading them aloud (evidently the missionaries carried copies of some sort and the ancient custom was to read aloud).[12] Aaron "began from the creation of Adam," reminding the king that "because of transgression man had fallen." Skillfully weaving a gospel tapestry, Aaron explained "the plan of redemption which was prepared from the foundation of the world, through Christ" (Alma 22:12–13). Using forceful imagery—he spoke of "breaking . . . bands" and "the sting of death" and being "swallowed up"—Aaron intoned that Jesus' "sufferings and death" generously offered not only atonement "for [the] sins" of those who repent but also the shattering of "the bands of death" for all, regardless of their status before God (22:14).

The response of the old king is astounding. The account is so vivid that an eyewitness must have written it—possibly Aaron. For "after Aaron had expounded these things unto him," the king asked, "What shall I do that I may have this eternal life?" The king continued, expressing himself in terms, particularly verbs, that reveal an eloquent command of language: "Yea, what shall I do that I may *be born* of God, having this wicked spirit *rooted out* of my breast . . . that I may *be filled* with joy, that I may not *be cast off* at the last day?" (Alma 22:15; emphasis added). His final wish plumbs the depth of his resolve, disclosing him to be a man of certitude and high principle: "I will give up all that I possess . . . that I may receive this great joy" (22:15). Plainly, he was more than a noble savage.

Aaron, a prince who was accustomed to dealing with people in high position, did not waver from his purpose. In reassuring tones, he pledged to the king that "If thou desirest this thing, if thou wilt bow down before God . . . then shalt thou receive the hope which thou desirest" (Alma 22:16). Again the response of the king is surprising, for he "did bow down before the Lord, upon his knees" (22:17). But he was being true to custom in his society. It was proper for a person to bow before royalty. Aaron too, when he and his companions had come to the king's residence, "bowed . . . before the king" (22:2). The king now took on a full outward form of humility before God, "even he did prostrate himself upon the earth." Raising his voice "mightily," the old monarch pleaded with God, approaching Him as if he did not know what he would find. "O God"—here we note the king's hesitation—"Aaron hath told me that there is a God" (22:17–18). Aaron? Yes. And the king believed.

The king really proceeded in a faith that rested upon Aaron's faith. He begged, "if there is a God, and if thou art God, wilt thou make thyself known unto me?" Next came the king's pledge, his part of the covenant: "I will give away all my sins to know thee." The king's hope, a term which Aaron had just mentioned (see Alma 22:16), was "that I may be raised from the dead, and be saved at the last day" (22:18). As if hit by lightening, the king "was struck as if he were dead" (22:18). At this point "his servants" dashed off "and told the queen all that had happened unto the king," with the result that we have already reviewed (22:19).

In the end, it was this aged king who turned the key opening Lamanite doors to the Nephite missionaries. They enjoyed unparalleled success during the remainder of their fourteen years in Lamanite lands. As a result of their unfettered access to Lamanite religious institutions, the missionaries became instruments of the Lord in converting the inhabitants of entire cities and adjoining regions of the country. Mormon, in fact, reproduced an impressive list of seven separate geographical areas that saw virtually all of their people convert to the Lord (see Alma 23:8–13). The most noticeable results were that these people "laid down . . . their weapons of war" (23:13), adopted a new name "Anti-Nephi-Lehies" that replaced their ethnic name Lamanities (23:16–17) and, after laying down their weapons, refused to "take up arms" again for self-defense or any other purpose (23:7; 24:6, 23). As a symbol not only of their repentance but also of their determination that they would never be guilty anew of taking the life of another person, they buried their weapons "deep in the earth" with a solemn covenant to leave them there (24:11–18).

Although the old king died years later as a beloved leader, over time his people had split and were already moving toward civil war at the moment of his death (see Alma 24:3–4). The reason for the division among his people had to do with a royal proclamation that he had issued long before. The proclamation had created a social and religious climate that allowed the missionaries to share the gospel undisturbed. For, according to this document, no citizen was to harrass the missionaries in any way. Further, the missionaries were to "have free access to their houses, and also their temples, and their sanctuaries" (Alma 23:2). Incidentally, the royal proclamation, which Lamanites had to obey, illustrates an important difference between Lamanite society and that of the Nephites. For when the elected chief judge of the Nephites wanted to take action on an important matter involving the Lamanite converts who had fled to Nephite lands for protection, he had to consult with his people (Alma 27:21). Under the terms of the Nephite democracy, the chief judge could not take unilateral action.

THE PROCLAMATION

When the king issued the proclamation that effectively gave the missionaries a free hand, the work of the missionaries leapt forward with almost furious speed (see Alma 22:27; 23:1–2). Of course, it was because "the king had been converted unto the Lord, and all his household . . . [that] he sent his proclamation . . . that the word of God might have no obstruction." The king also saw the practical and social advantages of convincing his people "that they were all brethren, and that they ought not to . . . commit any manner of wickedness"—Mormon even listed the kinds of wickedness that the king wished to rid from his society (Alma 23:3). The king was right. Eventually his people became "friendly with the [missionary] Nephites" and "did open a correspondence" with them (23:18; 24:8–9), presumably meaning that they willingly opened their homes and places of worship to the missionaries (23:2, 4). It may also indicate that, as time went on and the general social climate improved, other Nephite missionaries joined the original six men to assist in the work, although this possibility cannot be proven from the record.

The proclamation also meant that during the next few years "thousands were brought to the knowledge of the Lord." Moreover, these "thousands" came to "believe in the traditions of the Nephites" and learned of "the records and prophecies which were handed down" among the Nephites to that time (Alma 23:5). It was nothing short of a religious revolution! Entire parts of the population had stopped believing traditions that for generations had been handed down among their people, and started believing something else. Mormon fixes our minds on the sweep and depth of this conversion when, with an oath—"as the Lord liveth"—he declared, "as many of the Lamanites as . . . were converted unto the Lord, never did fall away. For they became a righteous people" (23:6–7). But this mass conversion brought a dark, deadly response from those who did not share their new view.

GEOGRAPHICAL ASIDE

Before examining the Amalekites and Amulonites, who galvanized the opposition to the missionaries into civil war, we should touch on a notable and important digression wherein Mormon tells us much about the geographical layout of the country. The subject arises because Mormon mentions that the old Lamanite king had sent his royal "proclamation throughout all the land . . . which was bordering even to the sea, on the east and on the west" (Alma 22:27). By describing the broad expanse of the kingdom of the Lamanities, Mormon introduces us to a number of details that characterized the countryside.[13]

The most important geographical feature that "divided" the Lamanite lands "from the land of Zarahemla" where the Nephites resided was "a narrow strip of wilderness" (Alma 22:27), presumably an almost impenetrable forest or jungle. In the past, many who had tried to traverse it had become lost or had experienced extreme difficulties (see Mosiah 7:4; 8:7–8; 9:3–4; Alma 17:7–9). Although Mormon termed this wilderness "a narrow strip," it seems to have formed an imposing barrier that took several days, even weeks in some instances, to cross.[14] It also seems that it was impossible for people to go around this wilderness region because it "ran from the sea east even to the sea west, and round about on the borders of the seashore." Significantly, it was within this wilderness that the headwaters "of the river Sidon" rose, which was one of the most important sources of water for the Nephites (Alma 22:27).

Mormon portrays Lamanite society as culturally very diverse. And part of his portrait arises in this section of his narrative. In addition to the high educational level that we glimpse in the royal house when Mormon rehearses the scene of Aaron and the old king, there was a part of the population that lived in cities and nearby agricultural areas. It was presumably within this sector of the populace that the missionaires saw most of their success. Those people, "rather than spend their days in idleness[,] . . . would labor abundantly with their hands" (Alma 24:18). Mormon also spoke of "the more idle part of the Lamanites" who "lived in the wilderness and dwelt in tents" (Alma 22:28). This portion of the citizenry seems to have been semi-nomadic. Their chief homeland lay in "the wilderness on the west, in the land of Nephi." They had spread "also on the west of the land of Zarahemla," effectively hemming in the Nephites from full access to the west sea. In addition, these tent-dwellers inhabited the area "by the seashore . . . in the place of their fathers' first inheritance" (22:28). Thus, it was these people who continued to reside in the region where the family of Lehi and Sariah came ashore and settled in the New World. (See 1 Ne. 18:23–25.)

Apparently the Lamanites had also established themselves "on the east by the seashore, whither the Nephites had driven them" (Alma 22:29). It must have been Nephite military action that had limited these eastern Lamanites in their territorial claims. The net effect of the Lamanites controlling the seacoast areas on the east and the west was that "the Nephites were nearly surrounded by the Lamanites" (22:29). The only exit for Nephites in case of a military disaster was to the north.

As a matter of course, "the Nephites had taken possession of all the northern parts of the land" that lay north of the "narrow strip of wilderness" (Alma 22:27, 29). The northern exposure of the land of Zarahemla reached as far as "the land which they called Bountiful," perhaps named Bountiful because it resembled in its climate and fruitfulness "the land of Bountiful" on the south seacoast of Arabia where the first family built its ship (1 Ne. 17:6–8; 18:1–4). Beyond Bountiful spread "the land which they called Desolation," which extended "northward . . . into the land which had been peopled and been destroyed . . . which was discovered by the people of Zarahemla" (Alma 22:30; Omni 1:21–22). The border area between Bountiful and Desolation was a lowland, for all references to traveling into that region speak of going "down" (see Morm. 3:7–8; 4:17; also Alma 22:31 ["up into the south wilderness"]).

It was in the area between Bountiful and Desolation that the Lamanites and Nephites encountered the most notable of all geographical features. Called variously "the small neck of land between the land northward and the land southward" (Alma 22:32), "the narrow neck" (Alma 63:5) and "the narrow pass" (Morm. 3:5), it was the narrowest point of land between the two oceans where "it was only the distance of a day and a half's journey for a Nephite" to travel from one ocean to the other (Alma 22:32). In later times, this spot would receive heavy Nephite fortifications to prevent Lamanite armies from overrunning the land northward, the only real refuge for Nephites in an emergency (see Alma 22:33–34; 52:9; Morm. 3:5–6).

Mormon adds one other important note in his geographical digression. He speaks of "the place of . . . first landing" of the people of Zarahemla (Alma 22:30). The ancestors of this people fled Jerusalem eleven or so years after Lehi and Sariah had left, "at the time that Zedekiah, king of Judah, was carried away captive into Babylon" (Omni 1:15). It is most likely that they had crossed the Atlantic Ocean and landed on the eastern seashore in the land northward (see Hel. 6:10). This group, accompanied by Zedekiah's son Mulek, was "brought by the hand of the Lord across the great waters" (Omni 1:16; Hel. 8:21). From their landing place they discovered that the surrounding territory, once inhabited, was littered with "bones" of the Jaredites (Omni 1:22; Alma 22:30). They then went "from there up into the south wilderness" (Alma 22:31), evidently the same wilderness as Mormon's "narrow strip of wilderness" (22:27). Perhaps finding the wilderness impenetrable, they retreated to a suitable place on the west bank of the Sidon River where they founded the city Zarahemla.

AMALEKITES AND AMULONITES

Mormon's narrative has preserved the origin of the Amulonites (see Mosiah 23:30–24:9). But the Amalekites remain something of a mystery. By the time that the Nephite missionaries arrived, both peoples had come to influence certain matters that affected Lamanite society, from military to education, from religion to establishing settlements.[15]

Mormon hints that the Amalekites were dissident Nephites or possibly Mulekites who had come under the influence of the religion of Nehor (see Alma 24:28, 30), a religious and political movement that had seemingly been infused with life after this man had suffered execution (Alma 1:15). Of the Amalekites, we can derive four characteristics from whispers in Mormon's report. First, because of the way that Mormon typically treated the names of groups, calling them after their original leader, we can safely assume that the person who was the moving force behind these people and their philosophy was a man named Amalek. Perhaps for good reason, Mormon never mentioned him in his account. Second, they were aggressive colonists who apparently never felt fully assimilated into Lamanite society. As an example, Mormon has exposed the clan-centered character of the society by delineating the lineage of those Lamanites converted after the slaughter of more than a thousand believers, specifying that "none who were Amalekites or Amulonites" were convinced of their error because of the killing. He then drew an even sharper distinction, saying that only "actual descendants of Laman and Lemuel" threw down their weapons in disgust and joined the survivors of the slaughter, the people of Anti-Nephi-Lehi (Alma 24:29). In this connection, it may be that the Amalekites' settlement activities were motivated in part because they remained largely unintegrated. We see their drive to colonize when they joined with others to settle the city of Jerusalem, "away joining the borders of Mormon," an area which had been uninhabited wilderness a generation or so earlier (Alma 21:1–2; Mosiah 18:4). Third, they must have shared some religious links to Nephites because they cofounded the city "Jerusalem, calling it after the land of their fathers' nativity," clearly honoring the early settlers in the New World and tying themselves to their ancestral place of origin (Alma 21:1). And fourth, like Nephites, they built "sanctuaries" in order to "assemble themselves together to worship" (Alma 22:7). Though by this time who or what they worshipped was clearly not who or what the Nephites worshipped. It was the Amalekites who openly sought to "stir up" their fellow citizens against the Nephite missionaries and their converts, including the king, leading to at least two blood baths and uncounted tortures of believers (Alma 24:1–2; 20–22; 27:2–3, 29).

Concerning the Amulonites, their origins are clearer. They took their rise from the surviving priests of King Noah who had abandoned their wives and children when a Lamanite army attacked their colony (see Mosiah 19:7–12, 18–21). Amulon, one of their number, took the lead among these defrocked priests when they later kidnaped twenty-four Lamanite women and settled themselves in a wilderness valley (see Mosiah 20:1–5; 23:30–32). After a wandering Lamanite army discovered them, the army apparently forced them to abandon their settlement until their status could be resolved because their actions with the Lamanite women had caused a war (see Mosiah 20:1–7; 23:35). In time, because of the Amulonites' skills and education, they moved into positions of influence in certain circles of Lamanite society (see Mosiah 23:39–24:6). However, as in the case of the Amalekites, there is reason to believe that Lamanite society never fully assimilated the Amulonites (see Mosiah 23:39: Amulon was appointed "a king and a ruler over *his* [Amulon's Nephite] people;" emphasis added). Along with the Amalekites, they founded the city of Jerusalem (see Alma 21:2) and, years later, made common military cause with this latter group against the converted king Anti-Nephi-Lehi and his people (Alma 24:1–2). We have to assume that by this time a second generation had grown up, children with their fathers. Together, when their murderous attack against the pacifist Anti-Nephi-Lehies backfired because the Lamanites among the attackers could not stomach the slaughter of their fellows (see 24:20–29), the Amulonites sought to quench their thirst for blood by overwhelming the renegade Nephite city of Ammonihah, annihilating its citizens to the last person (see Alma 16:1–3, 9–10; 25:1–2). It is one of the tragic ironies of the Book of Mormon that the Amulonites and Amalekites, who were largely of the religion of Nehor, led the Lamanite force that destroyed the city and citizens of Ammonihah, who were of the same religious order (see Alma 16:11; 21:4; 24:29).

In their flight from Ammonihah to avoid a counterattacking Nephite army, the remaining Amulonites became embroiled in a mutiny in the forest wherein many of the pure Lamanites in the force rebelled against the Amulonites who had tried to wrest control of their army. The Lamanites in the force overwhelmed the Amulonites, fathers and sons, killing many of them. The last that we hear of the Amulonites of that generation, probably from the record of the sons of Mosiah, is that "they are hunted at this day by the Lamanites" (Alma 25:3–9). From this point on, they disappear from Mormon's record. To be sure, the wives and younger children of the Amulonite families in the city of Jerusalem and elsewhere must have survived (see Alma 43:13). But these people seem never again to have influenced Lamanite affairs. When a short time later a Lamanite force again threatened the people of Anti-Nephi-Lehi, Mormon mentions only Amalekites as taking the lead in stirring "up the [Lamanite] people in anger against . . . the people of Anti-Nephi-Lehi," a role that the Amulonites had jointly played earlier in this era (see Alma 27:2; also 24:1; 43:6, 13). The Amulonite men, old and young, were all gone. It is a sad ending to a tale that began badly.[16]

NEPHITE ROYAL EDUCATION

We cannot end our review of the missionaries' experiences without touching on the matter of education as Mormon reveals it in his narrative. We must understand that it is almost impossible to learn about levels of education among the general populace, Nephite or Lamanite. To be sure, there are hints that literacy was rather widespread in some periods and within certain classes of people (see Mosiah 24:1, 4; 3 Ne. 6:12). But we are left with no concrete details. However, Mormon describes certain scenes in a way that we can learn, at least a little, about education within royal households.

On the Nephite side, we see only Aaron and Ammon in these chapters. From Aaron, Mormon has preserved little. But it may be enough to allow us to sense what seem to be his keen, refined abilities. They appear in the exchange with the old king. Here Aaron showed himself to be adept in dealing with another of royal stature, taking the part of the lowly servant when he requested on behalf of himself and his companions, "if thou wilt spare our lives, we will be thy servants" (Alma 22:3). We notice immediately two traits. First, Aaron knew that in the presence of a king, he should present himself as one of lesser status, here as a servant. Second—and this is a key point in grasping Aaron's ability to learn quickly about his Lamanite environment—he had come to understand Lamanite law. Although he had perhaps heard long before that Lamanite kings possessed the right to execute Nephites who wandered into their territory (see Alma 17:20), he and his brothers may also have found this out only after arriving. It is in Aaron's appeal to the king to "spare our lives" that he displays to our view his knowledge of this Lamanite custom (Alma 22:3). He was evidently a person who knew what to say on important occasions and who learned rapidly.

Furthermore, Aaron showed an impressive grasp of the literature of scripture when he taught the old king. Although Mormon was summarizing Aaron's words, he took up a lot of space doing so. Evidently, Aaron could speak in detail about scripture as well as read skillfully from it (see Alma 22:12–14). And we know from the earlier account of the education of King Benjamin's sons that princes learned such matters (Mosiah 1:2–3). But it is within Aaron's exposition of scripture that we catch a glimpse of his abilities with words. As with the old king, Aaron's vocal expressions carried force and conviction. We note some of his intense eloquence: "man . . . could not merit anything . . . but the sufferings . . . of Christ atone . . . he breaketh the bands . . . the grave shall have no victory . . . the sting of death should be swallowed up in the hopes of glory" (Alma 22:14). These words, evidently spoken without notes, reveal an eloquence that bespeaks a rich education and a humble faith that bespeaks constant companionship of the Holy Ghost.

Besides the scene in which Ammon taught King Lamoni, which bears similarities to the scene of Aaron teaching the old king and shows Ammon to possess comparable skills (see Alma 18:16–40), Mormon has recorded a short address of Ammon to his brothers that witnesses to a masterful control of imagery and a deft touch with poetic speech.[17]

Asking a series of rhetorical questions, Ammon began, "could we have supposed when we started . . . that God would have granted unto us such great blessings? . . . I ask, what great blessings has he bestowed upon us? Can ye tell?" Then he responded to his own questions: "I answer for you." Borrowing the language of light and darkness and mouthing expressions of love, he intoned that the Lamanites, "our dearly beloved brethren, who have so dearly beloved us," had been "in darkness, yea, even in the darkest abyss." In contrast, now "many of them are brought to behold the marvelous light of God [and] . . . thousands of them do rejoice." He punctuated this point by answering his earlier question, "And this is the blessing which hath been bestowed upon us" (Alma 26:1–4).

Within his use of imagery, Ammon's dominant motif was "the hands of God" that had moulded his fellow missionaries into "instruments" in order "to bring about this great work." This work made Lamanites "dearly beloved brethren" instead of "strangers to God" (Alma 26:3). Then turning to an agricultural motif, Ammon rhapsodized that these "hands" belong to "the Lord of the harvest" whose "field was ripe" and whose "sheaves . . . shall be gathered into the garners, that they are not wasted." There, the sheaves—the converts—"shall not be beaten down by the storm at the last day . . . neither shall they be driven with the fierce winds." Instead, "they are his [the Lord's]; and he [with his hands] will raise them up at the last day" (26:5–7).

The most impressive demonstration of Ammon's extraordinary skills with extemporaneous speech lies in the next two segments of his brief address. Remarkably, the next portion of his speech exhibits a visibly poetic character (see Alma 26:11–16). And Ammon seems to have made up these lines on the spot. Oddly, perhaps, he lapses into poetry at the words of mild criticism from his brother Aaron. For after Ammon had said, "let us sing to [God's] praise," Aaron appears to have heard enough and retorted, "I fear that thy joy doth carry thee away unto boasting" (Alma 26:8, 10). Picking up on Aaron's terms of joy and boasting, Ammon apparently improvised, falling into a rhythm of ideas that rest on parallelism characteristic of Hebrew poetry:

> I do not boast in my own strength,
>   nor in my own wisdom;
> but behold, my joy is full,
>   yea, my heart is brim with joy,
>   and I will rejoice in my God. (Alma 26:11.)

Reaching higher, Ammon followed his poetry with deep, reflective thoughts wherein he asked the ultimate question of a merciful God: Why spare me, O Lord? In high, lively prose, and echoing his earlier rhetorical question (see Alma 26:1), he asked his brothers, "Who could have supposed that our God would have been so merciful as to have snatched us from our awful, sinful, and polluted state?" God knew that "we went forth even in wrath . . . to destroy his church." The almost unutterable question was, "why did [God] not consign us to an awful destruction . . . and doom us to eternal despair? Oh," he groaned, "my soul . . . fleeth at the thought." Instead of angrily allowing "the sword of his justice [to] fall upon us," God "in his great mercy hath brought us over that everlasting gulf of death and misery, even to the salvation of our souls" (26:17–20).

Without pursuing Ammon's address further, for his lofty abilities are now evident, it is worth concluding that Ammon packed his short address with poetry and with a memorable review of the experiences that he and his fellow missionaries had undergone. In phrases that recall the exalted language of the biblical psalms, Ammon showed his stunning grasp on how one rounds off a sermonette. For he brought his words to an emotional close by once again returning to his brother's terms—*boasting* and *joy*. "Now if this is *boasting,* even so will I *boast;* for this is my life and my light, my *joy* and my salvation. . . . God is mindful of every people . . . and his bowels of mercy are over all the earth. Now this is my *joy,* and my great thanksgiving; yea, and I will give thanks unto my God forever" (Alma 26:36–37; emphasis added).

LAMANITE ROYAL EDUCATION

On the Lamanite side, we see three kings and two queens. We have already reviewed some of what we can say about the queens. As Mormon's narrative reveals them, both exhibit an impressive array of abilities. As for kings, Lamoni does not disappoint us. He seems to have been familiar with old customs, and he ruled with a sure hand. In addition, as we have seen, Lamoni's father displayed an impressively high benchmark of Lamanite royal education. While we have already concluded that he was a person of education, high principle, and noble qualities, there is more to notice. His ability to grasp the essence of an issue is just as impressive. For he had sensed that, in order to embrace the gospel message, he might have to give up everything that had made him who he was. And he had enough strength of character to make the decision. He confessed to Aaron, "I will give up all that I possess, yea, I will forsake my kingdom, that I may receive this great joy" (Alma 22:15).

We know the brother of Lamoni only by his throne name, Anti-Nephi-Lehi. He received this name from the old king, their father, at the time of his coronation. One assumes with good reason that the usual throne name was Laman, though this man descended from Ishmael (see Mosiah 17:21; 24:3). But the events that had lifted his people into the gospel realm must have suggested that the royal house break with past tradition. Anti-Nephi-Lehi would serve a co-regency with his father for only a few months (see Alma 24:3–4). Yet it is not in his rulership but in his impassioned speech about his beleaguered people that we can test his skills with words, and thus his education. Those with faith in Christ faced a national crisis wherein a certain segment of the populace, inspired by the always prickly Amalekites and Amulonites, had turned ruthlessly against the new converts—"their hatred became exceedingly sore"—and were threatening both civil war and their extermination on religious grounds (24:1–2, 5).

In the land of Ishmael, where the Nephite missionaries met with the two Lamanite king-brothers in "a council" under desperate conditions (Alma 24:5), King Anti-Nephi-Lehi spoke for his people by declaring that they would not oppose those who would exterminate them, no matter the cost (24:6, 16). Anti-Nephi-Lehi did not exhibit the elegant eloquence of his father. But in his short address he exhibited a capacity for clear, thoughtful reasoning. In addition, he filled the occasion with importance and heightened the moment by his skillful appeal to imagery.

The opening of his speech brims with formalized language that demonstrates his polished training.[18] But his ability to inspire and convince others with words appears in the second part. For example, in expressions that billow with meaning, he addressed the Nephite missionaries, his brother Lamoni, and possibly others: "it has been all that we could do . . . to repent of all our sins and the many murders which we have committed, and to get God to take them away from our hearts, for it was all we could do to repent sufficiently before God that he would take away our stain" (Alma 24:11). The hint of a long, difficult repentance is strong. And because that repentance was at last successful and "since God hath taken away our stains, and our swords have become bright, then let us stain our swords no more with . . . blood." Then drawing upon the striking imagery of the blood of Christ and its power to cleanse, he reasoned, "if we should stain our swords again they can no more be washed bright through the blood of the Son" (24:12–13). Next, waxing rhapsodic as well as touching on the cultural characteristic of hiding valuables in the earth for safekeeping (there were no banks), he drew multiple strands of thought together: "Oh, how merciful is our God! . . . [S]ince it has been as much as we could do to get our stains taken away from us, and our swords are made bright, let us hide them away that they may be kept bright, as a testimony to our God at the last day . . . that we have not stained our swords in the blood of our brethren. . . . [B]ehold, we will hide away our swords . . . we will bury them deep in the earth, that they may be . . . as a testimony that we have never used them" (24:15–16). Rich in imagery and forceful in conviction, his speech carried the day.

DELIVERANCE

The experiences of the Nephite missionaries close with a sudden and massive migration of tens of thousands of Lamanite converts. At base, it is a story of deliverance, a dominant theme of the Book of Mormon from its first chapter (see 1 Ne. 1:20). The account is at once mournful and triumphant. The mournful fiber lies exposed in the permanent displacing of these converts, now refugees all, from their homes and country. The triumphant strand knits them to the ancient Hebrews who under Moses received the gracious gift of God by entering a new land and creating a new life in relative peace and safety. Significantly, these Lamanites, in their new place of inheritance, became a bulwark of moral and spiritual strength to the larger Nephite society and, in particular, to the effort of church leaders to keep the faith burning brightly.

The Amalekites had stirred up certain elements of the Lamanite populace to such a pitch of anger and hatred toward the Anti-Nephi-

Lehies that these opponents "began *again* to destroy them" (Alma 27:2; emphasis added). These opponents probably arose among those who had never come to trust the Nephite missionaries, and there must have been many. When "Ammon and his brethren saw" the horrors that their converts were willing to endure, they urgently proposed to the king, "Let us gather together this people . . . and let us go down to the land of Zarahemla . . . and flee out of the hands of our enemies, that we be not destroyed" (27:4–5). Apparently, the Nephites' proposal to abandon hearth and home caught king Anti-Nephi-Lehi by surprise. For he objected that "the Nephites will destroy us" (27:6). But after the idea had taken root, the king sensed with Ammon the deep importance of making the right decision—to stay or flee. They agreed that Ammon would inquire of the Lord and the king would accept the Lord's word through him (see 27:7–11).

The Lord's response was forceful and urgent: "Get this people out of this land, that they perish not" (Alma 27:12). Plainly, the Lord considered the converts more valuable alive than dead. The Lord's further explanation is illuminating: "Satan has great hold on the hearts of the Amalekites, who do stir up the [other] Lamanites to anger" (27:12). In the end, the Lord promised, "I will preserve them" (27:12). The kings and missionaries must have hastily "gathered together all their people . . . and . . . all their flocks and herds, and departed out of the land" (27:14). All must have been well enough to travel, just as the psalmist sang about the fleeing children of Israel (Ps. 105:37).

But there was a problem. How would the Nephite nation respond? King Anti-Nephi-Lehi feared that his beleaguered people would go from one hot cauldron to another. But trusting the word of the Lord, he and his people started down toward Zarahemla. As they came closer to Nephite lands, rather than risk raising an alarm by appearing suddenly on the frontier, the Nephite missionaries volunteered to go and consult with the national authorities while the king's people remained out of sight, as it were (see Alma 27:15, 25). Then, when the missionaries' long-time friend Alma met them on the road and joined their purpose, the case was made. This small group of old Nephite friends now formed a formidable embassy. Alma had been the first elected Nephite head of state, and the four brothers were sons of the last reigning Nephite king. In a real sense, the current chief judge had no choice but to move quickly to a decision. When, with Alma, the brothers "went and told the chief judge all the things that had happened unto them in the land of Nephi," the chief judge immediately sent "a proclamation throughout all the land" asking citizens whether to welcome "their brethren, who were the people of Anti-Nephi-Lehi" (27:20–21). It is evident that such a proclamation among Nephites, unlike the proclamation issued years before by the old Lamanite king, could only seek the opinion of the populace whether to permit the Lamanite converts to settle in the land. The chief judge, as head of an elected government, was not free to make such a decision without consulting the citizens.

A positive answer came back. "Behold," said the Nephite majority, "we will give up the land of Jershon . . . for an inheritance" to the Lamanite refugees (Alma 27:22). These people would now have a home. It is perhaps significant that in Hebrew the root of the name Jershon means "to inherit."[19] Thus, those who had recently arrived were to settle in their new homeland as inheritors, never to leave (27:22, 24). But the generosity of the Nephites did not stop there. They had learned of the vow of the Anti-Nephi-Lehies not to take up arms against anyone. Hence, the Nephites charitably promised, "we will guard them from their enemies with our armies." There was only one condition: "that they will give us a portion of their substance to assist us that we may maintain our armies" (27:24).

These Lamanites seem not to have been assimilated socially by the Nephites. Their land of inheritance was "on the east by the sea" (Alma 27:22), a good distance from the capital city of Zarahemla. Mormon writes that "they were among the people of Nephi," but not that they were numbered among them. On the other hand, the converts were "*numbered* among the people who were of the church of God," apparently meaning that they enjoyed full fellowship in the church, even if not in civic and social affairs (27:27; emphasis added).

After the two kings, Anti-Nephi-Lehi and Lamoni, had departed from their country, the Lamanite royal succession must have collapsed into confusion. To be sure, someone wrested control. For, when we next glimpse inside the royal household five or so years later, a Lamanite king sat on the throne. But there is a strong hint that the populace never fully accepted the new successor. For, without serious opposition, a Nephite dissenter was able to ascend the throne after his supporters had assassinated the new monarch (see Alma 47).

In a different vein, the Lamanites who had fled were "distinguished for their zeal towards God." Moreover, "they were perfectly honest and upright in all things." Most importantly, "they were firm in the faith of Christ" (Alma 27:27). To signal their new beginning, they willingly accepted the name conferred on them by their new Nephite neighbors, "the people of Ammon," perhaps a signal that the two Lamanite kings had ceased to function as rulers (27:26). Thus the long, arduous effort of the six Nephite missionaries had paid eternal dividends. Those who came to Christ because of their efforts repaid them manifold by living exemplary lives. Indeed, the Nephite missionaries had brought deliverance—first spiritual and then temporal—to tens of thousands of their brothers and sisters, the Lamanites.[20]

NOTES TO CHAPTER FOUR

1. The names of the four brothers appear first in Mosiah 27:34. For the earliest mention of the names of the two companions, see Alma 20:2. Hints exist that others may have joined these six; see Alma 17:8 ("their numbers"), 12 ("those who were with them"); 21:11 ("and his brethren"), 13 ("a certain number of his brethren").
2. For brief treatments of Lamanite society, including mention of royalty, see John L. Sorenson, "Book of Mormon Peoples," in *Encyclopedia of Mormonism,* ed. Daniel H. Ludlow et al. (New York: Macmillan, 1992), 191–92; Daniel C. Peterson, "Lamanite Civilization," in *Book of Mormon Reference Companion,* ed. Dennis L. Largey et al. (Salt Lake City: Deseret Book, 2003), 495–96.
3. For a fuller discussion, see S. Kent Brown, *From Jerusalem to Zarahemla* (Provo, Utah: BYU Religious Studies Center, 1998), 59–65.
4. See the references collected by Matthew Roper, "Swords and Cimeters in the Book of Mormon," *Journal of Book of Mormon Studies* 8, no. 1 (Spring 1999): 34–43.
5. The Book of Mormon offers a translation—one of the few—of the distinctive title Rabbanah, saying that it meant "powerful or great king" (Alma 18:13). We do not know in what other contexts, formal or informal, this title may have been spoken. For the verb "to stay" in this passage, see Brown, *From Jerusalem to Zarahemla,* 65–67.

6. David Daube, *The Exodus Pattern in the Bible* (London: Faber and Faber, 1963), 39–46. Related legislation occurs in the law code of Hammurabi 32 (see James B. Pritchard, *Ancient Near Eastern Texts Relating to the Old Testament,* 3rd ed. [Princeton: Princeton University Press, 1969], 167; Martha T. Roth, *Law Collections from Mesopotamia and Asia Minor* [Atlanta, GA: Scholars Press, 1995], 87).

7. See chapter five of this volume as well as the observations of Brown, *From Jerusalem to Zarahemla,* 87–88, 161–166.

8. The verb "to grant," appearing six times in this passage, points to a covenantal act willingly initiated by the old king. The verb probably derives from, or is related to, the Hebrew verb *ntn* "to give," which appears in covenant contexts elsewhere, translated in KJV as "to make [a covenant]" (Genesis 9:12; 17:2; cf. Mosiah 19:15). See Michael L. Barré, "Treaties," in *The Anchor Bible Dictionary,* ed. D. N. Freedman et al., 6 vols. (New York: Doubleday, 1992), 6:654.

9. On Jerusalem's attraction for Lamanites and, chiefly, for Nephites, see Brown, *From Jerusalem to Zarahemla,* 12–17.

10. See endnote 8 for a brief discussion about the verb "to grant" as an indicator of a covenant or agreement.

11. Despite the general Lamanite rejection of the Nephite version of Lehi's journey (see Mosiah 10:12), the king's words reveal that he believed that God had "brought our fathers out of the land of Jerusalem" (Alma 22:9).

12. Compare the description of Lehi reading the book in his vision: "he read, *saying* . . ." (1 Ne. 1:13; emphasis added).

13. Important studies that rest on the information in Alma 22 include the brief treatment of John E. Clark, "Book of Mormon Geography," in *Encyclopedia of Mormonism,* 1:176–79, and the extensive treatment of John L. Sorenson, *An Ancient American Setting for the Book of Mormon* (Salt Lake City: Deseret Book and FARMS, 1985). See also Sorenson's *Mormon's Map* (Provo, Utah: FARMS, 2000).

14. John E. Clark estimates that the minimum time required to traverse this wilderness was nine days. See his "A Key for Evaluating Nephite Geographies," in *Review of Books on the Book of Mormon,* ed. Daniel C. Peterson (Provo, Utah: FARMS, 1989), 1:20–70, especially 50–56.

15. Brief treatments of the Amalekites and the Amulonites are those of John L. Sorenson, "Book of Mormon Peoples," in *Encyclopedia of Mormonism,* 194, and Craig K. Manscill, "Amalekites," and Keith J. Wilson, "Amulonites," both in *Book of Mormon Reference Companion,* 44–45 and 54–55 respectively.

16. For a reconstruction of events that affected the former priests of Noah and their families, see Brown, *From Jerusalem to Zarahemla,* 99–112. The prophet

Abinadi had prophesied that a terrible fate awaited those who had condemned him to death (see Mosiah 17:15–18); Mormon, of course, pointed out its fulfillment (see Alma 25:9–12).

17. For the poetic aspect, see Richard Dilworth Rust, *Feasting on the Word: The Literary Testimony of the Book of Mormon* (Salt Lake City: Deseret Book and FARMS, 1997), 75–77.
18. One notes especially the repeated thanksgivings, with slight variations, "I thank my God that he has . . ." in Alma 24:7, 8, 9, 10.
19. For the Hebrew root *yrš,* see Ernst Jenni and Claus Westermann, *Theological Lexicon of the Old Testament,* 3 vols. (Peabody, Mass.: Hendrickson Publishers, 1997), 2:578–81.
20. Throughout these chapters, the Nephite missionaries consistently labeled the Lamanites as "brethren." This tone is very different from the assessment that one finds occasionally, for example, from Mormon who, in his day, was facing Lamanite atrocities on the battlefield (see Alma 17:14–15; Morm. 4:14, 20–21; Moro. 9:7–8).

The Majestic Christ

CHAPTER FIVE

VOICES

Voices. A person could hear the voices of those who were arriving at the temple. These voices were excitedly pointing out the changes that had occurred all at once in and around the land of Bountiful. Then came the voice of God, hushing the other voices. At first His voice was incomprehensible, but finally, gradually, it became understandable. Out of the ensuing silence came the voice of God's Son, proclaiming the mystery of His death and Resurrection.

A DAY OF DAYS

The morning dawned as one of thanksgiving. But the day turned out unlike any that the gathering crowd had experienced. It seems that the rain held off, not falling during this day nor during the following two. People were gathering from miles around to the city of Bountiful for a celebration at the temple. As a rough count, there were "about two thousand and five hundred souls," including men, women and children (3 Ne. 17:25). They could not have anticipated the basic, fundamental changes that the Savior's teachings and miracles would introduce into their lives. For Jesus' visit would bring reassurance and healing, spiritual rejuvenation and clarity of purpose, stunning celestial displays and sublime revelation.

Months had passed, perhaps even a year, since the volcanoes erupted and the "great storm" roared to life, bringing widespread death and devastation, leaving only "the more righteous . . . people" as survivors (3 Ne. 10:12). Everyone remembered vividly the voice that had spoken out of the impenetrable darkness. That voice had rebuked them for their lack of faith and righteousness. The darkness had entombed them for three days, shutting out all light and trapping the harsh voice in their minds. After the storm and the voice and the darkness, the months had been filled with mourning as well as heroic efforts to bring routine back into people's lives. At last, after a successful harvest, people began to feel that their lives were on the upswing. Gathering at the temple would allow them to express their relief and their gratitude to God through song and word and deed.

On the day of celebration, the small, intense noise was unexpected. Almost immediately, a hush fell over the entire crowd. For "while they were . . . conversing one with another, they heard a voice as if it came out of heaven." This voice "was not a harsh voice, neither was it a loud voice; nevertheless . . . it did pierce them . . . to the center." As a matter of fact, "there was no part of their frame that [the voice] did not cause to quake . . . and [it] did cause their hearts to burn" (3 Ne. 11:3). But the crowd could not grasp whether it was just a noise or whether there were words. Soon the voice sounded again, but "they understood it not" (11:4). Finally, "the third time they did understand the voice" (11:6). Within the voice came the announcement of the ages, the announcement that would make this day the most memorable in their entire history: "Behold my Beloved Son, in whom I am well pleased, in whom I have glorified my name" (11:8). Lifting their eyes into the morning light, "they saw a Man descending out of heaven; and he was clothed in a white robe" (11:8). If it were possible, the silence grew even deeper, for "they durst not open their mouths" (11:8). All voices, including the one from heaven, were now hushed.

Even though the voices were still, we can imagine that the minds of everyone present were racing, asking questions. What does the voice mean? What does this descending man mean? What is going on? At first, as Mormon records, "they thought it was an angel that had appeared unto them" (11:8). They were wrong. The one who had descended among them was much more glorious and infinitely more loving. He was the Son of God—their Savior.

Not since God had descended onto Mount Sinai had so many people witnessed a divine epiphany. Remarkably, by His own words, the Son of God who came to Bountiful was the same who had descended onto Mount Sinai. For, He informed His listeners, "I am he that gave the law" to Moses and the former Hebrew slaves. Moreover, "I am he who covenanted with my people Israel," a covenant that forged the Hebrews into a nation, an entity that brought an enduring unity to their tribes and clans (see 3 Ne. 15:5). On this day of days, the Son of God would begin to instill a spirit—a spirit of peace and loving respect—into His audience that would unify tribes and clans whose rancorous relationships had mortally wounded national unity, particularly during recent years (see 3 Ne. 7:2, 14). The vibrant unifying force that He implanted would erase even the most nettlesome of boundaries, that which divided Nephites and Lamanites. The resulting condition was so remarkable that Mormon, the editor of the account, wrote not only in negative terms that carried hints of what had been the status quo for so long in the past, "there was no contention," but also in positive terms about the refreshing condition that unfolded after the three-day visit of God's Son, "they had all things common among them" and "the love of God . . . did dwell in the hearts of the people" (see 4 Ne. 1:2–3, 13, 15–17). Astonishingly, in the brief span of three days the Son of God infused such a spirit of unity among these people that it lasted for almost 200 years (see 4 Ne. 1:20–21). Not incidentally, He would also heal their hearts by dispelling a long-lingering insecurity about being cut off from the land of their first inheritance, the land of Jerusalem.

BEHOLD, I AM

The voice of God's Son now carried across the quieted gathering. In words that recalled the name that He had revealed to Moses on the holy mount almost thirteen centuries before, He declared, "Behold, I am . . ." (3 Ne. 11:10). Of course, as Mormon's account reminds us, He said more about Himself as He began to speak. But it seems important to pause long enough to understand what those in His audience may have sensed. At least the adults in the crowd knew the passage wherein Jehovah disclosed His title to Moses, *"I am that I am:* . . . Thus shalt thou say unto the children of Israel, *I am* hath sent me unto you" (Ex. 3:14; emphasis added). In light of this passage and in light of instances in the New Testament and elsewhere wherein Jesus spoke of Himself by repeating the expression "I am,"[1] it appears that He began His address to the hushed crowd with a firmly aimed reference to His identity as the God of the Israelite Exodus, an event which heretofore had stood as the unequaled demonstration of God's love for His people. That event had now been eclipsed, as Jesus would stress during His visit. His Atonement had supplanted and surpassed the Exodus as the grand proof of God's love.[2]

With a flourish of His right hand, the Savior introduced Himself to the crowd: "Behold, I am Jesus Christ, whom the prophets testified shall come into the world" (3 Ne. 11:10). We can imagine that at this news, people held their collective breath as feelings of unspeakable joy and reverence enveloped them. He immediately continued in compact yet revealing language to remind them what He had willingly done for them.

> And behold, I am the light and the life of the world; and I have drunk out of that bitter cup which the Father hath given me, and have glorified the Father in taking upon me the sins of the world, in the which I have suffered the will of the Father in all things from the beginning. (3 Ne. 11:11)

There it was, at last. The timeless declaration of the Atonement. Remarkably, this statement came from the lips of the Resurrected, Glorified Lord Himself rather than from one of the prophets who, from the first generation, had been promising both the Atonement and a visit by the Savior.[3] After this news, when opportunity arose a little later, the crowd's emotions poured out in song. Indeed, after inviting each person to come forward "to feel the prints of the nails in [his] hands and in [his] feet," Jesus promised them that they would "know that [he is] the God of Israel and the God of the whole earth, and [has] been slain for the sins of the world" (3 Ne. 11:14). He was right. For after "going forth one by one" and seeing "with their eyes" and feeling "with their hands," they "did know of a surety . . . that it was he, of whom it was written by the prophets, that should come." Then the gathered throng "did cry out with one accord"—the record reads here as if they were singing—forming words that recall Psalms 47 and 118: "Hosanna! Blessed be the name of the Most High God!" (11:15–17).[4]

The part of the day that saw the multitude come forward "one by one" to touch "the prints of the nails in his hands and in his feet," as well as the scar in the Savior's side, must have occupied several hours (3 Ne. 11:14–16). For example, if we calculate that each of the 2,500 persons spent an average of ten seconds kneeling to touch Jesus' feet and then standing to feel His hands and side, most likely also saying something such as "My Lord and my God," the total elapsed time is almost seven hours. Naturally, the children and infants would not have taken this much time because they were with their parents. Even so, it is safe to assume that as many as four or five hours passed from the time of Jesus' arrival until the multitude allowed their emotions to flow out into their song of praise.

PRIOR SUFFERINGS

We can only imagine what the previous months had been like for these people. Perhaps as much as a year had passed since the storm. Mormon recorded that the tempest and earthquake arose "in the thirty and fourth year, in the first month, on the fourth day of the month" and then wrote that Jesus came "in the ending of the thirty and fourth year" (3 Ne. 10:18).[5] The three terrifying days of darkness following the sudden, horrific storm only masked the devastation which the voice in the darkness had reeled off: "that great city Zarahemla have I burned with fire, . . . that great city Moroni have I caused to be sunk in the depths of the sea . . . that great city Moronihah have I covered with earth" (9:3–5). With the dawn of the fourth day, though the "earth did cleave together" (10:10), the sight of destruction must have been frightful and, worse, seemingly impossible to surmount. The immediate task for survivors would have been to find other survivors in the rubble of collapsed buildings and homes. Those so trapped would not have survived much longer. They had already spent three dreadful days pinched between fallen timbers and stones, and the coming heat of the fourth day would make their survival precarious at best.

It is possible that during the following anxiety-filled days people set aside their petty differences that had stripped their society of its political and social glue, and together worked feverishly to rescue those still alive in the tumbled structures. But even after pulling fortunate survivors from the storm's wreckage, people would have sought those skilled in the physician's arts to help loved ones and friends to heal. We suppose that there were many who received no skilled help to set broken limbs or to doctor gaping wounds. Some such unfortunates must have been among those "lame" persons whom Jesus would heal (3 Ne. 17:9; 26:15). After seeing to the needs and comfort of the injured and dying, people faced another daunting, physically taxing task—that of rebuilding homes and recovering seed to plant their fields. The tempestuous winds would have stripped fruits and nuts from trees, and flattened fields of corn and beans. But other plants not yet in blossom or not yet grown would have survived. In all, it was a tall order for people to wrest some sort of normal life from the ashes and debris lying at their feet. But they seem to have succeeded against the odds—a tribute to their combined character—because, when Jesus requested bread and wine for the sacrament, some was available, an indicator that people had enjoyed at least a moderately successful harvest (3 Ne. 18:1). Such success, doubtless brought about by unified efforts, formed a tangible prelude to Jesus' appeals for unity.

ORDINANCES

The Savior would say much that day. But His extended sermon would consist of more than principles for action and for thought, more than principles for probing our relationship to God and for testing our relationship to others, more than principles for examining ourselves and for standardizing our behavior. According to Jesus' discussion, such noble and important principles do not stand in cool isolation. Rather, Jesus drew the crowd's attention to ordinances as the essential companions to the principles, the one fitting hand-in-glove with the other. Moreover, as we shall see, Jesus meshed both principles and ordinances with practical action.

Initially, it was baptism that occupied the Savior's discussion and, at the very end of the first day, it was the Eucharist or the sacrament. Jesus' declarations about these ordinances bracket all else that He talked about that day. For after the crowd received their witness about Jesus' divinity by seeing Him, feeling Him, hearing Him, they listened to a sermon. Almost as a prelude to the main part of His remarks, which parallel the Sermon on the Mount, He turned the minds of the whole congregation to baptism by publicly conferring on Nephi, the head of the church, "the power . . . [to] baptize this people" (3 Ne. 11:21). We sense that this ordinance had become a fount of contention. For the Savior voiced His keen desire to the throng, and particularly to those eleven others whom He chose and empowered to baptize, that "there shall be no disputations among you" (11:22, 28). Jesus thereafter cleared the air by declaring both that a person needed to repent of sins and that there was a proper procedure for baptizing the repentant soul. He even repeated the words that those in authority were to say as they baptized an individual: "Having authority given me of Jesus Christ, I baptize you in the name of the Father, and of the Son, and of the Holy Ghost. Amen" (11:25).

According to the record, Jesus spoke the words "baptism" or "baptize" no fewer than thirteen times. The assembled audience could not have missed His emphasis. And, though He later turned to His chosen twelve disciples rather than to the assembly to instruct them about the sacrament, no one could miss the fact that this subject came at the end of the day, a position of emphasis because it would be fresh in the minds of the disciples when Jesus departed. Thus, His concern about ordinances—baptism and the sacrament—framed His other words that day, setting those words between sacred, saving ceremonies.

Concerning the sacrament, the Savior's declarations recall to our minds the lines which the Apostle Paul penned two dozen or so years later to church members in Corinth.[6] To His audience here, Jesus said that He was giving "another commandment . . . that ye [the disciples] shall not suffer any one knowingly to partake of my flesh and blood unworthily." Why not? Because, as Jesus explained in somber clarity, "whoso eateth and drinketh my flesh and blood unworthily eateth and drinketh damnation to his soul." As a result, Jesus firmly instructed the disciples, "if ye know that a man is unworthy to eat and drink of my flesh and blood ye shall forbid him" (3 Ne. 18:27–29). At this point, this commandment touches on a matter of church procedure. And Jesus' next words do as well: "Nevertheless, ye shall not cast him out from among you, but ye shall minister unto him and shall pray for him unto the Father in my name" (18:30). According to the Savior, there is a compelling reason to continue to work with the unworthy: "ye know not but what they will return and repent, and come unto me with full purpose of heart, and I shall heal them; and ye shall be the means of bringing salvation unto them" (18:32).

"THE SPIRIT OF CONTENTION IS NOT OF ME"

One of the bold threads of Jesus' instructions on that first day concerned "disputations" and "contentions." He first mentioned these fractious evils in connection with baptism. But His teaching about such evils spread out to include more than the possible staining of an ordinance. And we can see how Jesus widened the principle. At first, He states that He was instructing His disciples in baptismal procedures so that "there shall be no disputations among you" (3 Ne. 11:22). After reviewing the procedures, including the words of the baptismal prayer and the fact that baptism is performed by immersion, He affirms that He has clarified procedural matters so that there would be no "disputations among you concerning the points of my doctrine, as there have hitherto been" (11:28). Why? Because among the members of the Godhead there is unity, and disputations among their worshipers heap scorn on that spirit of unity: "verily I say unto you, that the Father, and the Son, and the Holy Ghost are one; and I am in the Father, and the Father in me, and the Father and I are one" (11:27). In stark contrast to this divine unity, which should be reflected in the earthly church, stands "the spirit of contention" which "is not of me, but is of the devil, who is the father of contention, and he stirreth up the hearts of men to contend with anger, one with another" (11:29). Thus, those who impenitently pursue courses of "contention" and "anger" shove themselves away from the Savior, one of the important points that He stressed this first day.

The issue of unity versus "contentions" and "disputations" was not minor. Throughout the generations following the rupture between the brothers Laman and Nephi, lack of unity had bedeviled the entire Book of Mormon society, leading to skirmishes and raids, murder and war. And as one contentious dispute followed another, distrust and hatred continued to fester as an unhealed canker just beneath the surface of people's lives. Finally, less than a half-dozen years before the Savior's appearance, national unity—such as it was in both the Lamanite and Nephite hegemonies—simply disintegrated. The result was that many small states came to consist of tribes and extended families whose only common cause was "not to go to war with another." Jesus deplored the whole situation: "they . . . did destroy the peace of my people and the government of the land" (3 Ne. 9:9). He knew their fractious history and knew that the divisions would eventually lead again to bloodshed and suffering.

The unity that the Savior pled for was simple and, seemingly, limited to believers. It had to do not only with the way that church members should practice essential ordinances within the church—baptism and the sacrament—but also with the way that they should treat each other as fellow saints—"Judge not that ye be not judged," and so forth (3 Ne. 14:1). But Jesus would have known that such manifestations of unity within the church would burst beyond the membership of the church, spilling into the lives of all citizens, whether church members or not. Moreover, its effect would be stunning in its strength, introducing an era of peace and goodwill unequaled in the annals of this earth. To be sure, people had come together in common cause following the devastating storm. But their efforts of rescuing others and rebuilding their lives were born out of necessity. And there was no guarantee that, after the crisis had receded, they would not turn back to what they had been—hopelessly divided into tribes. But then Jesus came. The unity that He offered was infinitely more potent and everlastingly more durable. Why? Because this unity arose out of individuals' inner willingness to cooperate and pull together, sharing a palpable joy at having "all things common" with neighbors and family (3 Ne. 26:19; 4 Ne. 1:3). It is this tie to the inner soul of each person that made this unity succeed and made it endure.[7]

MY DOCTRINE

The Savior's reference to "disputations . . . concerning the points of my doctrine" deftly steered his audience to His next major teaching, namely, to "declare . . . my doctrine" (3 Ne. 11:28, 31). Importantly, His doctrine consists of several interlocking parts. Introducing it, He specifies that His doctrine comes from "the Father" and that it emanates from the Godhead. As the spokesman for the Godhead, "the Father commandeth all men, everywhere, to repent and believe in [the Son]" (11:32). Thus, the first two parts of the doctrine are belief or faith in the Son, and repentance. Jesus goes on to say that "whoso believeth in me, and is baptized, the same shall be saved" (11:33). Hence, the third part of His doctrine consists of baptism. To the person who "believeth in me" and "believeth in the Father also . . . will the Father bear record of me, for he will visit him with fire and with the Holy Ghost" (11:35). In this light, it becomes evident that the fourth dimension of Jesus' doctrine has to do "with fire and with the Holy Ghost," which come from the Father. There are two further aspects of Jesus' doctrine. He uncovers the first in the following words: "I say unto you, ye must repent, and become as a little child, and be baptized in my name. . . . And again I say unto you, ye must repent, and be baptized in my name, and become as a little child" (11:37–38). Besides two elements that we have already seen—repentance and baptism—the aspect that rises afresh is that of becoming "as a little child." The Savior repeats this point twice for accentuation. Moreover, He intentionally places this point both before and after the requirement to "be baptized," thus underscoring its essential importance both before baptism and afterwards. He then summarizes, introducing the final aspect: "this is my doctrine, and whoso buildeth upon this buildeth upon my rock." The fortifying result for those who accept and build upon the deep-seated elements of Jesus' doctrine is that the "gates of hell shall not prevail against them" (11:39).[8]

But there is a further warning. It has to do with adding to or subtracting from Jesus' doctrine, even in the most minute ways. For "whoso shall declare more or less than this, and establish it for my doctrine, the same cometh of evil, and is not built upon my rock" (3 Ne. 11:40). Later, near the end of that first day, the Savior voiced a similar warning after blessing and then causing the elements of the sacrament to be distributed to the crowd: "whoso among you shall do more or less than these are not built upon my rock" (3 Ne. 18:13). Instead, one in authority was "to do, even as I have done, even as I have broken bread and blessed it and given it unto you" (18:6). We detect in Jesus' words that even the slightest variation from what He has set as a standard is wholly unacceptable and, more ominously, leaves the tampering perpetrator without defense against the raging tempests of evil, as if "built upon a sandy foundation" (18:13).

THE SERMON AT THE TEMPLE

Commentators have treated in ample detail the next part of Jesus' sermon whereas, by comparison, the rest has drawn scant interest. Why? Because this upcoming section of Jesus' sermon is almost identical to the Sermon on the Mount, one of His paramount addresses concerning what He expects of His followers.[9] Hence, the modern interest. Without trying to cover ground that is already well compacted, we observe that two features of this sermon immediately stand forth. The first has to do with its long introduction which, unlike the Sermon on the Mount in Matthew's Gospel, molds a framework around Jesus' remarks. The second is its Christocentric character, that is, Jesus takes over center stage. Let us explore each of these dimensions.

The long introduction clarifies that Jesus aimed His remarks at church members, those who "believe in [the] words" of Jesus' chosen twelve "and come down into the depths of humility" and are baptized "with water" and "with fire and with the Holy Ghost," thereby receiving "a remission of their sins" (3 Ne. 12:1–2). Of these individuals, "blessed are the poor in spirit who come unto me, for theirs is the kingdom of heaven," and so on (12:3). The law of the gospel, as a person could term this sermon, is not for just anyone. It is chiefly for insiders. This disclosure sheds greater light on the Sermon on the Mount which, in Matthew's gospel, begins rather abruptly, almost as if it were addressed to anyone. To be sure, Matthew records that Jesus was teaching His "disciples," His followers. But He offers no more context than this (see Matt. 5:1–2). In what appears to be a more complete account in Third Nephi, because apparently disciples recorded it almost immediately after Jesus delivered the sermon,[10] we grasp the fact that Jesus was addressing church members who had been baptized and had received a remission of sins.

The passage quoted above— "blessed are the poor in spirit who come unto me, for theirs is the kingdom of heaven"—draws out the second point, the Christocentric nature of the sermon (3 Ne. 12:3). The relative clause "who come unto me" does not appear in Matthew's record. It occurs only in the Book of Mormon account.[11] Its presence, along with other similar expressions, lifts Jesus as it were into the center of His own words.

In an impressive array of alterations to Matthew's record that persist from one end of the sermon to the other, the Savior draws attention to Himself as the resurrected, glorified Son of God, constantly reminding His hearers that He alone opens the door to salvation. For example, in Matthew's version, Jesus says "Ye are the salt of the earth" (Matt. 5:13). To these people in the New World, Jesus specified that *"I give unto you* to be the salt of the earth," underlining that it is He who empowers those whose influence will be as savoring salt (3 Ne. 12:13; emphasis added). In another instance, Matthew records Jesus as saying, "one jot or one tittle shall in no wise pass from the law, till all be fulfilled " (Matt. 5:18). In mild contrast, to this group of people He declares in words that tie to His redemptive work: "one jot nor one tittle hath not passed away from the law, but *in me* it hath all been fulfilled" (3 Ne. 12:18; emphasis added). With such changes, Jesus Himself stands in the foreground of the sermon. In Matthew's recounting, Jesus said, "If thou bring thy gift to the altar, and there rememberest that thy brother hath ought against thee; Leave there thy gift . . . first be reconciled to thy brother, and then come and offer thy gift" (Matt. 5:23–24). To His audience in the New World, Jesus holds the focus on Himself: "if ye shall *come unto me,* or shall desire to come unto me, and rememberest that thy brother hath aught against thee . . . first be reconciled to thy brother, and then *come unto me* . . . and *I will receive you"* (3 Ne. 12:23–24; emphasis added). According to Matthew, at the end of this part of the sermon, Jesus commanded His hearers in Galilee: "Be ye therefore perfect, even as your Father which is in heaven is perfect" (Matt. 5:48). The significant change in Jesus' wording in the New World sermon follows the pattern of Jesus becoming the center of His own words: "Therefore I would that ye should be perfect *even as I,* or your Father who is in heaven is perfect" (3 Ne. 12:48; emphasis added).

SELF AND OTHERS

All of these Christocentric examples appear in the first part of the sermon wherein the Savior changes or replaces provisions of the law of Moses, purposely placing Himself amidst the new law. Adjustments also appear throughout the other two segments or chapters. In both sections, Jesus touches on subjects that have everything to do with His overriding agenda, that of unity. In the first of these segments in chapter 13 of Third Nephi, Jesus focuses on an individual's public style versus personal substance, a substantial shift from His concerns about the law of Moses in the previous chapter (3 Ne. 13; see Matt. 6).[12] He effectively raises the bar for His hearers by dealing initially with right action before God, whether public or private (3 Ne. 13:1–18). Jesus' examples—almsgiving, praying, and fasting—point to attempts to aggrandize oneself in God's sight which, if insincere, fail miserably and therefore seem to raise the individual only in the estimation of fellow humans. Jesus' point seems to be that we cannot somehow elevate ourselves in God's all-seeing estimation except by sincere action. Even the last segment, which has to do with our response to this world (treasures, masters, bodily needs), draws our attention to the connections with the divine world as the real measure of all our actions (see 13:19–34). From beginning to end, we can read chapeter thirteen as a statement about the tension between public and heavenly recognition; that is, about right motives, about sincerity, about visible style and invisible substance. In effect, Jesus' focus rests on how we respond to our achievements or our own actions. To the Prophet Joseph Smith the Savior issued a similar caution to those who "undertake to cover [their] sins, or to gratify [their] pride [and their] vain ambition." From such dispirited individuals "the heavens withdraw themselves." And because of their dismal future prospects, "the Spirit of the Lord is grieved" (D&C 121:37).

At this point in the sermon, the Savior augmented His commandments about how persons respond to their own motives, wants, and desires. He adds the dimension of how they should respond to the actions of others, that is, to actions or events external to themselves (3 Ne. 14; see Matt. 7). Two examples will illustrate. Although Jesus' new concern does not appear in every verse, it stands forth prominently in His directive, "Judge not, that ye be not judged" (3 Ne. 14:1). This warning rests on a legal principle that the Savior highlights elsewhere: "Judge not, and ye shall not be judged: condemn not and ye shall not be condemned" (Luke 6:37).[13] Then Jesus melds the two concerns together—motives and responses—in His very positive command: "Therefore, all things whatsoever ye would that men should do to you, do ye even so to them, for this is the law and the prophets" (3 Ne. 14:12). Here, Jesus tightly summarizes the essential character of the law and the prophets, kneading their intent into a very few words about how we treat one another. By so doing He adroitly brings together His concerns about motives and responses.

Jesus brings these concerns to a stunning culmination by condemning how a person uses outwardly noble motives to mask a lack of inner obedience and conviction: "Not everyone that saith unto me, Lord, Lord, shall enter into the kingdom of heaven; but he that doeth the will of my Father who is in heaven. Many will say . . . have we not prophesied . . . and . . . cast out devils, and . . . done many wonderful works? And then I will profess . . . depart from me, ye that work iniquity" (3 Ne. 14:21–23).

At the literal core of this set of issues stands the kingdom of God. The Savior's directive in 3 Nephi 13:33 forms a midpoint in the latter two sections of the sermon: "seek ye first the kingdom of God and his righteousness." Thus, according to the Savior's words, we can enter the kingdom only after we have garnished ourselves in right motives both when dealing with our inner selves and, equally, when dealing with others. For God measures all of these dimensions of our lives. At the end of this segment, Jesus declares, "whoso heareth these sayings of mine and doeth them, I will liken him unto a wise man, who built his house upon a rock—And the rain descended, and the floods came, and the winds blew . . . and it fell not, for it was founded upon a rock" (3 Ne. 14:24–25).

In sum, Jesus' ringing appeals for personal changes in matters of integrity and social interaction fit snugly within His larger agenda of unity. For only with the genuine personal effort of each individual to overcome both inner unrighteous desires and peevish relationships with others could these hearers realize His vision for celestial-like unity within their society.

I AM THE LAW

The Savior's hearers—at least "some among them"—found it difficult to grasp that "the law is fulfilled that was given unto Moses" (3 Ne. 15:2, 4; also 12:18–19). This inability was nothing new. His Old World followers also experienced difficulty with aspects of the Mosaic law. To them He had said, "Do not commit adultery, Do not kill, Do not steal, Do not bear false witness, Honour thy father and thy mother" (Luke 18:20). Plainly, Jesus exhibits a deep respect for this part of the law. Moreover, in order to illustrate the importance of the commandment "thou shalt love thy neighbor as thyself" (Lev. 19:18), Jesus recited the parable of the good Samaritan, one of His most memorable stories (Luke 10:30–37). On the other hand, Jesus was critical of certain aspects of the law. For example, the Savior stood firm against the particular aspect that we call *lex talionis,* the legal facet that allowed a person to exact revenge against another by taking "eye for eye, tooth for tooth."[14] Instead, as Jesus admonished His disciples in both the Old and New Worlds, a person is to "love your enemies, bless them that curse you, do good to them that hate you, and pray for them which despitefully use you and persecute you" (Matt. 5:44; 3 Ne. 12:44). In this case, Jesus does not merely affirm or even adjust the law; He effectively dismisses it, replacing it with a command to love enemies. Thus, in Jesus' view, the law seems both to stand and not to stand. And this apparent ambiguity may have led to the confusion that Jesus seeks to solve for His New World hearers.

Truth be told, the Savior had already declared to the assembled crowd both that "the law . . . hath all been fulfilled" and that "old things are done away, and all things have become new" (3 Ne. 12:18, 47). Even so, "some among them . . . understood not" that "the law," which points to the coming Messiah, "is fulfilled" (3 Ne. 15:2, 4). To clarify completely, Jesus drew together two concepts that associate him directly with the law of Moses: *"I am he* that gave the law" and "the law *in me* is fulfilled" (15:5; emphasis added). Besides the allusion to Himself as Jehovah who called Moses[15]—within the divine name I am—He placed himself once again in the center of the picture: "I have come to fulfill the law; therefore it hath an end" (15:5). Moreover, "the law which was given unto Moses hath an end *in me*" (15:8; emphasis added). In contrast, now "I am the [new] law, and the light. Look unto me, and endure to the end, and ye shall live" (15:9).

With this declaration, the Savior had moved to fresh ground. The new law which He embodied—His body bore its tokens in the scars or "prints of the nails" (3 Ne. 11:14)—rested on His following "the will of the Father in all things from the beginning" and thereby submitting Himself to be "slain for the sins of the world" (11:11, 14). He thus became the exemplar of submission to God. He was also the keeper of the covenant and the giver of its commandments. For in contrast to the now defunct law, "*the covenant which I have made* with my people is not all fulfilled" (3 Ne. 15:8; emphasis added). Since its fulfillment lies yet in future, there is much to do: "therefore keep my commandments" (15:10). Those who follow Him follow His example in submitting themselves to God. And that means keeping the commandments of the new law of the Son.

"THIS IS THE LAND"

Inspired teachers had taught the idea of a promised land for centuries. More than 600 years before the Savior's appearance, the prophets Lehi and Nephi had learned that their family would "be led [by the Lord] to a land of promise; yea, even a land which I have prepared for you . . . which is choice above all other lands" (1 Ne. 2:20).[16] After arriving in the New World, Lehi declared that "this land is consecrated unto him whom [God] shall bring" (2 Ne. 1:7). But not everyone seems to have been thoroughly convinced, including some descendants of Nephi who were not inclined to accept the New World as their promised land, their new God-given home. A review of key passages leads us to think that these people, who were Israelites, longed for the original homeland granted to their people by the Lord.[17] To those in the crowd that day who might have harbored any doubts, the Risen Jesus spoke directly: "this is the land of your inheritance; and the Father hath given it unto you" (3 Ne. 15:13). Later, during the second day of His three-day visit, Jesus would say that "the Father hath commanded me that I should give unto you this land, for your inheritance" (3 Ne. 20:14). From these passages it seems plain first that Jesus had led their forebears from Jerusalem to the New World in their memorable exodus, and next that He was offering reassurances to His audience that grew out of His own past actions.

But there was a more immediate issue at hand which the Savior's gentle assurances were apparently designed to meet. It was that of the crippling impact of the terrible storm months ago. We can almost hear people saying then, "If this is a promised land, then I don't want to stay in it. It is wrecked beyond repair." And, "I lost my husband and children when our home collapsed, and the place seems cursed." Further, "If God cares so much about this land, I am not sure that I can please Him." It was Jesus' task to lift, to raise the spirits of His hearers. And one of the best evidences for the demanding urgency to lift the crowd's morale is the fact that He stopped his discourse on His covenant with the house of Israel, saving its conclusion for the next day (see 3 Ne. 16, 20–22). Instead of finishing His discourse, He remarked: "I have compassion upon you; my bowels are filled with mercy." He then healed "their sick and their afflicted, and their lame" (3 Ne. 17:7, 9). Why did the Savior stop His discourse and heal the afflicted? Because, as He said, "I perceive that ye desire that I should show unto you what I have done unto your brethren at Jerusalem, for I see that your faith is sufficient that I should heal you" (17:8). Jesus here ties His expression "what I have done . . . at Jerusalem" to healing, an observation that underscores firmly what people in the crowd acutely needed at that moment. And, not surprisingly, Jesus was responsive to their needs rather than continuing His discourse.

To be sure, the Savior's presence alone hoisted their spirits, much as the presence of an important person will do for any of us. Further, the strong, reaffirming spiritual witness that each received when touching Him added an enlivening buoyancy to people's morale. But He called His audience "weak" and unable to "understand all my words" (3 Ne. 17:2). Even in His presence, as the hours began to wear away, their hearts and minds evidently ran to other concerns. Those concerns dissipated, at least in part, when "he did heal them every one" (17:9). And there is more.

LITTLE CHILDREN

The Savior created one of the most memorable scenes in the Book of Mormon when, right after healing people in the crowd, "he commanded that their little children should be brought" to Him (3 Ne. 17:11). In what follows, Jesus brings the crowd closer to a full healing, a complete lifting of their spirits.

In response to Jesus' directive, parents "brought their children" forward "and set them down upon the ground round about him, and Jesus stood in the midst" (3 Ne. 17:12). In the process, the "multitude gave way" and then the Savior "commanded the multitude that they should kneel upon the ground" (17:12–13). At this point, we can imagine Jesus standing in the middle of the seated children who were surrounded by the kneeling adults. Jesus then prayed.

His prayer was beyond words to describe. Jesus began by groaning "within himself," a sound that people would not have expected (3 Ne. 17:14). We can only imagine what it was like to hear the Son of God groaning aloud. Then immediately out of His mouth came the words, "Father, I am troubled because of the wickedness of the people of the house of Israel" (17:14). The crowd, of course, consisted of "people of the house of Israel." So Jesus includes them within these opening words of His prayer. But even though they are infused with "wickedness," He calls down the blessings of heaven in a stunning way.

At some point after this first day, the people present bore "record" of the occasion (see 3 Ne. 17:16). We are tempted to believe that officials created a permanent record by inscribing the following words perhaps on metal or stone. The record exhibits a poetic character that points to care when creating it. We read the following:

And after this manner do they bear record:

The eye hath never seen,
neither hath the ear heard, before,
so great and marvelous things
as we saw and heard Jesus speak
unto the Father;

And no tongue can speak,
neither can there be written by any man,
neither can the hearts of men conceive
so great and marvelous things
as we both saw and heard Jesus speak;

and no one can conceive of the joy which filled our souls
at the time we heard him pray for us
unto the Father. (3 Ne. 17:16–17)[18]

We read that "so great was the joy of the multitude" at hearing the Savior's prayer "that they were overcome" (3 Ne. 17:18). Even so, "Jesus . . . bade them arise" from the ground (17:19). He had not finished, and they obeyed. Uttering words that uncover a notable change of His feelings from being "troubled" to joy, Jesus confesses, "now behold, my joy is full" (17:14, 20). Then "he wept . . . and he took their little children, one by one, and blessed them, and prayed unto the Father for them" (17:21). The crowd was enthralled. But they could not have anticipated what happened next. For after saying to the multitude, "Behold your little ones," they raised their eyes from the children "toward heaven" and "saw angels descending out of heaven as it were in the midst of fire" (17:23–24). From the language of the record, it seems clear that people found difficulty in trying to describe what they were seeing, whether it was fire or something similar. In any event, they beheld that angels "came down and encircled those little ones about, and they were encircled about with fire." Moreover, "the angels did minister unto them" (17:24). It seems that the angels ministered both to the children and to the adults. It was a never-to-be-forgotten moment.

We must explore one more aspect in this scene. It has to do with how we picture the setting of these events that touched the children. We start with the Savior. As the most Holy One, He was standing "in the midst," at the sacred center (3 Ne. 17:12, 13). The children sat "upon the ground round about him" (17:12). When the angels "came down," they "encircled those little ones about." In their place next to the children, the angels themselves "were encircled about with fire" (17:24). On the edge stood the adults. And beyond them was what we might term profane space which stretched away from this holy scene. If we understand that the Risen Jesus was the most holy Person in this setting, and that holiness somehow diminishes as one moves away from the Savior, then the children sat in the next most holy place, namely, next to Him. Next to them were the angels who "did minister unto [the children]" (17:24). Beyond them was the celestial fire; beyond the fire, the adults. Was there not a visual message to the adults about the special status of children in Jesus' eyes? Is there not a message for us?

ARCHITECTURE OF THE TEMPLE

The previous set of scenes illumine physical characteristics of the temple. At the beginning of the day, Jesus had arrived and "stood in the midst of them" (3 Ne. 11:8). Where was Jesus standing? He had arrived that day while people were "gathered together . . . round about the temple . . . in the land Bountiful" (11:1). We further note that when Jesus came down, He "stood" so that "the eyes of the whole multitude were turned upon him" (11:8; cf. 17:5). We conclude either that Jesus was standing on an elevated spot so that all could see Him or that the crowd was perched on elevated ground that surrounded at least a section of the temple, thus allowing them to look down on Him without obstruction. Which was it? This and the other accounts seem to point to Jesus standing above the crowd, not below. How so? On two occasions, the eyes of the crowd were drawn to heaven, both when Jesus first appeared and when the angels came down (see 11:5; 17:24). If the temple structure rose above the gathering crowd as they heard the voice, their eyes would naturally follow the prominence of the temple upward toward the voice and subsequently to the descending Jesus. Similarly, it is natural to think that the crowd was already looking upward at Jesus rather than downward when they "cast their eyes towards heaven" and saw "angels descending" toward the children (3 Ne. 17:24).

Moreover, there are hints that the crowd stood in an open space, which itself was not covered with stone or masonry. For instance, we read that "the whole multitude fell *to the earth*" after the Savior introduced Himself (3 Ne. 11:12; emphasis added). In addition, Jesus later instructed these same people to "kneel down *upon the ground*" as He prepared to pray for them. Moreover, after He had prayed for them, "they arose *from the earth*" (17:13, 20; emphasis added). What can we conclude thus far? These notices seem to say that the people were standing on ground just outside of the structure of the edifice and were not standing on stonework.

What did the edifice itself consist of? None of the passages that we have reviewed to this point describe the Savior's movements within or near a masonry structure. Instead, they all seem to point to an earthen structure, perhaps made of beaten earth. Of course, the temple may have consisted of an earthen core with a masonry facing added at certain points. Such masonry, for instance, could have formed a stairway or a retaining wall or a platform resting atop a small earthen hill or pyramid. But nothing in the accounts hints at any stonework. To be sure, the earliest temple built in the city of Nephi bore resemblances to the temple of Solomon, which itself was erected of stones (see 2 Ne. 5:16; 1 Kgs. 6:7; 1 Chr. 22:2, 14–15). We are therefore justified in believing that this first temple included stonework. But we cannot know whether stoneworking skills were ever applied to the temple structure in Bountiful where Jesus appeared. In fact, all passages that speak of the physical context of Jesus' visit repeat terms such as "earth" and "ground" rather than stones. If this is so, where was Jesus standing?

As we have seen, it seems evident that the Savior started His visit by standing on an elevated spot. But where? It is most likely that He positioned Himself inside the structure of the temple, perhaps on a stairway or on a raised platform. Much later in the day, He may have moved from that spot to a place next to the crowd. For, as He was praying for the multitude, "he himself also knelt *upon the earth*" as the crowd was doing (3 Ne. 17:15; emphasis added). We surmise that He stepped outside the structure of the temple before He knelt, perhaps kneeling next to the crowd. In fact, we read that the multitude had already retreated a little, effectively allowing Him to join them where they were. For people had moved back when "they brought their little children" so that Jesus could bless them, implying that the children did not gather on the temple structure itself: "and the multitude gave way till [the children] had all been brought unto him" (17:12). Further, when the parents brought their children forward for the blessing, "they . . . set [their children] down *upon the ground* round about him" (17:12; emphasis added). It seems evident that, wherever

Jesus was standing or sitting, people could still see Him. For they knew when He arose from the ground and when He wept and when He blessed the children (17:18, 21). From these passages, then, we conclude that Jesus apparently stepped outside the temple structure in order to join the crowd before blessing the children. If this is so, it speaks volumes about Jesus' interest to mingle and touch and bless people rather than to stay within the confines of an edifice, however sacred it might be.

SACRED SPACE

The terminology that underlies the images of Jesus descending from the temple to bless the people also highlights the sacred character of the temple. We read that, at the beginning of his visit, the Savior "stood in the midst of them" so that "the eyes of the whole multitude were turned upon him" (3 Ne. 11:8). Later, in the scene that we have just described, He "stood in the midst" of the children (3 Ne. 17:12). Then, when the angels appeared, they descended "out of heaven as it were in the midst of fire" (17:24). We note that each of these passages introduces the word "midst," a word that can carry a sacred meaning. For it can point to a sacred center.[19] A couple of examples will illustrate.

In a passage quoted from Isaiah, we read a few lines from the Lord's song of praise that He dictates for the suppliant:

> Cry out and shout, thou inhabitant of Zion;
> for great is the Holy One of Israel in the midst of thee.
> (2 Ne. 22:6; Isa. 12:6)

We notice immediately the expression "in the midst," which mirrors the Book of Mormon record.[20] In this quotation, it is evident that "the Holy One of Israel" is "in the midst" of His people. Where would that be? In Isaiah's day, the Lord was thought to inhabit His house, His temple. In another passage, wherein the Savior quotes a warning from the prophet Micah, a similar notion arises:

> Thy graven images I will also cut off, and thy standing images out of the midst of thee, and thou shalt no more worship the

> works of thy hands: And I will pluck up thy groves out of the midst of thee. (3 Ne. 21:17–18; Micah 5:13–14)

Micah's references to "the midst" connect to the temple of his day where the "graven images" and "standing images" stood. In addition, the "groves" evidently consisted of trees or bushes that represented the goddess Asherah at her altar or sanctuary.[21] In light of these passages from Isaiah and Micah, it is apparent that the expression "the midst" often points to a temple or to a sanctuary which, in a symbolic sense, stands in "the midst" of God's people. This is not all.

If we are correct in surmising that the Savior came to an earthen temple in Bountiful, there may be a conceptual tie between such a temple and the primordial mountain or primordial hill. This might help explain why the Nephites in this region may have chosen not to build their temple with stone. (It is also possible that stone was difficult to transport to the site.) According to ancient sources, temples stood atop mountains or hills to commemorate the place where, during creation, the earth first pushed up out of the watery chaos and began to give form to the created earth.[22] We see the connection between temples and mountains in the famous prophecy of both Isaiah and Micah:

> And it shall come to pass in the last days, that *the mountain of the Lord's house* shall be established in the top of the mountains. . . . And many people shall go and say, Come ye, and let us go up to *the mountain* of the Lord, to *the house* of the God of Jacob. (Isa. 2:2–3; Micah 4:1–2; emphasis added)

This prophecy establishes a firm conceptual bond between a mountain and the Lord's house, the temple. It would therefore not have been out of character for the edifice in Bountiful to have been mostly or entirely made of earth.

There is one additional notation about the setting of the temple. It has to do with a nearby source of water. On the second day, the crowd had grown so large that there was "an exceedingly great number" of people "in the place where Jesus should show himself" (3 Ne. 19:3). Presumably, that "place" was near the temple. Further, because "the multitude was so great," the twelve disciples "separated [the crowd] into twelve bodies" in order to "teach" them "those same words which Jesus had spoken" the prior day (19:5–6, 8). After rehearsing Jesus' instructions to the twelve groups, the twelve disciples "went down unto the water's edge" where "Nephi went down into the water and was baptized" (19:10–11). Thereafter, Nephi "baptized" the rest of the twelve (19:12). The point? It is evident that there was a source of water nearby that was deep enough to baptize an adult person. What is not clear is whether it was a running stream, such as a river, or whether it was a standing source, such as a pond or seashore. It is also not clear whether the setting for the temple was chosen because of the nearness of water or whether the builders had excavated a channel that brought water to the temple grounds. In any case, the water would presumably have allowed the cultivation of a garden in the vicinity of the temple. Not surprisingly, both water and greenery are features common to ancient sacred sites.[23]

THE COVENANT—SCATTERING AND GATHERING

Frequently, it is the simple gesture or act, rather than a major event, that plants a meaning deep in people's lives. Such simple, seemingly minor actions may mean the difference between softened emotions or hardened hearts, between calm understanding or chafed feelings. Months before, the people in the Savior's audience had felt the chastening sting of the voice in the darkness after the storm. That voice had rubbed emotions until they were raw by accusing the storm's survivors of "iniquity and abominations," which brought the devil to laugh and "his angels [to] rejoice" (3 Ne. 9:2, 12). But, besides the chafed feelings and devastated emotions that needed healing, there was a deeper insecurity running through the society that also needed to be resolved, an insecurity about being cut off from the land of Jerusalem, from the land promised to the ancestors of Jesus' audience. For there is evidence from the first generation to the last that people pined for Jerusalem. We see this longing not only lingering behind the pep-talks of Nephi (see 1 Ne. 19 and 22), but also within the mournful lines of Jacob—"we being a lonesome and a solemn people, wanderers, cast out from Jerusalem" (Jacob 7:26)—as well as in Moroni's parting words, "awake, and arise from the dust, O

Jerusalem" (Moro. 10:31, paraphrasing Isa. 52:1–2).[24] In order to salve such raw feelings and to douse smoldering insecurities, the Savior rehearsed the important place of His hearers and their descendants in God's grand plans, plans that reached far ahead to the last days. The reason for their important place in these plans went back to ancient covenants. And Jesus' simple, low-key approach went far in reassuring the people in His audience of their lofty status in God's eyes, both now and in the future. In addition, one of the sublime elements accompanying Jesus' words was the setting: He was offering sacred reassurances to them in the shadows of the temple in Bountiful.

On the first day of His visit, as we recall, the Savior broke off His sermon in order to meet the unspoken but desperate needs of His listeners, acknowledging their destitution with His words: "I perceive that ye desire that I should show unto you what I have done unto your brethren at Jerusalem" (3 Ne. 17:8). Before that moment, He had been speaking about fulfilling "the covenant which the Father hath made unto all the people of the house of Israel" (3 Ne. 16:5). The next day, Jesus drew His audience back to the subject: "now I finish the commandment which the Father hath commanded me concerning this people, who are a remnant of the house of Israel" (3 Ne. 20:10). He had already taken up the Mosaic law and the broad issue of inheritance on the first day.[25] Now He turned to the future of the house of Israel and also of the Gentiles. Why? Because people do not live in a vacuum. The future of the descendants of these New World hearers was tied tightly to that of their neighboring Gentiles.

For the rest of chapter 20 in Third Nephi, and the next two chapters, the Savior held the crowd's collective focus on three important aspects of God's plans. They are (1) the scattering and subsequent gathering of the house of Israel, (2) the role of the Gentiles, and (3) the spiritual transformation of both Israelites and Gentiles so that they "believe in me, that I am Jesus Christ, the Son of God" (3 Ne. 20:31; also 20:13).

The Savior gave to the gathered throng a sense of God's timing. There is to be "a sign," Jesus declared, "that ye may know the time when these things shall be about to take place, that I shall gather in . . . my people" (3 Ne. 21:1). What is that sign? It is to appear "when the words of Isaiah should be fulfilled" (3 Ne. 20:11–12; also 16:17). A commingling of certain events will constitute the sign. Specifically, "when these things which I declare unto you . . . shall be made known unto the Gentiles that they may know concerning this people," and "when these things [which Jesus teaches] . . . shall come forth of the Father from them [the Gentiles] unto you," and lastly "when . . . thy seed shall begin to know these things," then "it shall be a sign unto them . . . that the work of the Father hath already commenced unto the fulfilling of the covenant which he hath made unto . . . the house of Israel" (3 Ne. 21:2–3, 7). Said another way, the record of Jesus' declarations at the Bountiful temple will come to the Gentiles and, in turn, from the Gentiles to the descendants of those in the audience. The appearance of this record will constitute the sign, thus fulfilling a prophecy of Isaiah. What is that prophecy? Jesus alluded to it almost immediately: "in that day . . . shall the Father work a work, which shall be a great and a marvelous work among them; and there shall be among them those who will not believe it" (21:9). This scripture reminds us of the following lines from Isaiah: "behold, I will proceed to do a marvelous work among this people, even a marvelous work and a wonder;" and further, "this people draw near me with their mouth, . . . but have removed their heart far from me," a circumstance of unbelief (Isa. 29:14, 13).

But before God gathers the house of Israel, an act to be heralded by the record of Jesus' words in the New World, there was to be a scattering. That scattering took place in stages and, in two instances, involved God's choice to move people away from Jerusalem. In other cases, it took the form of punishment for wicked acts. All such events, past and future, begin in the Old World, in and around Jerusalem. For, as Jesus pointed out, the forebears of His New World hearers "were separated from among them [the people in Jerusalem] because of their iniquity." Moreover, "other tribes hath the Father separated from them; and it is because of their iniquity that they know not of them" (3 Ne. 15:19–20). Hence, God chose to separate remnants or groups specific to the house of Israel from those in the Old World. We know about three separations. The first involved a large population from the northern kingdom of Israel which the Assyrians took captive in 721 B.C. According to the Old Testament, this separation resulted from sin (2 Kgs. 17:6–19).[26] The second group, whom God led, consisted of the party of Lehi and Sariah who left Jerusalem soon after 600 B.C.[27] To the New World, God also directed a third group, that of Mulek, son of Zedekiah, the last Judahite king (597–586 B.C.; see Omni 1:14–16; Hel. 6:10).

Two other scatterings were to come much later. The first was to be a scattering of Jews following the death of Jesus. Speaking prophetically, Nephi of old had declared that "they shall be scattered among all nations" and "shall wander in the flesh, and perish" (1 Ne. 22:5; 19:14). The second was to be that of the descendants of the crowd listening to Jesus. These later people of the New World, "because of [their] unbelief," would be scattered by the Gentiles and "cast out from among them" (3 Ne. 16:7–8; also 20:15, 27–28; 21:2, 24).

As these latter two groups would suffer at the hands of Gentiles, so they would later receive aid from Gentiles who will "assist my people" to gather (3 Ne. 21:23), the one to "the land of their fathers . . . which is the land of Jerusalem"[28] and the other to the "New Jerusalem" where "the powers of heaven will be."[29] In order for the gathering to go forward, the Gentiles "should be established in this land, and be set up as a free people by the power of the Father, that these things might come forth from them" (21:4). In fact, if the Gentiles did not prepare themselves to assist in this monumental effort, God's people would punish them for their insolence.[30]

Notably, the Savior paints the events of the gathering in the colorful language of the Second Exodus, an image that Isaiah makes vivid. Drawing on Isaiah's inspired reframing of the Exodus experience, Jesus intones,

> And then shall a cry go forth: Depart ye, depart ye, go ye out from thence, touch not that which is unclean; go ye out of the midst of her; be ye clean that bear the vessels of the Lord. For ye shall not go out with haste nor go by flight; for the Lord will go before you, and the God of Israel shall be your rearward. (3 Ne. 20:41–42; Isa. 52:11–12)

Introducing an important change, the Savior refers again to this passage from Isaiah, adjusting the focus onto the Father: "and they shall not go out in haste, nor go by flight, for *I will go* before them, *saith the Father,* and *I will be* their rearward" (3 Ne. 21:29; emphasis added; Isa. 52:12). Thus, it is the Father who will guide events of the gathering, a point that amply illustrates its importance.[31]

THE COVENANT—THE ROLE OF THE GENTILES

It does not come as a surprise that Gentiles would be involved in events that also touch remnants of the house of Israel. After all, people only rarely avoid influences and contacts from others. Hence, Gentiles figure prominently in the Savior's prophecies about later events at a juncture that He calls "the fullness of the Gentiles" (3 Ne. 16:4). As such, they stand both as recipients and as dispensers of God's blessings.

As a portent of the gathering, the record of the Savior's words to His New World hearers is to come through the Gentiles to the house of Israel. He declared that "these sayings which ye shall write [in the record] shall be . . . manifest unto the Gentiles, that through . . . the Gentiles, the remnant of their seed [of the Nephites and Lamanites] . . . may be brought in" (3 Ne. 16:4). To begin the process, the Savior instructed His hearers to "write the things which I have told you; and according to the time and the will of the Father they shall go forth unto the Gentiles" so that "these works [in the record] . . . shall come forth from the Gentiles, unto your seed" (3 Ne. 23:4; 21:5; also 23:4).

For the remnants of the house of Israel, the blessing that flows to them from the record is that, "when these things come to pass that thy seed shall begin to know these things—it shall be a sign unto them, that they may know that the work of the Father hath already commenced" (3 Ne. 21:7). Moreover, the record comes through the Gentiles so that "the remnant of their seed [of the house of Israel], who shall be scattered . . . may be brought in, or may be brought to a knowledge of me, their Redeemer" (3 Ne. 16:4). Thus, the blessings of the record are both temporal and spiritual. That is, the gathering which follows the appearance of the record is to be both physical and spiritual.

In God's plans, blessings are also destined to come to the Gentiles because of the record and because of their role in the gathering. The fact that the Father chooses Gentiles to be His agents for bringing forth the record means that they have received "the blessing" and "the mercies of the Father" (3 Ne. 20:15; 16:9). Such blessing and mercies "shall make them mighty above all, unto the scattering of [God's] people" (20:27). In their role, the Gentiles later become the instrument to "assist my people that they may be gathered in, who are scattered upon all the face of the land" (3 Ne. 21:24).

By the Father boldly extending His mercies to the Gentiles in scattering and then in gathering His people, as well as in bringing forth the record, He will "show forth his power unto the Gentiles . . . that they may repent and come unto [Jesus] and be baptized . . . that they may be numbered among my people" (3 Ne. 21:6).[32] Thus, events in the wider world will lead attentive Gentiles to change their lives. Upon those Gentiles who believe, God will pour out "the Holy Ghost through [Jesus] . . . which blessing upon the Gentiles shall make them mighty" (3 Ne. 20:27). For it is "the Holy Ghost, which witnesses unto them of me and of the Father" (3 Ne. 16:6; also 15:22–23). The happy result for the Gentiles, "if they will repent and hearken unto my words, and harden not their hearts," is that the Savior "will establish [his] church among them, and they shall come in unto the covenant" of the Father (3 Ne. 21:22).

As one might expect, the Resurrected Lord issues a stern warning to Gentiles who do not believe and respond as He hopes. Quoting His Father, Jesus warns, "wo, saith the Father, unto the unbelieving of the Gentiles," for "behold, saith the Father, I will bring the fulness of my gospel from among them" (3 Ne. 16:8, 10). The warning then grows sharper. Referring to Himself, Jesus proclaims that "whosoever will not believe in my words . . . shall be cut off from among my people" (3 Ne. 21:11). As a next horrifying step, His Father threatens that "I will execute vengeance and fury upon them, even as upon the heathen, such as they have not heard" (21:21). In another quotation from His Father, Jesus mournfully warns that "if they [the Gentiles] shall harden their hearts against me I will return their iniquities upon their own heads, saith the Father" (20:28). Through the Son, the Father had listed such iniquities. Specifically, He warned that He would take these drastic actions if the Gentiles "shall sin against my gospel . . . and shall be lifted up in the pride of their hearts above all nations . . . and shall be filled with all manner of lyings, and of deceits, and of mischiefs, and all manner of hypocrisy, and murders, and priestcrafts, and whoredoms, and of secret combinations" (16:10; also 30:2). In sum, the threats to the Gentiles are aimed not only at sinful acts but also at unresponsive disbelief.

THE COVENANT—COMING TO CHRIST

Significantly, missteps by the Gentiles would bring heartening consequences for the house of Israel. For, as the Father promises, if He has to "bring the fulness of my gospel from among" the Gentiles, "then will I remember my covenant which I have made unto my people, O house of Israel, and I will bring my gospel unto them" (3 Ne. 16:10–12).[33] The Savior repeats this promise of future spiritual favors throughout His sermon. We read that "the remnants which shall be scattered abroad . . . [shall] be gathered in from the east and from the west, and from the south and from the north; and they shall be brought to the knowledge of the Lord their God, who hath redeemed them" (3 Ne. 20:13). More precisely, "the fulness of my gospel shall be preached unto them; and they shall believe in me, that I am Jesus Christ, the Son of God" (20:30–31).[34]

Such inspiring proceedings, the Savior affirms, tie to the covenant that God made with Abraham and then renewed with his grandson Jacob. To be sure, the covenant applied not only to themselves but also to their descendants, to "all the people of the house of Israel" (3 Ne. 16:5). Addressing His hearers, Jesus announced that "ye are of the house of Israel; and ye are of the covenant which the Father made with your fathers, saying unto Abraham: And in thy seed shall all the kindreds of the earth be blessed" (3 Ne. 20:25).[35] In fact, Jesus had earlier declared, "this people will I establish in this land, unto the fulfilling of the covenant which I made with your father Jacob" (20:22). But, as we have seen, descendants of the house of Israel are not the only people who are to receive such blessings. Referring again to Abraham, Jesus turns the focus of His hearers toward Gentiles. In the process of fulfilling "the covenant which he made with Abraham," the Father will pour out "the Holy Ghost through [Christ] upon the Gentiles" (20:27).

It is in light of such reassuring prophecies that the Savior quotes the splendid promises that appear among the lines of Isaiah, chapter 54, a chapter that opens by featuring the symbol of a barren woman and ends with a promise of God's protection for "the servants of the Lord" (3 Ne. 22:17).[36] Amidst these lines we read of the tent of the Lord which expands generously to accommodate a flood of "the children of the desolate . . . wife" (22:1). "Enlarge the place of thy tent," runs the prophecy, "and let them stretch forth the curtains of thy habitations" (22:2). Then, speaking of the faithful people of God's covenant, the prophet writes, "thy seed shall . . . make the desolate cities to be inhabited" (22:3), an allusion to the return of God's people. Speaking of the scattering and gathering, the Lord intones, "For a small moment have I forsaken thee, but with great mercies will I gather thee" (22:7). After the long-awaited gathering, "all thy children shall be taught of the Lord; and great shall be the peace of thy children" (22:13). Following the gathering, however, troubles will sprout up. Enemies "shall surely gather together against thee;" but "whosoever shall gather together against thee shall fall" (22:15). Says the prophet in encouraging tones, "No weapon that is formed against thee shall prosper. . . . This is the heritage of the servants of the Lord" (22:17).

These heartening promises lead us to notice one other pledge in Jesus' sermon. It concerns the redemption of Jerusalem, a prospect that intertwines with the gathering and its associated events. The Savior quotes the Father as declaring, "I will remember the covenant which I have made with my people . . . that I would gather them together in mine own due time, that I would give unto them again the land of their fathers for their inheritance, which is the land of Jerusalem" (3 Ne. 20:29). Said another way, when "they shall believe in me, that I am Jesus Christ, the Son of God . . . then will the Father gather them together again, and give unto them Jerusalem . . . for their inheritance" (20:31, 33; also 20:46). Therewith, God's people will respond with song: "Break forth into joy, sing together, ye waste places of Jerusalem; for the Lord hath comforted his people, he hath redeemed Jerusalem" (3 Ne. 16:19; quoting Isa. 52:9). Thus Jerusalem will again become a spiritual center which, along with New Jerusalem in the New World, will allow the Lord to be "in the midst" of His people (3 Ne. 20:22; 21:25).[37]

And what will allow "the power of heaven [to] come down among them" and the Lord to "be in the midst" of his people (3 Ne. 21:25)? It is repentance. This immovable principle lies in the words of the

Savior to His hearers in the New World: "the Father . . . sent me to bless you in turning away every one of you from his iniquities" (3 Ne. 20:26; see Abr. 2:6). In that state, those returning to Jerusalem "shall believe in me, that I am Jesus Christ, the Son of God, and shall pray unto the Father in my name" (3 Ne. 20:31).

The grand, resulting condition, of course, is that of unity. Quoting lines from Isaiah, the Savior declared on both days that "thy watchmen . . . shall see eye to eye when the Lord shall bring again Zion" (3 Ne. 16:18; also 20:32; Isa. 52:8). Elsewhere, Isaiah writes that people will "sing together" in unity (3 Ne. 16:19; 20:34; Isa. 52:9). It is important to recognize that this theme strikes a chord that Jesus had struck when He spoke about "one fold, and one shepherd" (3 Ne. 15:17, 21; 16:3). In that instance, the Savior had been stressing the unity between His Old World disciples, His New World followers, and "the other tribes . . . [which] the Father separated from them" (3 Ne. 15:20; see 16:1–3). On the first day of His visit, Jesus had also underscored the need for unity among His followers by declaring that "the Father, and the Son, and the Holy Ghost are one; and I am in the Father, and the Father in me, and the Father and I are one" (3 Ne. 11:27). Then, on the second day when He was addressing matters concerning the house of Israel and the Gentiles, the Savior returned to this point. Paraphrasing Isaiah's words, Jesus declared that "the Father . . . hath redeemed Jerusalem" and thereby "hath made bare his holy arm in the eyes of the nations" so that "all the ends of the earth shall see the salvation of the Father" (3 Ne. 20:34–35). When "the nations" perceive "the salvation of the Father" and the accompanying redemption of Jerusalem, "the nations" will also see that "the Father and I are one" (20:35). It will be a moment of bright illumination when "the nations" understand the unity of the Father and the Son.

DAY TWO AND THE TWELVE

The Savior's reassuring sermon on the future of the house of Israel and the Gentiles, as we have seen, stretched from day one into day two. We now need to back up and examine how day two began, for it was certainly different from the beginning of day one. By now, the twelve disciples had joined the Savior at center stage. In addition, because news of Jesus' visit had spread, the multitude had grown to "an exceedingly great number" who had traveled hard "all that night, that they might be on the morrow in the place where Jesus should show himself" (3 Ne. 19:3). The Savior's visit on the second day was no surprise. Anticipation was running high.

We can safely assume that the place of meeting was again at the temple in Bountiful, because the account gives no hint that the Savior asked for a change in meeting locale. One of the pieces of information that newcomers to the temple would have soon learned was Jesus' choice of twelve disciples, whom He had empowered to baptize, to administer the sacrament, and to confer the gift of the Holy Ghost (see 3 Ne. 11:18–22; 18:5–6, 10–12, 36–37). Hence, it is not surprising that the expanded multitude willingly allowed themselves to be "separated into twelve bodies" wherein "the twelve [disciples] did teach" (3 Ne. 19:5–6). It is to their credit that the people recognized and responded positively to the authority which Jesus had invested in these twelve men. On their part, the twelve showed their keen spiritual skills by teaching "those same words which Jesus had spoken" on the first day, "nothing varying from the words which Jesus had spoken" (19:8).

This teaching session drew the multitude into a Pentecost-like experience. And it was tied to an ordinance. For, after the twelve repeated "those same words which Jesus had spoken," they then "knelt . . . and prayed to the Father . . . that the Holy Ghost should be given unto them" (3 Ne. 19:8–9). As on the first day when angels and "fire" descended "out of heaven" and then "encircled" the children (3 Ne. 17:24), so on the second day, following the baptism of the twelve, "the Holy Ghost did fall upon them." At the same time, the twelve were "encircled about as if . . . by fire; and it came down from heaven . . . and angels did come down out of heaven and . . . minister unto" the twelve (3 Ne. 19:13–14). All of this awe-inspiring activity, which "the multitude did witness" (19:14), formed a most solemn and sacred introduction to the Savior. For, "while the angels were ministering to the disciples, behold, Jesus came and stood in the midst, and ministered unto them [the twelve]" (19:15). On their own initiative, the people in the crowd "all knelt down upon the earth" (19:17). Even with the arrival of the Savior, the multitude would not have missed the centrality of the twelve as recipients first of the ministration of angels and then of the Savior Himself.

Following these events that spotlighted the twelve, there was to be another. This one also flowed to them from the Savior, securing the lofty position of the twelve in the sight of the multitude. At base, there was a need for the Savior to show unity between Himself and the twelve. Hence, in addition to praying for the twelve (see 3 Ne. 19:16–20), Jesus affirmed the oneness by His words and then demonstrated that unity by an extraordinary display. For, referring to the twelve and those whom they would convert, Jesus prayed aloud for oneness, "that I may be in them as thou, Father, art in me, that we may be one" (3 Ne. 19:23). Next came the miracle of unity whose wonder everyone could behold. With subdued awe Mormon records that "Jesus blessed [the twelve] . . . and the light of his countenance did shine upon them, and behold they were as white as the countenance and also the garments of Jesus" (19:25). So that readers do not miss the visual significance of this scene, Mormon declares that "the whiteness [of Jesus' countenance and garments] did exceed all the whiteness . . . upon earth" (19:25). To add emphasis, he later reports that the twelve "were white, even as Jesus" (19:30). In sum, no one could disregard the visual and auditory signals of unity between the Savior and His twelve disciples.

Within these scenes that involved the twelve disciples, a fundamental change was taking place. The Savior had come to people in the New World to make a difference in the way that they lived their lives. Particularly for the past few years, these people had been saddled with leaders who held onto authority by appealing to tribal loyalties (see 3 Ne. 7:1–14). While Jesus did not directly discourage such loyalties during His visit, He raised to view a higher loyalty that gained its height and strength from His celestial approval.[38] That loyalty was to center in the twelve disciples whose ministry would eventually unite people under the banner of heaven, as it were. From that moment on, the effective government of these people would rest within the church, specifically among the twelve disciples. By pressing forward while suffering indignities and afflictions, the twelve overcame old prejudices and replaced them with a religious and social unity that glued the society together as never before (see 3 Ne. 28:18–22). In fact, it appears that in time all persons "were converted unto the Lord, and were united to the church of Christ," effectively creating a theocracy or religious government (28:23).[39] As we shall see below, the new economy of this way of life rested on holding "all things common among them" (3 Ne. 26:19), a teaching that the Savior introduced on the third day.

THE SACRAMENT

The Savior's acts of blessing and passing the emblems of His body and blood occurred on the first two days of His visit. And they involved miracles. He may have repeated them on day three as well, although Mormon does not preserve a record of such. Taken by themselves, the sacramental ordinances of the first two days are significant. The major difference between the two days lies in how Jesus approached the ordinance. At the end of the first day, He "commanded His disciples that they should bring forth some bread and wine" for the sacrament (3 Ne. 18:1). None was available at the temple, so they went to obtain some, probably in the town. As we have already seen, the account hints that enough time had passed since the terrible storm—perhaps a full year—to allow people to harvest grains and fruits and to repair their mills and other food processing apparatus.[40] Although we do not know exactly where the disciples obtained the bread and wine, "when the disciples had come . . . [Jesus] took of the bread and brake and blessed it" (18:3). Then came the first miracle. After the disciples had eaten their fill of bread, at Jesus' command they gave bread "unto the multitude" who also ate "and were filled" (18:4–5). Similarly, all partook of the wine and "were filled" (18:9). It is astonishing that a crowd of 2,500, having passed the day without a meal since morning, would be filled by eating a little bread and drinking some wine. The miracle, of course, recalls Jesus' feeding of the 5,000 during his ministry in the Old World.[41]

On day two, the result was similar. Naturally, the crowd was much larger, effectively magnifying the miracle that the Savior performed. In this instance, most of the newcomers "did labor exceedingly all that night" in order to reach "the place where Jesus should show himself" (3 Ne. 19:3). We can imagine that, when people learned of Jesus' first visit and of His plan to return, they simply dropped everything and, with family members, immediately began the trek to Bountiful. We can further imagine that most arrived hungry and tired. Thus, when Jesus provided bread and wine early in the day so that they "were filled" (3 Ne. 20:9), He was responding to a basic human need as well as to their spiritual needs.

There were two notable differences between these experiences with the sacrament. First, we read that, on day two, instead of the crowd simply being "filled" by partaking of bread and wine, the people in the multitude "were filled with the Spirit" after eating and drinking (3 Ne. 20:9). Perhaps Mormon meant this note to imply that a similar manifestation had occurred during the first ministration of the bread and wine on day one. We cannot know this, though it is well within the realm of possibility. The second difference is more remarkable. On the first day, "Jesus commanded his disciples that they should bring forth some bread and wine" (3 Ne. 18:1). But on day two, "there had been no bread, neither wine, brought by the disciples, neither by the multitude" (3 Ne. 20:6). Even so, Jesus "truly gave unto them bread to eat and also wine to drink" (20:7). Hence, the sacramental miracle on day two was more remarkable than that on day one. It seems evident that the manifestation of the Savior's powers was growing day by day.

Similarly, the Savior's instructions that accompanied each sacrament build one upon another. For example, on the second day He characterized the acts of eating and drinking in the following way: "he that eateth this bread eateth of my body to his soul; and he that drinketh of this wine drinketh of my blood to his soul; and his soul shall never hunger nor thirst, but shall be filled" (3 Ne. 20:8). Such an act, He affirmed as He initially unfolded its significance on the first day, is done "in remembrance of my blood, which I have shed for you." Moreover, by eating and drinking in this way, a person witnesses "unto the Father that ye do always remember me." Such remembrance brings "my Spirit to be with you," the worshiper (3 Ne. 18:7, 11). There is an additional component. For the one who partakes, "this is fulfilling my commandments, and this doth witness unto the Father that ye are willing to do that which I have commanded you" (18:10). That is, the worshiper who partakes of the bread and wine is being obedient to "my commandments" and thereby expressing a willingness to do whatever else Jesus has commanded.

To those who administer the sacrament, Jesus gave firm directions, including the words of the prayers,[42] and even threatened penalties. To the twelve He said, "this shall ye always observe to do, *even as I have done*" (3 Ne. 18:6; emphasis added). What is more, "whoso among you shall do more or less than these are not built upon my rock . . . and the gates of hell are ready open to receive them" (18:13). In this light, there was to be no adjustment or change to the way that Jesus had performed the ordinance. For persons to make changes, it would be as if building "upon a sandy foundation; and . . . they shall fall" (18:13). In conclusion, changes to the ordinance were unacceptable; offering the sacrament to unworthy persons was unacceptable; but assisting and praying for those who need to repent was acceptable—even commanded.

SETTING THE RECORD STRAIGHT

Jesus turned from His detailed prophecy about the house of Israel and the Gentiles, and from the sacrament, to the testimonials of His Resurrection. Indeed, His mere presence among the crowd constituted a testimony of His Resurrection. But He wanted the record, which was to appear among the Gentiles, to certify that there had been many witnesses not only of His own Resurrection but also of the resurrection of other people. Jesus' return from the dead had loosed the bands of death for them too. To this end, He now would correct an omission in the record. Turning to Nephi, he directed him to bring "the record which ye have kept" (3 Ne. 23:7). Jesus began browsing through the record—we read that "he cast his eyes upon them" (23:8), the word "them" offering a hint that the record consisted of leaves rather than a roll. The Savior then cited the prophecy of Samuel the Lamanite wherein the prophet predicted that, at the time of Jesus' Resurrection, "there were many saints who should arise from the dead, and should appear unto many, and should minister unto them" (23:9; citing Hel. 14:25). "Was it not so?" Jesus asked. One suspects that there was a moment of silent embarrassment before Nephi and his fellow disciples replied: "Yea, Lord, Samuel did prophesy according to thy words, and they were all fulfilled" (3 Ne. 23:9–10). With Jesus coaxing him, Nephi the record keeper "remembered that this thing [the fulfilling of Samuel's words] had not been written" (23:12). Jesus then "commanded that it should be written" (23:13). This aspect of the record would now be complete.

Two important points arise within this account. First, the Resurrection formed the grand proof that the Savior had broken the bands of death. This proof lay not only in His own resurrected body, which bore "the prints of the nails in [his] hands and in [his] feet" (3 Ne. 11:14), but also in the bodies of the others who had risen from the grave. Second, there were "many" witnesses of the Resurrection—some were probably standing in the multitude—because a number of those who rose from their graves had then appeared to these people and "did minister unto them" (3 Ne. 23:11). The written affirmations of these resurrections, His and theirs—the voice of witnesses—were to be a part of the record whose appearance would signal the beginning of the gathering of God's people in accord with ancient covenants.

TO THE END OF TIME

In a reference to a largely unrecorded set of instructions from day two, we read that the Savior "expounded all the scriptures unto [the multitude] which they had received" (3 Ne. 23:6). On one level, of course, Jesus' Resurrection would help to make sense of important parts of these scriptural records "which they had received" (23:6). But the Savior was not finished. There were "other scriptures," Jesus declared, "that ye have not." These documents, he said, "I would that ye should write" (23:6). We infer that the disciples must have enjoyed access to writing materials at the moment, perhaps from an archive associated with the temple, the likely place of storage for the records that Jesus had just examined. Turning to His twelve disciples, "he commanded them that they should write the words which the Father had given unto Malachi," the Old Testament prophet whose ministry occurred long after the departure of Lehi and Sariah from Jerusalem.[43] At that moment, Jesus began dictating chapters 3 and 4 of Malachi's book. Malachi's chapters are now part of the Book of Mormon record (see 3 Ne. 24–25).

The Savior underlined the importance of these two chapters by saying that "the Father commanded that I should give [these chapters] unto you; for it was wisdom in him that they should be given unto future generations" (3 Ne. 26:2). Why? It is very possible that the "future generations" were those yet to be born among the Nephites and Lamanites. On this view, the immediate posterity of the multitude were to be the beneficiaries of Jesus' dictated words from Malachi. But it is also possible that such "generations" were to be part of a much later audience as well. For the Savior seems to tie the prophecies of these two chapters to events of the last days.[44] Such a tie would help to explain their importance. How so? Immediately after repeating Jesus' words about "future generations," the account records that "he did expound all things, even from the beginning until *the time that he should come* in his glory—yea, even *all things which should come* upon the face of the earth, even until . . . the heavens and the earth should pass away" (26:3; emphasis added).

The Savior went on to teach concerning the final judgment, "even unto the great and last day, when all people . . . shall stand before God, to be judged of their works" (26:4). Evidently, Jesus' quotation of Malachi 3 and 4 served as the springboard for a long discussion of events "from the beginning . . . unto the great and last day" (3 Ne. 26:3–4). For those in the crowd, it must have been a mind-expanding, awe-inspiring moment. For Mormon, the recorder of this account, he would inscribe that he "was about to write" a full recitation of Jesus' words about the last days "but the Lord forbade it." Why? The Lord's response was that "I will try the faith of my people" (26:11). More specifically, if the distant descendants of "this people" who were listening to the Savior that day "shall believe these things," which Mormon has recorded, "then shall the greater things" of Jesus' sermon on the last days "be manifested unto them" (26:8–9). Thus, belief in the words recorded in the record will lead to deeper enlightenment. However, if "they will not believe these things" which are in the record, "then shall the greater things be withheld from them, unto their condemnation" (26:10). In this light, disbelief in the Savior's message given on this occasion would serve as grounds for divine condemnation.

CHILDREN SPEAK

Just as Mormon offers only a short summary of Jesus' words about the last days, he likewise briefly mentions an extraordinary phenomenon on day two: Jesus inspiring children so that "they did speak unto their fathers great and marvelous things" (3 Ne. 26:14). The scene must have followed the Savior's exposition of "all things even from the beginning . . . unto the great and last day" (26:3–4). The key passage reads:

> [H]e did teach and minister unto the children of the multitude . . . and he did loose their tongues, and they did speak unto their fathers great and marvelous things, even greater than he had revealed unto the people. (26:14)

At a later point in the narrative, Mormon draws our attention to a similar phenomenon that occurred on the third and last day of Jesus' visit. He summarizes thus: "on the morrow . . . the multitude . . . both saw and heard these children; yea, even babes did open their mouths and utter marvelous things" (26:16; emphasis added). On this latter occasion, Jesus obviously took matters to a new level by involving infants in the miracle. In each account, people heard the voices of children, voices that carried important messages.

From the events that involved children on day one (see 3 Ne. 17:11–24) and from these two events of the second and third days, it seems evident that each day Jesus deliberately chose to interact with children in the presence of their parents and other adults. Two reasons for His interaction spring to mind. First, because of the purity and innocence of the children, He could show His power through them. But a more important reason may go back to a pair of declarations that He voiced rather early in His visit on day one. On that occasion, as we have seen, He asserted that people "must repent, and become as a little child, and be baptized in my name" (3 Ne. 11:37). Plainly, according to Jesus' words, one is to become "as a little child" in order to receive baptism. The Savior next repeated the same concepts, but He switched the order, declaring that people "must repent, and be baptized in my name, and become as a little child" (11:38). We detect a conscious shift in emphasis. In this latter case, a person is to be "as a little child" following baptism; otherwise, warned the Savior, the individual "can in nowise inherit the kingdom of God" (11:38). As already mentioned, Jesus' interactions with children during the days of His visit held up children as examples for adults and as objects for adults' concern. But that is not all.

There appears to be an important sequence in the kinds of blessings that the Savior showered on the children. On day one, the children were the object of Jesus' blessings and, immediately thereafter, of angels' ministrations (3 Ne. 17:21–24). On the second day, "he did loose their tongues" so that "they did speak . . . great and marvelous things" (3 Ne. 26:14). On the third day, he endowed "even babes" with the power to "utter marvelous things" (26:16). Clearly, the Savior had made them agents for instruction and revelation. While this observation is important in and of itself, we must not forget a lesson that seems to lie just beneath the surface of these manifestations through children. It is a lesson tied to the brass ball that served as a guide to Lehi and Sariah during their journey across deserts and oceans. In the words of Nephi, who was a participant in that journey, "we see that by small means [or, the brass ball] the Lord can bring about great things" (1 Ne. 16:29; also Alma 37:38–41). The fact that children are young and small has little to do with their abilities to instruct in spiritual matters and to receive revelation if the Lord chooses to use them in this way.

DAY THREE

Mormon writes much more briefly about events of the third day of the Savior's visit than the previous two. Mormon's brevity may have been due in part to the Lord forbidding him to repeat Jesus' words on day two about the end of time (see 3 Ne. 26:11). It may also have grown out of the extremely sacred character of the teachings and events of that last day, almost as if there were a crescendo building through the first two days, which reached its zenith on the third. As a support for this last point, from Mormon's summary we learn that the words of the "babes" were especially sacred because their utterances "were forbidden that . . . any man write them" (26:16). In contrast, on the first day, "the multitude did see and hear and bear record" of what happened to the children, thus preserving a report (3 Ne. 17:25). Although Mormon does not mention a record of events that involved children on day two, we can safely presume that one existed. For he had to learn from some source about the "great and marvelous things" the children uttered, a process which led him to judge that such words were "even greater than [what Jesus] had revealed unto the people" (3 Ne. 26:14). It was only on day three that the words coming from infants "were forbidden that . . . any man write them" (26:16), thus underscoring their unusual holiness.

ALL THINGS IN COMMON

In the long run, it was not enough that the Savior had drawn the adults' attention to children by turning them into mouthpieces for divine teaching; it was not enough that He had brought the new law that would replace the old, complete with ordinances and officials authorized to perform those ordinances; it was not enough to renew promises that the covenants made by the Father to the house of Israel would find fulfillment in the appearance of a sacred record and the gathering of Israelite remnants and believing Gentiles to lands and cities of promise; it was not enough that the Savior's hearers learn about the course of events until the final judgment of all humankind. As Mormon's summary of day three illustrates, there was more. There was a need for Jesus to teach those people how to live together in peace and harmony. For centuries, wars and tribal conflict had plagued them and their ancestors. For long stretches of their history, warfare and factionalism and feuding had been a way of life. Only the Savior could turn back this old and debilitating tide. And He did it with simple economics.[45]

It is one of the Savior's enduring legacies that He taught and evidently provided the organizational means for holding all things in common. Mormon offers only the scantiest of summaries. But it is instructive. He wrote that, following Jesus' three-day visit and the beginning of the ministry of the twelve disciples, people "had all things common among them" (3 Ne. 26:19; also 4 Ne. 1:3).[46] We do not know what mechanisms Jesus instituted that allowed people to share goods. But we do know that this commonality of goods persisted within the general populace until about A.D. 200 when people "did have their goods and their substance no more common among them" (4 Ne. 1:25). The force of Jesus' teachings on this subject obviously made such a deep impact on His hearers that they kept the system in place for almost 170 years.

THE MISSION OF THE TWELVE

Besides the miracle of the infants and Jesus' teaching about all things in common, the third day evidently saw the formal beginning of the mission and ministry of the twelve disciples. Mormon writes that "the disciples whom Jesus had chosen began from that time forth to baptize and to teach as many as did come unto them" (3 Ne. 26:17). One suspects that the crowd on the third day was even larger than the gathered multitude of the second day. Hence, as the twelve had divided and taught the multitude at the beginning of day two (see 3 Ne. 19:5–6), so they likely would have been involved in teaching the ever-expanding numbers of people on the third day. In addition, as Mormon affirms, "the disciples . . . began . . . to baptize" (3 Ne. 26:17). Day three may well have offered opportunity for them to undertake this part of their ministry since they had received authority to baptize and had so far only baptized themselves (see 3 Ne. 11:21–22; 19:11–12). We suspect that by the end of day three the disciples were on their way to teach and baptize among those who had not been present for Jesus' visit. Perhaps the miracles that accompanied their preaching began even before they left the city and land of Bountiful (see 4 Ne. 1:5). For Mormon records that "many of" those whom the twelve taught "saw and heard unspeakable things, which are not lawful to be written" (3 Ne. 26:18).[47] Hence, armed with authority and power, the twelve set off "to baptize and to teach as many as did come unto them" (26:17), inaugurating an era when people "had all things common" and each person dealt "justly, one with another" (26:19). There was to be an extended period of peace and prosperity (see 4 Ne. 1:2–3, 7, 18, 23).

CONCLUSION

The impact of Jesus' visit in the land of Bountiful is unequaled in all of sacred literature. For three days He held multitudes of people spellbound both with His words and with His miracles. He was able to teach and perform acts that He had been unable to do among followers in the Old World because of their unbelief (see 3 Ne. 19:35). His New World hearers seem to have been eager to receive anything that He would offer to them. Because of "their faith," He was able to show them the depths and heights of His powers, even blessing "babes" that they could "utter marvelous things" (3 Ne. 26:16). As impressive as were the events of Jesus' visit, it is a witness to the enduring legacy of His teachings and to the empowering impact of the Holy Ghost on believers that for more that one and one-half centuries, people dealt justly with one another and held all things in common. A unity of spiritual and temporal purpose lay across the land as rays of a golden sun. It all began with a voice from heaven, a voice which then introduced the Son of God to a crowd of 2,500 at the temple in Bountiful. By the end of His three-day visit, there arose a combined voice of testimony from those who had witnessed His words and acts. That combined voice set in motion an era of peace and prosperity unparalleled among the peoples of God.

NOTES TO CHAPTER FIVE

1. Consult particularly Matt. 28:20; Mark 14:62; John 4:26 (Greek text); 6:20 (Greek text), 35, 48, 51; 8:12, 18, 23–24, 28, 58; 10:9, 11, 14; 11:25; 15:1, 5; 18:5. For such statements by Jesus as the resurrected, glorified Lord, see 3 Ne. 15:5, 9; 18:16; 20:19, 23, 31; 27:27; though the following study would benefit from access to the Greek text of the New Testament, consult James R. Harris, "The 'I Am' Passages in the Gospels and in 3 Nephi," in *The New Testament and the Latter-day Saints,* ed. H. Dean Garrett (Orem, Utah: Randall Book Co., 1987), 89–113.
2. See Brown, *From Jerusalem to Zarahemla: Literary and Historical Studies of the Book of Mormon,* 157–67.
3. On early references to the Atonement, consult 1 Ne. 1:19; 10:4–6, 11; 11:33; on the Savior's promised post-resurrection appearance, see 1 Ne. 12:6; 13:35.
4. The term "Hosanna" provides a temple tie. The meaning is "save us, we beseech thee" and was sung as part of the liturgy at the Feast of Tabernacles in the temple (the so-called "Hallel;" see Ps. 118:25) with pilgrims waving their lulab, consisting of branches of myrtle or willow or a palm branch (see George A. Buttrick et al., eds., *The Interpreter's Dictionary of the Bible,* 4 vols. and suppl. [Nashville: Abingdon Press, 1962, 1976], 2:648; and David Noel Freedman et al., eds., *The Anchor Bible Dictionary,* 6 vols. [New York: Doubleday, 1992], 3:290–91; also 3:30). The expression "the most high God" recalls this title in Psalm 47:2 ("the Lord most high is terrible; he is a great King over all the earth"). Consult also *The Anchor Bible Dictionary* 4:1004 and Gen. 14:19–20, 22; 2 Sam. 22:14; Ps. 7:17; 9:2; 18:13; 21:7. Incidentally, the

cry of the crowd recalls that of the Spirit who appeared to Nephi (see 1 Ne. 11:6, "Hosanna to the Lord, the most high God").

5. On the length of time between the storm and Jesus' arrival, consult Brown, *From Jerusalem to Zarahemla,* 146–56. On the nature of the storm, see Bart J. Kowallis, "In the Thirty and Fourth Year: A Geologist's View of the Great Destruction in 3 Nephi," *BYU Studies* 37, no. 3 (1997–1998): 137–190.

6. About A.D. 57, Paul wrote: "whosoever shall eat this bread, and drink this cup of the Lord, unworthily, shall be guilty of the body and blood of the Lord. But let a man examine himself and so let him eat of that bread, and drink of that cup" (1 Cor. 11:27–28). On the date of the composition of 1 Corinthians, see Richard L. Anderson, *Understanding Paul* (Salt Lake City: Deseret Book, 1983), 395 (chronological chart).

7. See Joseph Fielding McConkie, Robert L. Millet, and Brent L. Top, *Doctrinal Commentary on the Book of Mormon,* 4 vols. (Salt Lake City: Bookcraft, 1992), 4:173; and Andrew C. Skinner, "Zion Gained and Lost: Fourth Nephi as the Quintessential Model," in *The Book of Mormon: Fourth Nephi through Moroni, From Zion to Destruction,* ed. Monte S. Nyman and Charles D. Tate Jr. (Provo, Utah: BYU Religious Studies Center, 1995), 295–96.

8. A rock as a metaphor for the Savior or some other spiritual reality is frequent (e.g., Moses 7:53; Deut. 32:15; Matt. 16:18; 2 Ne. 4:30; D&C 6:34). The principle that "the gates of hell shall not prevail against" a person is difficult to explain, unless one sees such gates in the same way that one sees the gates or doors of heaven—the spot from which inspiration and angelic messengers emerge.

9. Krister Stendahl, "The Sermon on the Mount and Third Nephi," in *Reflections on Mormonism: Judaeo-Christian Parallels,* ed. Truman G. Madsen (Provo, Utah: BYU Religious Studies Center, 1978), 139–54; Stanley R. Larson, "The Sermon on the Mount: What Its Textual History Discloses concerning the Historicity of the Book of Mormon," *Trinity Journal* 7, no. 1 (Spring 1986): 23–43; John W. Welch, *The Sermon at the Temple and the Sermon on the Mount: A Latter-day Saint Approach* (Salt Lake City: Deseret Book, 1990); *Illuminating the Sermon at the Temple and Sermon on the Mount: An Approach to 3 Nephi 11–18 and Matthew 5–7* (Provo, Utah: FARMS, 1999); Victor L. Ludlow, "Covenant Teachings of the Book of Mormon," in *The Disciple as Scholar: Essays on Scripture and the Ancient World in Honor of Richard L. Anderson,* ed. Stephen D. Ricks, Donald W. Parry, and Andrew H. Hedges, (Provo, Utah: FARMS, 2000), 85–90.

10. The series of literary seams formed by such expressions as "when Jesus had spoken these words," etc., hints that a scribe (or scribes) copied down Jesus' words after His sermon rather than during His speech. Most probably, the sermon was written during the night following the first day of His visit, a

pattern that may have persisted through the next two days (see 3 Ne. 12:1; 13:25; 14:1; 15:1, 2; 17:1, 5, 15; 18:17, 26, 36), although we do know that disciples wrote down Mal. 3 and 4 at Jesus' dictation (see 3 Ne. 24:1).

11. This clause also occurs in the Joseph Smith Translation of Matthew 5:3. Since the prior verses in this version show an influence from the Book of Mormon record, one assumes that this latter was the inspiration for many changes in the JST Matthean text. See the discussion of Robert A. Cloward, "The Sermon on the Mount in the JST and the Book of Mormon," in *The Joseph Smith Translation: The Restoration of Plain and Precious Things,* Monte S. Nyman and Robert L. Millet, eds. (Provo, Utah: BYU Religious Studies Center, 1985), 163–200.

12. John Welch has argued persuasively for a unity within the sermon that is based on apparent temple connections throughout. While on one level his suggestion is compelling, on another there really are substantial differences between the three main segments of the sermon. And one should allow Jesus to change directions. See Welch, *Illuminating the Sermon at the Temple,* 23–104.

13. This sort of principle underlies the story of the fate of Daniel's accusers (see Dan. 6:24). See the discussion on the Sermon on the Mount by Willoughby C. Allen, *A Critical and Exegetical Commentary on the Gospel according to S. Matthew,* 3rd ed. (Edinburg: T. & T. Clark, 1977), 65–66. Also consult McConkie, Millet, and Top, *Doctrinal Commentary on the Book of Mormon,* 4:90.

14. See Ex. 21:24; Lev. 24:20; Deut. 19:21; also Matt. 5:38–42; Luke 6:29–30; 3 Ne. 12:38–42.

15. On the issue of connections in 3 Nephi to Moses and the Exodus, see Brown, *From Jerusalem,* 157–67.

16. On the land of promise, see also 1 Ne. 5:5; 7:13; 10:13; 12:1, 4; 13:12, 14, 30; 17:38; 18:8, 22–23, 25; 2 Ne. 1:3, 5–11; 3:2; etc.

17. Concerning the anxiety that people felt after they were far from Jerusalem and the land of their forebears, consult Brown, *From Jerusalem,* 12–17.

18. The repeating refrains throughout the piece point to its poetic character. The general tone of the first stanza is made more specific and emphatic in the second, as well as in its third section. The final resolution and expression of joy and wonder had come in the prayer of Jesus for those in attendance, a point emphasized by placing this notation at the end. An important question is: where was this testimony preserved? Did it appear in a public place, such as on a plaque, or on a stela?

19. For studies on the sacred center, see *Mircea Eliade, Cosmos and History: The Myth of the Eternal Return* (New York: Harper & Row, 1959), 12–17; Hugh Nibley, "What is a Temple?" in *The Temple in Antiquity,* ed. Truman G. Madsen (Provo, UT: BYU Religious Studies Center, 1984), 22–25.

20. The Hebrew term "midst" comes from a root with the meaning "inner." See Ernst Jenni and Claus Westermann, eds., *Theological Lexicon of the Old Testament,* 3 vols. (Peabody, Mass.: Hendrickson Publishers, Inc., 1997), 3:1164. This root stands at the base of the expressions in Isa. 12:6 and Micah 5:13–14.

21. The masculine plural "asherîm" is the term translated "groves" in this passage. On the sacred symbols of Asherah, see G. Johannes Botterweck and Helmer Ringgren, eds., *Theological Dictionary of the Old Testament,* 11 vols. (Grand Rapids, MI: Eerdmans, 1974–2001), 1:438–444; Tilde Binger, *Asherah: Goddesses in Ugarit, Israel and the Old Testament* (Sheffield: Sheffield Academic Press, 1997); Judith M. Hadley, *The Cult of Asherah in Ancient Israel and Judah* (Cambridge: Cambridge University Press, 2000); also Daniel C. Peterson, "Nephi and his Asherah," *Journal of Book of Mormon Studies* 9, no. 2 (2000): 16–25.

22. For information on the primordial mountain, see Eliade, *Cosmos and History,* 12–16; John M. Lundquist, "The Common Temple Ideology of the Ancient Near East," in *The Temple in Antiquity,* 54–66.

23. For water and greenery at temple sites, see *Eliade, Cosmos and History,* 6–10; Hugh Nibley, "What Is a Temple?", 20–28.

24. On the lamentations of Nephite writers over Jerusalem, see Brown, *From Jerusalem to Zarahemla,* 12–17.

25. On the Mosaic law, see 3 Ne. 12:17–48; 15:2–10; on the land of inheritance, consult 3 Ne. 15:13 and 16:16 as well as 20:14, 22; 21:22.

26. The record for the first year of the Assyrian king Sargon II (721–705 B.C.) sets the number of people taken captive from the northern kingdom of Israel at 27,290 (see James B. Pritchard, ed., *Ancient Near Eastern Texts Relating to the Old Testament,* 3rd ed. with suppl. [Princeton: Princeton University Press, 1969], 284–85).

27. Consult S. Kent Brown and David R. Seely, "Jeremiah's Imprisonment and the Date of Lehi's Departure," *The Religious Educator* 2:1 (2001): 15–32.

28. On the gathering, see 3 Ne. 16:5; 20:13, 18, 29, 33; 21:1, 27–29; concerning the return to "the land of their fathers," see 3 Ne. 20:29, 46; on the redemption of Jerusalem, consult 3 Ne. 16:19; 20:29, 33–34, 36–38, 46.

29. Concerning New Jerusalem, consult 3 Ne. 20:22; 21:23–24; New Jerusalem is to belong to members of the house of Israel who inherit "this land" in the New World (3 Ne. 15:13; 16:16; 20:14, 22; 21:22, 28; compare 16:8).

30. All of the Savior's stern warnings rest on language quoted or adapted from the prophet Micah; see 3 Ne. 16:14–15 (Micah 5:8); 20:16–19 (Micah 5:8–9; 4:12–13); 21:12–18 (Micah 5:8–14).

31. The question arises whether the Savior is referring to Himself or to His Father when He speaks of "the Father" in such passages (e.g., 3 Ne. 20:10, 12, 14,

19–20, 25–29, 31, 33–35, 46; 21:2–4, 6–7, 9, 11, 14, 20, 26–29). Nothing appears in the account that settles this matter.

32. The promise of the Gentiles being "numbered" within the covenant also appears in 3 Ne. 16:13 and 21:22.

33. The pattern of the gospel going from the Gentiles to the Jews in the last days is a theme in Paul's Epistle to the Romans (see Rom. 9–11); see also the study by Johannes Munck, *Christ and Israel: An Interpretation of Romans 9–11* (Philadelphia: Fortress Press, 1967).

34. In this connection, consult also 3 Ne. 20:39–40 and 21:27. We could cite numerous other passages within the Book of Mormon.

35. This passage quotes the Lord's words to Abraham in Gen. 22:18; see also Gen. 12:3; 18:18; Abr. 2:9–11; the Lord repeated this promise in turn to Isaac and Jacob (consult Gen. 26:4 and 28:14).

36. See Cynthia Hallen's fine treatment of Isaiah 54, "Redeeming the Desolate Woman: The Message of Isaiah 54 and 3 Nephi 22," *Journal of Book of Mormon Studies* 7, no. 1 (1998): 40–47.

37. There must be a similar notion lying behind the concept of the Lord establishing his "people" (3 Ne. 20:21–22) and establishing "again among them my Zion" (3 Ne. 21:1).

38. Through the "voice" that was "heard among all the inhabitants . . . upon all the face of this land," survivors of the storm learned that the "city Jacobugath, which was inhabited by the people of king Jacob" had been "burned with fire because of their sins . . . for it was they that did destroy the peace of my people and the government of the land" (3 Ne. 9:1, 9). Thus, the Savior apparently had little reason to scold His hearers over earlier, tribal loyalties.

39. That the twelve continued as an identifiable institution appears in 4 Ne. 1:14.

40. For a discussion of the evidences for the passage of time between the storm and Jesus' visit, see Brown, *From Jerusalem to Zarahemla,* 146–56.

41. For the feeding of the 5,000, see the accounts in all four Gospels: Matt. 14:13–21; Mark 6:32–44; Luke 9:11–17; John 6:5–14; for the feeding of the 4,000, consult Matt. 15:32–38; Mark 8:1–9.

42. The prayers over the bread and wine, which Jesus entrusted to the twelve, are preserved by Moroni (see Moro. 3–4).

43. On the dating and message of Malachi, consult Roland Kenneth Harrison, *Introduction to the Old Testament* (Grand Rapids, MI: Eerdmans, 1969), 958–62.

44. Consult Sidney B. Sperry, *Book of Mormon Compendium* (Salt Lake City: Bookcraft, 1968), 425–26.

45. Several writers have spoken about a "Zion society," but have pursued the matter no further. Consult Skinner, "Zion Gained and Lost", 295–296;

McConkie, Millet, and Top, *Doctrinal Commentary on the Book of Mormon,* 4:197.

46. An important study of this era of peace is that of Andrew C. Skinner, "Zion Gained and Lost", 289–301.

47. A person might think that the expression "many of them" in 3 Ne. 26:18 refers to the twelve. But it seems to point to those whom they taught. Why? Because apparently all of the twelve, not "many" of them, experienced their own heavenly blessings that they could not talk about (see 3 Ne. 28:13–16).

Moroni

CHAPTER SIX

"I have but few things to write"—Mormon 8:1

Silence had become Moroni's trusted companion. Sound was now unsettling, for he lived in fear of being discovered by enemies. Gone was his mother, who had died in the Lamanite attack on the city of Jordan. Gone were his dear wife and children, who perished in the flames that had engulfed the city called Desolation. Gone were his three sisters and their families. He was completely alone.

Years before, he had beheld 10,000 soldiers under his command perish in a single day. Worse, that day had seen the deaths of almost a million of his fellow citizens as they were swept down by a relentless, experienced force of Lamanite fighters, though the Lamanites too had paid an awful price in the battle. Moroni, when he allowed himself to think about the end of that fateful day, recalled that from his perch on the side of a hill he could see countless corpses—men, women, children—lying beneath him in the gray grasp of death. His own father then lay near death.

At this moment Moroni sat on a high ridge scanning intently the valley below. He had learned to keep to high ground, for he could see more from such places. Then he spotted a Lamanite scouting party in the tall grass near the valley stream. He did not want them to know of his presence, for they would surely follow and kill him. So he turned and crept higher into the trees, clutching his bundle of precious plates and translation aids close to his chest. He knew the general direction that he was to go—northward. He had known for several months that he must bury the plates and leave them in the protection of God.

Moroni is one of the most tantalizing characters in scripture. His life bridges two eras: one that spanned the last decades of his civilization, ending with its utter annihilation, and one in which the only civilizing influences were those of his enemies. But these influences proved too weak to unite his enemies for, as Moroni writes, "the Lamanites are at war one with another . . . and no one knoweth the end of the war" (Morm. 8:8). Whatever the fate of his enemies, Moroni had been "commanded by my father [Mormon]" to finish the record whose contents were "to show unto the remnant of the House of Israel what great things the Lord hath done for their fathers" (Morm. 8:1; title page of the Book of Mormon). In choosing what to write on the last pages of the record, Moroni was moved "by the spirit of prophecy and of revelation" (title page). We also suspect that his choices of topics also grew—in a major way—out of his sometimes harrowing, horrifying experiences. In all, his future audience was the Lamanites, his enemies, or at least their descendants. But to write to them he had to keep out of their grasp.

MORONI'S STORY

Although Moroni was raised in one of the most notable families of his era, it made little difference. It was the worst of times. And, if possible, matters only grew worse as Moroni grew older. On the broader canvas, as long as people in his society had each other to hate, tribes and clans and secret societies and governments descended willfully and consciously into the carnage of war and revenge. Rape, pillaging, and wholesale slaughter were the defining marks of the age. Above all, hate smoldered, then seethed, then flared into horrible actions that created rivers of blood. While Moroni was born into this dark and hopeless age, remarkably he seems little tainted by the human storms that swirled around him first as a lad, and then as an adult. Instead, with divine aid he kept his faith, his hopes, his sanity.[1]

In truth, we know little about Moroni's life. Most of what we know comes from his writings that focus principally on other people and on important gospel principles. Hence, we are left to reconstruct his world—and his life within it—from hints that either he or someone else has left in the record. What is clear is that he lived on a grand stage whereon the unspeakable, obliterating destiny of his civilization was played out. He was one of a few surviving witnesses of the utter destruction of his people. Few have ever witnessed what Moroni did, and survived. His world was filled with terrible acts of torture and slaughter, alleviated only rarely with unexpected acts of compassion and assistance, which were almost all directed toward women, children, and the elderly.[2]

Moroni's grandfather, a man named Mormon, relocated from the "land northward" to the "land southward" about A.D. 322 when Moroni's father, also Mormon by name, was eleven years old (see Morm. 1:5–7). By doing so, this grandfather apparently gave up life in a rural setting for one closer to the settled communities of his people in the south, perhaps for economic reasons. It is impossible to say, of course, whether a series of bad harvests on the family homestead had influenced the decision to move. But that is certainly a possibility in a largely agrarian society. During prior centuries, people had been moving into the "land northward" because of the availability of land and associated opportunities, and because they could escape the general area of the border with the Lamanites, which had often been the setting for international conflict and tension (see Alma 63:4–9; Morm. 1:10). And still others had moved north because there was no rule of law (see 3 Ne. 7:12).

We presume that Moroni's father married in his late teens or early twenties, as did most young men in ancient cultures. There is no hint in any account whether Mormon married Moroni's mother before or after he took command of the Nephite armies at the very youthful age of fifteen (Morm. 2:1–2). Because Mormon retained his rank as commander in chief of the Nephite armies for about thirty-six years, until his temporary retirement of thirteen years,[3] it is evident that Moroni was born into and raised in a family whose father was often away for long periods of time. In this light, Moroni's mother would have exerted the largest influence on him during his preteen years. And he may well have been the only son born to his parents, because he calls himself "*the son* of Mormon" (Morm. 8:13; emphasis added).[4] His education likely included the skills of reading and writing in two languages, Hebrew and "reformed Egyptian" (Morm. 9:32–33).[5]

Life in the military carries its own set of attractions, at least initially, and Moroni would likely have been drawn to his father's adopted profession rather early in his life. Whether Moroni also took up a vocation or pursued a business, such as trade, remains unknown. We know only that he was experienced enough as a soldier to serve as a military commander of 10,000 armed men during the last stand of his people (see Morm. 6:12).

If Moroni was the oldest child in his family, he was probably born between A.D. 332 and 335, when his father was in his early twenties. He was named for the famous Captain Moroni who had served his people at a time of severe national crisis many generations earlier.[6] If Moroni was born soon after A.D. 332, he was in his early fifties when he led his 10,000 into the last battle in 385. Since he lived until A.D. 421, he apparently reached his later eighties by the time he last added materials to the plates.[7]

In addition to his military duties, it is also evident that at some point, and perhaps often, Moroni held a responsible position within the church of his day, in addition to his military duties, for his father writes to him: "Jesus Christ . . . hath called you to his ministry" (Moro. 8:2). It is also obvious that Moroni's father was the head of the church, for when he went to the Lord in prayer about a serious ecclesiastical matter, the Lord responded as if Mormon was in charge (see 8:7–9). Then, after learning the will of the Lord—and here is the important part for Moroni—his father instructed him to set the matter right: "my son, I desire that ye should labor diligently, that this gross error should be removed from among you [in the church]" (8:6). Moroni also reported to his father when his father was absent so that he knew what was going on in the church (see 8:5, 7, 27).

In this connection, it is apparent that from time to time, church members suffered persecution, a blight that would have touched Moroni and his own family. Even those church members close to his father during his days as the chief military officer of the Nephite armies, and who therefore should have enjoyed some immunity from harassment, were objects of persecution. Mormon writes that unbelieving Nephites "in this part of the land . . . are also seeking to put down all power and authority which cometh from God" (Moro. 8:28). The "power and authority" which they sought "to put down" would have rested within the membership of the church where Mormon was then campaigning.

THE DARKEST DAY

From a careful reading of Moroni's words whereby he finishes his father's book (see Morm. 8–9), we sense the anger and frustration and pain that still punctuated Moroni's memories of that horrible, fateful day now fifteen years in the past (see Morm. 8:6). After the crushing of his society, his culture, Moroni did not enjoy the luxury of an armistice or, more importantly, a peace that followed the last, defining battle, a peace that would have allowed his jangled feelings and jagged memories to heal. Instead, in one day he became a fugitive rather than a trusted citizen, a hunted man rather than a faithful church member, an outcast rather than a general. Though he and his father had foreseen these results because of mounting troubles, Moroni still would not have been prepared to witness the complete annihilation of his people or known the empty feeling of being without friend or family.

It is Moroni's father who is our chief source for contemporary events, offering to readers a small glimpse of the terrors that beset their society as it rushed headlong over the precipice that divided enlightened civilization from benighted chaos. Not since the Canaanite tribes—then the covenant people of God—slid into a debilitating apostasy had a people fallen so precipitously into the grasp of satanic behavior.[8] In Mormon's words, the people "do not repent, and Satan stirreth them up continually to anger one with another" (Moro. 9:3).

The speed wherewith all came to an end must have surprised and unnerved the few survivors. No one could have anticipated that in a single day the Nephite civilization—its literature and music, its agriculture and architecture, its military and manufacturing skills, its men, women, and children—would simply cease to exist. So complete was the defeat that only twenty-four persons survived and were left to survey the hundreds of thousands whose bodies "lay upon the face of the earth . . . to crumble and to return to their mother earth" (Morm. 6:11, 15). And we do not learn whether any others among the twenty-four had sustained life-threatening wounds as apparently Mormon had. For his wounds were severe enough that he was left for dead—"[the Lamanites] passed by me that they did not put an end to my life" (6:10). Apparently, Mormon soon died of his wounds because Moroni records that his "father hath been slain in battle" (Morm. 8:5). Hence, we are left to wonder whether Mormon was able himself to pen the last part of his own record, which followed the battle, or whether he dictated this section to Moroni, perhaps with difficulty (see Morm. 6–7).

Thus it was "at an instant suddenly," in the words of Isaiah, that an entire civilization had become "like small dust" and "as chaff that passeth away" (Isa. 29:5). We can only guess at the feelings and thoughts that surged through Moroni as he surveyed the bloody, mangled wreckage of his people and mourned the loss of his father "and all [his] kinsfolk" (Morm. 8:5). Some fifteen dreary years later, we also sense a quieted anxiety when he writes that "I have not . . . whither to go; and how long the Lord will suffer that I may live I know not" (8:5). Notably, his expression "the Lord will suffer that I may live" displays the sentiments of a person who, over time, has become completely submissive to the will of God. In this way, Moroni stands as the antithesis of those who perished. They were, in the words of Mormon, "fair ones" who had "rejected that Jesus, who stood with open arms to receive [them]." Knowing his people, Mormon then lamented that "if ye had not done this, ye would not have fallen" (Morm. 6:17–18). In contrast to those who died together in battle, Moroni survived alone. Why? To "finish the record" that his father had been writing and editing by bearing witness to "the sad tale of the destruction of my people" (Morm. 8:1, 3).

By completing the record of the annihilation of his people—a "commandment of my father" (Morm. 8:3)—and by abridging the book of Ether, the record of the Jaredite people who had also been obliterated, Moroni hands to readers a double testimony of the fate of the wicked who deliberately turn from the Savior (see Moro. 9:22–23). (The Jaredites were a people who had come from Asia to the New World—their land of promise too—and had prospered, then experienced the complete destruction of their society by civil war.) Of course, the story of the end of Moroni's people also has to have a beginning and a middle in order to be understandable. And these prior parts, edited by his father, lift to our view the enduring joys, both mortal and eternal, that played out in the lives of real people who embraced the Savior and His teachings.

Moroni thus brings to final fruition the effective intent of his father Mormon to hold up a mirror and allow readers to see themselves, even to measure themselves, against those of the past. The work of Mormon, which Moroni continues and completes, was to provide a righteous standard to readers by which readers could measure themselves. He did so by retelling the stories of other persons' lives who had lived both wickedly and righteously. And the life that Mormon and Moroni seek for their readers includes a strong belief in and a fidelity to Jesus Christ.

SOUTHWARD FLIGHT, THEN NORTHWARD

It is not clear why Moroni or any other survivor of that terrible battle would have headed south. But the tantalizing possibility that he and others fled in that direction grows out of his account. Since the agreement of A.D. 350, when Moroni was perhaps in his middle or late teens, the "land southward" had been the domain of the Lamanites (see Morm. 2:28–29). Because this region included the old Nephite capital city, Zarahemla, Nephites would naturally have been curious about any tidings concerning their former territory and properties. Perhaps when news or rumor reached Nephites during intervening years (A.D. 360–385), that the Lamanites had moved into the Zarahemla region, Nephites assumed that Lamanites had essentially abandoned their original settlement called the city of Nephi.[9] Perhaps the few Nephite survivors thought that if they could go south beyond the territory controlled by Lamanites, they would be out of harm's way. Perhaps they judged that the Lamanites, who had come into the "land northward" to fight the final battle, would remain in the north to explore and to homestead and to root out any pockets of Nephite resistance. After all, for years the Lamanites had sought to push into the "land northward" both for economic reasons and for the strategic advantages of hemming in Nephites on both the south and north.[10]

Whatever the case, it seems evident that Moroni first fled south and then reversed his course, traveling north. Traveling south had apparently been a mistake.

How do we reach this conclusion? Because, writing as an eyewitness, Moroni laments that "the Nephites who had escaped into the country southward were hunted by the Lamanites until they were all destroyed" (Morm. 8:2).[11] How else can a person understand Moroni's words? It is possible, of course, that Moroni learned about the fate of these fugitives from other escapees who had gone southward and then turned back north where, by chance or by prior arrangement for a rendezvous, they met Moroni and gave him the news. But such a hypothesis seems to contradict Moroni's spare narrative. His remark that "they were all destroyed" seems to disclose that no one known to him who had fled southward survived. We surmise that the Lamanite search for Nephite survivors was so palpably intense, allowing no opportunity for survivors to rest, whether in the north or the south, that Moroni and his fellows were always and literally on the run. At least by turning back to the north country, Moroni would put himself into territory that was more familiar to him than to any Lamanite pursuers. After all, he had not been in the southland since he was a youth and, as we have noted, he was then about fifty-two or fifty-three years old.

That Nephite survivors "were hunted by the Lamanites" after fleeing "into the country southward" and "were all destroyed" can mean only one thing (Morm. 8:2). The Lamanites went home. To be sure, many would have remained to explore and homestead in the northern territories. But enough people—the majority it seems—returned to their homes and towns. Such an observation would logically point to a Lamanite people who were exhausted by the long, twenty-four-year war and who wished to return to normal lives.[12] But instead, as Moroni, the unobserved observer, writes of the years immediately following the last battle, "the Lamanites" fell into "war one with another." He laments, "the whole face of this land is one continual round of murder and bloodshed; and no one knoweth the end of the war" (Morm. 8:8). Even after thirty-five years, "their wars are exceedingly fierce among themselves" (Moro. 1:2). It seems apparent that what Moroni was witnessing was the explosion of clan and tribal warfare. After all, the Book of Mormon society had divided itself into clans in the past when some overarching national interest did not unite it.[13] As long as the Lamanites, a group of clans united under a king, were struggling against the Nephites, there was a pressing reason to unite in a common cause. But soon after the Nephites were gone, strong-willed clan leaders apparently turned to other causes that created friction within the larger Lamanite society and drew themselves and their clans down into regional and national conflicts, effectively plunging the broader society into civil war. We can only imagine what life was like for Lamanite women and children during these tempestuous years.

LAMANITES

It is Moroni's language about the Lamanites, his enemies, that betrays his exasperation and ache. His words lose their edge, however, when he incises his final entries in the record. But some fifteen years after the final battle, he is still filled with tormenting anguish and injury. Even when he speaks of Lamanites who had converted to God in an earlier era, he effectively withholds credit from them and instead gives credit to the Nephite missionaries, reporting that "it was the faith of Nephi and Lehi that wrought the change upon the Lamanites" and "it was the faith of Ammon and his brethren which wrought so great a miracle among the Lamanites" (Ether 12:14–15). Moreover, he puts a hard edge on his narrative of events from his own day. For instance, with a sad memory of the fate of his own people he writes that "the Lamanites have hunted my people . . . from city to city and from place to place, even until they are no more" (Morm. 8:7). What is worse, "my father . . . was killed by them" and "all my kinsfolk," so that "I have not friends nor whither to go" (8:3, 5). As a result, "I . . . remain alone to write the sad tale of the destruction of my people" (8:3). He might have added that he could not have anticipated that he alone would survive—"I am alone" (8:5)—and that none of his family would be with him. Instead, his future was dauntingly unclear—"how long the Lord will suffer that I may live I know not" (8:5). It is a woeful tale. And while he sees the punishing hand of God within events that swept down his people (see 8:8), the Lamanites stand accused of the atrocities that had crushed Moroni's world.

Perhaps his pique is measured by what he does not say as much as by what he chooses to say about his enemies. For very few of his words seem aimed at the members of the house of Israel who would descend from the Lamanite tribes, at least initially. Instead, he seems purposely to direct his words more broadly to the larger group of descendants from Abraham, though Lamanites would have been in the back of his mind. In speaking of "this record," which he was finishing, he prophesies that "none can have power to bring it to light save it be given him of God . . . [for] the welfare of the ancient and long dispersed covenant people of the Lord" (Morm. 8:14–15).[14] Later, he warns in fierce, clipped tones that those who "shall breathe out wrath . . . against the covenant people of the Lord who are the house of Israel . . . the same is in danger to be hewn down and cast into the fire" (8:21). Yet, when he writes condemningly about "those who do not believe in Christ" and "who deny the revelations [and miracles] of God," we suspect that in his mind he aims his words toward the Lamanites (Morm. 9:1, 7).

Not surprisingly, Moroni mirrors his father whose editorializing at times betrays the severe difficulties with enemies that he had been facing before working on the plates. One of Mormon's major opportunities to write and edit seems to have arisen during the dozen years between his victory over the forces of the Lamanite king Aaron in A.D. 333 and the renewal of hostilities which led to Nephite retreats to the cities of Jashon and Shem (see Morm. 2:9, 16, 20–21). Another would have come during his thirteen-year retirement from military service, from A.D. 362 to 375 (see Morm. 3:11, 16; 5:1). Surrounding these periods were numerous minor skirmishes and major battles with Lamanite forces, which left Mormon's soldiers wounded, dying, and dead, and their families in desperate straits. Hence, when he introduces readers to the mission of the four sons of King Mosiah, Mormon preserves the warm language of the missionaries' record that speaks of Lamanites as "brethren" (Alma 17:9, 11). But he also adds editorial notes atop the account wherein he coldly characterizes Lamanites as "a wild and a hardened and a ferocious people" who were "very indolent" and "did worship idols," thus bringing on themselves "the curse of God" (Alma 17:14–15).[15]

It is only many years later, just as Moroni is about to slide the record into its final resting place, that he adopts a fully conciliatory tone toward Lamanites and their descendants, seeking the blessings of God for them. He composes his last lines by declaring "I write unto *my brethren,* the Lamanites" (Moro. 10:1; emphasis added). For the next few verses he specifically addresses them: "I would exhort you . . . that ye would remember how merciful the Lord hath been . . . [and] I would exhort you that ye would ask God . . . if these things are not true. . . . And by the power of the Holy Ghost ye may know the truth of all things" (10:3–5). There is more. Almost as a parent, he bears witness that "ye may know that he [God] is, by the power of the Holy Ghost." Further, in words now shaped with kindness, "I would exhort you, *my beloved brethren,* that ye remember that every good gift cometh of Christ" (10:7, 18; emphasis added). Thus, all of Moroni's final urgings in the last chapter of his own book are directed to Lamanites. Only when he plainly changes audiences are his words cast more broadly: "And now I speak unto all the ends of the earth . . ." (10:24). What seems clear is that Moroni has come to terms with the now distant but raw, chafing memories of Lamanite atrocities against his family and against his people, and he has genuinely forgiven them. Perhaps Moroni lives as long as he does to allow him to come to peace within himself. It has taken almost thirty-five years.

Choosing the Most Important Matters

Naturally, as we have seen, Moroni holds the Lamanites near the top of his list of concerns, for both spiritual and personal reasons. Even though they are his enemies and have devastated his world, he knows well enough that they are a people of prophetic destiny, as the Risen Savior had reminded His New World hearers generations earlier.[16] Hence, it is not surprising that at the end of his father's book, Moroni wrestles down his inflamed feelings and offers almost a prayer on their behalf—"these things . . . we have desired concerning our brethren [the Lamanites], yea, even their restoration to the knowledge of Christ" (Morm. 9:36).

Indeed, it is the set of topics that Moroni chooses to raise into the light that leads us into his deepest thoughts. At the top of his priorities stands the record entrusted to him by his father. It is ever with him. When he travels, he carries it. When he camps, he hides it.

When he wakes, he thinks of it. Its safety is always the primary concern for him. In addition, Lamanites constantly press themselves into Moroni's consciousness. For the sake of the preservation of the record and for the sake of his own safety, he must avoid them. And his memory would not dismiss their atrocities. Yet, ironically, the record he must now keep from them will become the very instrument for "their restoration to the knowledge of Christ" (Morm. 9:36). Those are not his only concerns. The record also shows Moroni's third major concern, that of a lack of faith in Christ. He worries compassionately over "those who do not believe in Christ" because they "deny the revelations of God" as well as the attending spiritual gifts (9:1, 7). The very existence of the record will prove both the reality of Christ and the fact that "the Lord hath spoken it [the record]" (Morm. 8:26). In addition, the record will offer proofs that spiritual powers and gifts are palpably real, reporting that people of faith could "remove mountains . . . [and] cause prisons to tumble to the earth" (8:24).

In this connection, we have to acknowledge that Moroni's impoverished situation must have also influenced his thinking and ordering of priorities, particularly as he had opportunity to write. After all, he has been reduced to the very minimum in life. Everything of value has been shorn from him, including his family members, his home, and his way of life. The only mortal treasure not ripped from his grasp is his own life. He is not weighed down by any concerns except his own safety and the safety of the record. As a result, we see a man writing about what matters most rather than taking up the limited space on his few plates for less important items.

THE RECORD AND ITS TRANSLATOR

First on Moroni's list of things he must do is to finish the record. We know he is to complete it because of "the commandment of my father" (Morm. 8:3). But there is much more. We find Moroni drawing up instructions for the eventual recipient and translator of the plates, then joining his prayers with others for that individual, and finally prophesying about the state of mankind and condition of the world when the record is brought forth. Let us explore these dimensions.

Moroni's first piece of advice to the translator is that "the [gold] plates" on which the record is inscribed "are of no worth." Why?

Because "no one shall have them to get gain." On the other hand, because of its content "the record [itself] is of great worth." Moreover, the person who "shall bring it to light, him will the Lord bless" (Morm. 8:14). Moroni then informs the eventual translator that "God wills that [the translation] shall be done with an eye single to his [God's] glory," because the record is created in large measure for "the welfare of the ancient and long dispersed covenant people of the Lord" (8:15). Hence, the translator will reap no self-aggrandizement in the process. Through the process the translator will come to know that the task "shall be done by the power of God." Even so, the process may introduce mistakes, what Moroni terms "faults of a man." But any person who therefore condemns the record must "be aware [of God's power in the process] lest he shall be in danger of hell fire" (8:16–17). In a more positive vein, "whoso receiveth this record, and shall not condemn it because of the imperfections . . . the same shall know greater things than these," which are noted in the record (8:12). This statement forms Moroni's first prophetic declaration that the record itself will lead readers to know that it is true and that it forms a gate of sorts to invisible yet real spiritual powers.

Most interesting, and the second point Mroni wishes to emphasize is that many of "those saints who have gone before me, who have possessed this land," have prayed specifically "in behalf of him [whom] the Lord should suffer to bring these things forth" (Morm. 8:23, 25). As a companion effort in their prayers, those very saints have prayed "in behalf of their brethren"—the Lamanites and others—so that the Lord would "remember the covenant which he hath made with them."[17] The intensity of their prayers has been as a "cry, yea, even from the dust [of the earth]" (8:24, 23). Moroni then brings forward proofs that their prayers will be effective "in behalf of him" who will "bring these things [the record] forth" by declaring that through prayer "in [God's] name could they remove mountains; and in his name could they cause the earth to shake." Further, because of their prayers, "even the fiery furnace could not harm them, neither wild beasts nor poisonous serpents" (8:24–25). Such instances of raw, divine power underscore for Moroni the assurance that, with God's help and because of the prayers of many, the translator will succeed even though some would "breathe out wrath and strifes against the work of the Lord" (8:21).

MATERIALISM

Thus far, Moroni's concerns have centered chiefly on the translator of the record. The third matter he discusses leads into a widening vision of the future; it has to do with us and our situation. For, as he reminds his future readers, "I speak unto you as if ye were present" because in vision "Jesus Christ hath shown you unto me, and I know your doing" (Morm. 8:35). He really does view our world and our time because the vision ties to "that day when these things [the record] shall come forth among you" (8:34). And after he sees our era, what does he write about? What has captured his attention? Standing squarely in the middle of his concerns for us is materialism, a love of property and its ability to confer a deceiving sense of well-being and even of importance. Next to materialism stands its usual companion, a warped perception of spiritual strength which, in fact, denies sacred realities and paints God as One who rewards righteous behavior by bestowing material blessings. Moroni's response to this bleak future looms in the form of a warning. And his warning does not distinguish between people of the covenant and those outside.

Conditions of materialism and vacant spirituality, of course, do not arise in a blink of time. They result from a process. Moroni does not focus on the process but rather on its enfeebling results for individuals who willingly embrace what he sees as an empty mirage. In addition, such conditions go hand in dirty hand with social injustices. In Moroni's words, the record itself forms the true measure of these matters. That is, "the plates," though made of a precious metal, astonishingly "are of no worth." Rather, it is "the record [that] is of great worth" (Morm. 8:14). This set of observations informs us about his fundamental point of view. The value placed on material goods must be significantly less than that placed on spiritual matters. After all, we recall, Moroni's life had been stripped bare of all comforts and amenities. He has come to know in a day-to-day manner about matters of real value—and they do not consist of material goods.

More to the point, Moroni writes that "I know that ye [his readers and others] do walk in the pride of your hearts . . . unto the wearing of very fine apparel, unto envying . . . and all manner of iniquities" (Morm. 8:36). Indeed, "ye do love money and your substance, and your fine apparel" to the point that "ye adorn yourselves with that which hath no life." The lamentable result is that such people "suffer the hungry, and the needy . . . to pass by you, and notice them not" (8:37, 39). Thus, materialism links to a perverting and disabling laxity in social justice and, more broadly, in simple acts of charity.

Materialism also brings its captives to a false view of their spiritual state. Instead of caring for "the poor and the needy, and sick and the afflicted," they come to value "the adorning of . . . churches" (Morm. 8:37). Such blighted persons earn Moroni's strongest condemnation: "ye pollutions, ye hypocrites . . . who sell yourselves for that which will canker." It is they who have "polluted the holy church of God" and are "ashamed to take upon [themselves] the name of Christ" while all about them people suffer (8:38).

As we might expect, this gangrenous material and spiritual condition blinds its adherents to a situation that, surprisingly to them, threatens to undo their world. For Moroni adds that these individuals "build up . . . secret abominations to get gain" while "widows . . . and also orphans . . . mourn before the Lord." Furthermore, "the blood of their fathers and their husbands . . . cry unto the Lord from the ground, for vengeance upon [their persecutors'] heads" (Morm. 8:40). From Moroni's words, we sense that certain people have embraced the damnable view that reckons the lives of certain persons to be expendable, to be less valuable than wealth. For those whose ambitious actions lead to the death of another, Moroni warns that "the sword of vengeance hangeth over you" and "the time soon cometh that [God] avengeth the blood of the saints upon you," a terribly vivid imagery of the guilty spattered with blood (8:41).

As if to reinforce his words, Moroni addresses this topic again when editing the book of Ether. There, in the context of reporting the stunning demise of an entire civilization, he warns his readers that "this secret combination which shall be among you" is "built up to get power and gain," an obvious grab for political and economic control (Ether 8:23–24). Hence, its ultimate object is power—"to overthrow the freedom of all lands, nations, and countries." Predictably, at its base stands "the devil, who is the father of all lies." As a matter of fact, from "the beginning"—here is Moroni's proof from the past that problems will become deadly serious in that future era when the record appears—the devil has regularly inspired those who have "hardened [their] hearts" and "have murdered the prophets, and stoned them" (8:25). What is Moroni's advice to those who live in such a terrible age? They are to "repent of [their] sins, and suffer not that these murderous combinations shall get above [them]," because they bring about "the work of destruction," both social and religious (8:23). Those who perpetrate such heinous acts draw the unwanted, vanquishing attention of God to themselves. In Moroni's words, in time "the sword of the justice of the Eternal God shall fall upon [them]," a terrible but deserved end (8:23).

What is more, institutionalized religion bears some of the blame for the paralyzing moral vacuum that is to exist when the record comes forth. The record "shall come in a day when . . . churches become defiled" and are "built up . . . to get gain." How so? Because practitioners have "transfigured the holy word of God." Worse, on a personal level, the "leaders of churches and teachers shall rise in the pride of their hearts, even to the envying of them who belong to their churches" (Morm. 8:28, 33). It is in such a disquieting period of spiritual turbulence and misdirection that the record will appear, bringing clarity and celestial purpose to those who will receive it.

SPIRITUAL GIFTS

Moroni's concern with the disorderly spiritual tapestry of that future era ties firmly to his deep anxiety about the accompanying absence of spiritual gifts, a vacuous condition that he would have observed in his own society. On Moroni's part, it is not clear whether a direct, vivid experience raised his anxiety about this matter. It may simply have grown out of his vision wherein "Jesus Christ hath shown you unto me" (Morm. 8:35). Or it may have grown out of some other circumstance. We do not know. But his deep concern is obvious because of the space that he devotes to the topic of spiritual gifts on the few plates that are at his disposal.

After Moroni's long discussion about the record and the disheartening circumstances surrounding its appearance in modern times, he turns to the matter of belief that is tightly centered in Christ. It is this principle, that of an unshakable belief in Christ, that determines whether spiritual gifts can be manifest. Perhaps oddly, he introduces readers to the set of issues in a negative way: "I speak also concerning *those who do not believe in Christ*" (Morm. 9:1; emphasis added). For such people, the vivid proof of the reality of Jesus will appear in the inevitable, engulfing events at the end of time: "will ye believe [in Christ] in the day of your visitation . . . when the Lord shall come . . . when the earth shall be rolled together as a scroll . . . when ye shall be brought to stand before the Lamb of God—then will ye say that there is no God?" (Morm. 9:2). For the "unbelieving" there is still a chance for reaching a redemptive haven. But it will require that they "cry mightily unto the Father in the name of Jesus, that perhaps ye may be found spotless . . . having been cleansed by the blood of the Lamb, at that great and last day" (9:6). But for those who continue stubbornly in unbelief, no spiritual gifts can be manifest to sweeten their lives: "all these gifts . . . are spiritual, [and] never will be done away . . . only according to the unbelief . . . of men" (Moro. 10:19). Said another way, "the reason why [God] ceaseth to do miracles among . . . men is because that they dwindle in unbelief, and depart from the right way" (Morm. 9:20).

The first gift that Moroni points to is revelation. Why? Because with this queen of gifts come all the others, including "prophecies . . . healing . . . speaking with tongues, and the interpretation of tongues" (Morm. 9:7). His language is firm, almost strident: "I speak unto you who deny the revelations of God, and say that they are done away" (9:7). For Moroni, nothing could be further from the truth: "he that denieth these things knoweth not the gospel of Christ" (9:8). But there is more to not knowing than mere ignorance. It means knowingly claiming that the "God who created the heavens and the earth" by miraculous means has somehow changed.[18] This point draws in Moroni's second gift, that of miracles. Quoting a source known only to him, perhaps from the brass plates, Moroni asks, "do we not read that God is the same yesterday, today, and forever?" (9:9).[19] Citing notable, miraculous actions of the past, such as God's creation of "the heavens and the earth" and Jesus' "many mighty miracles" (9:11, 18), Moroni again asks, "if there were miracles wrought then, why has God ceased to be a God of miracles? . . . behold, I say unto you he changeth not; if so he would cease to be God" (Morm. 9:19). It is this concept—which, at God's core, He wants to work remedying miracles for His children—that drives Moroni to object strenuously to those who would deny God's powers: "the reason why he [God] ceaseth to do miracles among . . . men is because [of] . . . unbelief" (9:20). It is not because of any inability on God's part, a point that we have already mentioned.

Later, just as Moroni is closing the record before hiding it in the earth, he brings readers back to the matter of spiritual gifts, placing his discussion at the end, a place of emphasis. At this point he makes a catalogue of spiritual gifts, much like that of the Apostle Paul,[20] wherein he brings forward each of them so that readers can appreciate the breadth of God's gifts. While his listing lies within the section addressed directly "unto my brethren, the Lamanites" (Moro. 10:1), perhaps forming Moroni's acknowledgment of their unusual spiritual sensitivities, it seems plain that all readers are to benefit from the discussion. Moroni knows that he is raising the issue a second time: "*again,* I exhort you, my brethren, that ye deny not the gifts of God, *for they are many.*" Such gifts come to people "by the manifestations of the Spirit of God, to profit them" (10:8; emphasis added). After reviewing each of the gifts, Moroni then aptly summarizes by predicting that God "is the same yesterday, today, and forever, and . . . all these gifts . . . never will be done away, even as long as the world shall stand." In some way, just as bestowing these gifts is a part of God's nature, so their appearance among people on earth is a part of the intended natural order. They only disappear because of "the unbelief of the children of men" (10:19).

FAITH, HOPE, AND CHARITY

It is fortunate that Moroni does not stop after writing about the record and the Lamanites and faith in Christ. Other topics occupied his mind during his long years alone. One of the most prominent clusters of principles sketched by Moroni mirrors his father's sermon on faith, hope, and charity (see Moro. 7).[21] It seems abundantly apparent that Mormon's views influenced directly and measurably those of Moroni. This influence naturally leads Moroni to include the text of his father's sermon as an important piece in his own book.

For both authors, faith means fundamentally "faith in Christ" (Moro. 10:4). Although Moroni defines faith broadly as "things which are hoped for and not seen" (Ether 12:6), faith, as it ties to celestial matters, must be linked to Christ. On one level faith forms a quiet, almost invisible aspect of individuals' lives, such as "they of old [who] were called after the holy order of God." As an example, Moroni points to the missionaries Nephi and Lehi through whose faith came "the change upon the Lamanites, that they were baptized with fire and with the Holy Ghost" (12:10, 14).[22] But the robust exercise of faith has also led to the occasional dramatic release of divine aid for the benefit of God's servants. For instance, "it was the faith of Alma and Amulek that caused the prison to tumble to the earth" (12:13). In addition, because of the faith of the brother of Jared, "when God put forth his finger he could not hide it from the sight of the brother of Jared." In fact, "the Lord could not withhold anything from his sight; wherefore he showed him all things" (12:20–21). Belief in this enlivening faith forms the energetic counterpoint to the disbelief that smothers spiritual gifts.

However, faith does not stand alone. Its immediate, abiding companion is hope. As Moroni reminds his readers, individuals cannot "be saved in the kingdom of God if ye have not faith; neither can ye if ye have no hope" (Moro. 10:21). Said another way, "without faith there cannot be any hope" (Moro. 7:42). But hope in what? The response of Mormon and Moroni centers hope on the eventual outcome of a person's life, that is, on future events that in mortal life are only promised. For example, some "have obtained a sufficient hope by which ye can enter into the rest of the Lord" in this life *"until ye shall rest with him in heaven"* (7:3; emphasis added). Again, "what is it that ye shall hope for? Behold I say unto you that ye shall have hope through the atonement of Christ . . . *to be raised unto life eternal . . . according to the promise"* (7:41; emphasis added). Sadly, for the person who lives without this hope in eventual, celestial realities, "ye must needs be in despair" (Moro. 10:22).

The third of the three virtues is charity. As the crown of personal virtues, it always stands with faith and hope and ever seems to be preceded by them. But perhaps in contrast to them, charity is more of a gift than they are. For, as Mormon observes, it is "bestowed" by God "upon all who are true followers of his Son, Jesus Christ" (Moro. 7:48). In a memorable, revelatory exchange between Moroni and the Lord, Moroni intones in one of his prayers, "I remember that thou hast said that thou hast loved the world, even unto the laying down of thy life. . . . And now I know that this love which thou hast had for the children of men is charity." In fact, this charity, in a generous and legal manner, makes it possible for persons to "inherit that place which thou hast prepared in the mansions of thy Father" (Ether 12:33–34). Hence, charity possesses both a this-worldly dimension, as seen in Jesus' atoning act, and an other-worldly aspect, which eventually allows those who have received it to inherit "the mansions of [the] Father." For, "except ye have charity ye can in nowise be saved in the kingdom of God" (Moro. 10:21). And worse, in God's sight, if a person "have not charity he is nothing" (Moro. 7:44).

Charity, of course, unfolds to its recipients a galaxy of virtues that continue to grace their lives. In one of Mormon's most memorable lines, he writes that "charity suffereth long, and is kind, and envieth not, and is not puffed up, seeketh not her own, is not easily provoked, thinketh no evil, and rejoiceth not in iniquity but rejoiceth in the truth, beareth all things, believeth all things, hopeth all things, endureth all things" (Moro. 7:45). How does a person become a recipient of these divinely bestowed traits? Through prayer. As Mormon admonishes the hearers of his sermon, doubtless from his own experience, "my beloved brethren, pray unto the Father with all the energy of heart, that ye may be filled with this love" (7:48). Again, its results are both terrestrial and celestial. Terrestrial aspects manifest themselves in a person's treatment of others in "pure love" (7:47). Concerning celestial aspects, individuals are to pray for charity "that ye may become the sons of God; that when he shall appear we shall be like him . . . that we may be purified even as he is pure" (7:48). For "charity is the pure love of Christ, and it endureth forever" (7:47).

What is the source for such doctrinal principles, particularly as they are configured in the thoughts of Moroni and his father?[23] One key may lie in the first part of Mormon's sermon on faith, hope, and charity (see Moro. 7). Here Mormon turns attention to the opposites good and evil, especially as they apply to works and gifts. Mormon introduces his hearers to the topic by paraphrasing a scriptural source: "I remember the word of God which saith by their works ye shall know them." What is not clear is whether the next line goes back to the source or whether it forms Mormon's commentary: "if [people's] works be good, then they are good also" (Moro. 7:5). Whichever the case, Mormon has shown that, at least for the initial part of his sermon, he has a scriptural source in mind. What might it be? Because Mormon is evidently paraphrasing a passage from memory, we need not find a perfect fit. The closest fit comes from the words of the Resurrected Jesus when He says, "by their fruits ye shall know them" (3 Ne. 14:20). While the difference between Mormon's term "works" and Jesus word "fruits" might discourage the view that Mormon had Jesus' words in mind, there is further evidence that this might very well be the source.

As Mormon continues, he declares that "if a man being evil giveth a gift, he doeth it grudgingly; wherefore it is counted unto him the same as if he had retained the gift" (Moro. 7:8). This line too recalls words spoken by Jesus on the same occasion and at an almost identical place in His sermon:

> [W]hat man is there of you, who, if his son ask bread, will give him a stone? Or if he ask a fish, will he give him a serpent? If ye then, being evil, know how to give good gifts unto your children, how much more shall your Father who is in heaven give good things to them that ask him? (3 Ne. 14:9–11)

While there is resemblance between Mormon's point and that of Jesus, it is not certain that Mormon fully depends on the Savior's words. The manifest tie comes in another passage wherein Mormon goes on to deal with meaningless, insincere prayer: "likewise also is it counted evil unto a man, if he shall pray and not with real intent of heart; yea, and it profiteth him nothing, for God receiveth none such" (Moro. 7:9). Similarly, Jesus dealt with insincere prayer in the very sermon that Mormon seems to be alluding to:

> [W]hen thou prayest thou shalt not do as the hypocrites, for they love to pray, standing in the synagogues and in the corners of the streets, that they may be seen of men. Verily I say unto you, they have their reward [of praise from others]. (3 Ne. 13:5)

A quick comparison of Mormon's words with these words of Jesus indicates that Mormon evidently had in mind this part of the Savior's sermon given in the New World. This observation leads us to deduce that Mormon and later Moroni were likely resting their concepts about faith, hope, and charity on the words of Jesus, even though we do not possess them. Instead, they must lie in the sections of the report of Jesus' words that Mormon did not record in the book of Third Nephi. After all, Mormon writes that "there cannot be written in this book even a hundredth part of the things which Jesus did truly teach unto the people" during His three-day visit (3 Ne. 26:6).[24]

MORONI'S REVELATIONS AS PROOFS

As already noted, Moroni writes strong words to those "who deny the revelations of God, and say that . . . there are no revelations, nor prophecies." To such persons Moroni announces, "he that denieth these things knoweth not the gospel of Christ" (Morm. 9:7–8). But these are not mere words. Moroni's own experience has taught him the reality of special spiritual disclosures. For example, when he writes of the three "disciples of Jesus, who did tarry" in the flesh, but had long since departed at the Lord's behest, he reports that "my father and I have seen them, and they have ministered unto us" (Morm. 8:10–11).[25] More important, in the second of his farewells, tucked in the abridged record of the Jaredites, Moroni says to his readers that "we shall meet before the judgment-seat of Christ. . . . And then shall ye know that I have seen Jesus, and that he hath talked with me face to face" (Ether 12:38–39).[26]

Besides these two impressive experiences, Moroni records a personal sequence of prayer and responding heavenly revelation, which demonstrates both the actuality of revelation in Moroni's life as well as the love that the Lord lavishes on those who seek Him in prayer. Translating and abridging the book of Ether leaves a deep impression on Moroni. What is that impression? It is that "the things which [the brother of Jared] wrote were mighty even as thou [God] art, unto the overpowering of man to read them" (Ether 12:24). Discovering the literary skill of an author from another culture, saturated with spiritual power, brings Moroni to a startling conclusion—that his own literary skills are weak in comparison. And this conclusion leads him to worry aloud in prayer that the recipients of the record, "the Gentiles," will come to "mock at these things, because of our weakness in writing," a concern that he raises elsewhere.[27] Perceiving clearly that the Lord had somehow assisted the brother of Jared, Moroni laments that the Lord "made us that we could write but little, because of the awkwardness of our hands [and] . . . because of the placing of our words" (12:23–25). In a gentle, comforting response to Moroni's lament, the Lord assures him that "if men come unto me I will show unto them their weakness. I give unto men weakness that they may be humble; and my grace is sufficient for all" (12:27). Concerning those who may mock, the Lord says abruptly, "Fools mock, but they shall mourn" (12:26).

In his own words, "I, Moroni, having heard these words, was comforted" (Ether 12:29). But Moroni does not stop his prayer because, it seems, the Lord's warning to the mocker has caught in Moroni's mind and has begun to worry him. Thus he continues his prayer, an exercise of his own faith, by reminding himself and the Lord about the wonderous works that have come about because of people's faith: "I know that thou workest unto the children of men according to their faith" (12:29). Then after rehearsing a number of miraculous occurrences owing to faith (see Ether 12:30–34), Moroni reaches the heart of his concern: "I know by this thing which thou hast said, that if the Gentiles have not charity, because of our weakness [in writing], that thou wilt prove them, and take away their talent" (12:35). Evidently, it has pained Moroni that his inability to express himself with power in writing might become a reason for recipients of his record not to take it seriously or, worse, thereby to become cursed by God. Therefore he "prayed unto the Lord that he would give unto the Gentiles grace, that they might have charity" toward one another which would affect the way that they view the record and its authors (12:36). The Lord's answer is instructive. He does not assure Moroni that He will do as Moroni has asked. Instead, He seeks to reassure Moroni about his own future: "If they have not charity it mattereth not unto thee, thou has been faithful; wherefore, thy garments shall be made clean . . . even unto the sitting down in the place which I have prepared" (12:37). What is the outcome? These verses demonstrate that Moroni enjoys a relationship with the Lord that includes revelations that both instruct Moroni and comfort him in his lonely mission.

AGRAPHA

As we have now seen, Moroni's account rests partly on his own revelatory experiences. And it stands partly—even mostly—on records from the past. He identifies most of these records, such as those which derive from the Jaredites (the book of Ether) and from his father (a sermon and two letters). But there are some sources that he does not identify, and we are left to speculate about their place within his own scriptural record. The common scholarly term for such unidentified sources is "agrapha" (singular, agraphon), which means not written in a known text. For instance, King Limhi quotes three sayings from God that are not found in any known ancient source (see Mosiah 7:29–31).[28] These sayings therefore are agrapha. Similarly, Moroni quotes sayings or alludes to incidents whose origins are unknown to us, unexpectedly adding to what we sense about the character and breadth of scripture among his people.

The first occurrence in Moroni's writings is the following: "Behold what the scripture says—man shall not smite, neither shall he judge; for judgment is mine, saith the Lord, and vengeance is mine also, and I will repay" (Morm. 8:20). While a person might see Isaiah 47:3 as lying behind this saying, it does not offer a good match: "I will take vengeance, and I will not meet thee as a man." The second instance finds a parallel in the New Testament Gospel of Mark. But this text cannot be a source because Moroni would not have enjoyed access to it. Hence, the words of Jesus recorded in Mormon 9:22–25, which show both similarities and differences with Mark 16:15–18, must go back to the three-day visit of the Resurrected Savior.

The next consists of a pair of paraphrased sayings also attributed to the Risen Lord. Moroni recalls the two sayings within his prayer for grace to be with the Gentiles:[29] "I . . . remember that thou hast said that *thou hast prepared a house for man, yea, even among the mansions of thy Father*" (Ether 12:32; emphasis added). It may be significant that Moroni utters the term "man" rather than "Gentiles" or "house of Israel" in an effort to express a broad plea that God's grace extend to all. The second he cites as follows, for a similar reason: "And again, I remember that thou hast said that *thou hast loved the world, even unto the laying down of thy life for the world."* Though a paraphrase, Moroni takes up Jesus' term "the world" as a possible point of emphasis in his prayer that God's grace be available to all people, "the children of men" as he calls them (Ether 12:33; emphasis added).

The final agraphon consists in Moroni's quotation of words of Christ and comes almost at the end of the record: "If ye have faith ye can do all things which are expedient unto me [Christ]" (Moro. 10:23). This saying is very similar to one quoted by Mormon: "If ye will have faith in me ye shall have power to do whatsoever thing is expedient in me" (Moro. 7:33). Each of them expresses the certain idea that the one who exercises faith can perform the Lord's tasks. Moroni's version could be considered to be a variant of the version quoted by his father, but it need not be so. Either or both might be thought of as deriving from the following words of the Risen Jesus, though it is unlikely: "whatsoever ye shall ask the Father in my name, which is right, believing that ye shall receive, behold it shall be given unto you" (3 Ne. 18:20). The similarities between the two sayings quoted by Moroni and Mormon are striking enough to suggest a common source. In each case, the author probably quoted from memory rather than from a written text, thus accounting for the modest differences. But the dissimilarities between their quotes and that from Third Nephi are significant enough to discourage any suggestion of dependence on this saying by the Resurrected Jesus. Instead, we have to postulate that both Moroni and Mormon are thinking of a saying of Jesus that is preserved among the records not included elsewhere in the Book of Mormon text.

THE HOUSE OF ISRAEL

It should not surprise a reader that Moroni expresses interest in the house of Israel. He is, after all, an Israelite. In fact, Moroni presents his pedigree: "I am the son of Mormon, and my father was a descendant of Nephi" who, like his father, as we learn from another source, "was a descendant of Manasseh, who was the son of Joseph who was sold into Egypt" (Morm. 8:13; Alma 10:3). Thus Moroni possesses a natural reason to be interested in the fate of his people. But that is not all.

When giving directions to the future translator of the record, Moroni makes a most interesting equivalency: "for God wills that [the translation] shall be done with an eye single to his glory, or the welfare of the ancient and long dispersed covenant people of the Lord" who "are the house of Israel" (Morm. 8:15, 21). It seems apparent that, for Moroni, God's will and God's glory are intimately tied to "the welfare of the . . . covenant people." In an adjoining passage, he links the "covenant which he [God] hath made unto the house of Israel" with "the eternal purposes of the Lord" (8:21–22). Moroni is not creating this linkage simply because he is an Israelite. This tie is divine. For in the midst of a subsequent revelation, the Lord Himself pleads,

> Come unto me, O ye house of Israel, and it shall be made manifest unto you how great things the Father hath laid up for you, from the foundation of the world. . . . Behold, when ye shall rend that veil of unbelief [and] . . . when ye shall call upon the Father in my name, . . . then shall ye know that the Father hath remembered the covenant which he made unto your fathers. (Ether 4:14–15)

Finally, at the very end of the record, and thus in a place of high emphasis, Moroni borrows the language of Isaiah and makes an impassioned plea to his fellow Israelites:

> [A]wake, and arise from the dust, O Jerusalem; yea, and put on thy beautiful garments, O daughter of Zion . . . that thou mayest no more be confounded, that the covenants of the Eternal Father which he hath made unto thee, O house of Israel, may be fulfilled. (Moro. 10:31; compare Isa. 52:1; 54:2)

Two points of interest arise from this passage. First, Jerusalem and, by extension, its citizens have been in the hearts and minds of Moroni and his people since the first generation departed Jerusalem.[30] We can almost hear something like the Passover expression "Next year in Jerusalem!" spoken by Nephites over the years. Second, the covenants that God made with the ancestors of the Israelites are to be fulfilled, including those that have to do with posterity and priesthood rights and land.[31] And the appearance of the record is to herald that coming fulfillment.

ORDINANCES

Readers are deeply indebted to Moroni for preserving details about important saving ordinances of the gospel. All of what he preserves has now taken its place in the modern Church.[32] Moroni could not have missed the clarity of the Risen Savior's words to "all his disciples, in the hearing of the multitude" during His three-day visit—which Moroni now quotes: "he that believeth *and is baptized* shall be saved" (Morm. 9:22–23; emphasis added). On that same occasion, pointing to another ordinance, the Savior had cautioned His authorized disciples that they "not suffer any one knowingly to partake of my flesh and blood unworthily" (3 Ne. 18:28). Moroni adheres to this lead and counsels readers accordingly: "See that ye are not baptized unworthily; see that ye partake not of the sacrament of Christ unworthily; but see that ye do all things in worthiness, and do it in the name of Jesus Christ" (Morm. 9:29). Moroni's words thus capture the sense of holiness that accompanies the ordinances performed "in the name of Jesus Christ" which is to be matched by the worthiness of the recipient and the officiator. This sense of holiness flows through all of Moroni's description of the ordinances.

One occasion for mentioning ordinances, and particularly how they are performed, arises when Moroni is about to bury the record. He expresses surprise at still being alive: "I have not as yet perished; and I make not myself known to the Lamanites lest they should destroy me" (Moro. 1:1). It next becomes clear that he is thinking chiefly of future readers, specifically Lamanites, when he writes about ordinances: "I write a few more things, that perhaps they may be of worth unto my brethren, the Lamanites, in some future day" (1:4). In a way, he is handing to readers a template that will fit the true church.

While writing his last entries in the record, as we have seen, Moroni touches on baptism. What is next? Confirmation. And that is what we find. His ultimate source for this ordinance, and the others, was the occasion when "Christ spake these words unto [the twelve disciples] at the time of his first appearing," that is, on the first of his three days in the New World (Moro. 2:3). It becomes evident here that Moroni has chosen to incorporate items that his father had not included in his abridgment of Third Nephi. Why? We go back to a prior point. Moroni is offering a peek at the workings of the true church to future readers. The ordinance of confirmation, which will be present in the true church, involves first calling "on the Father in [Jesus'] name, in mighty prayer." As a result, "*ye shall have power* that to him upon whom ye shall lay your hands, ye shall give the Holy Ghost" (2:2–3; emphasis added). Receiving divine power stands as a demonstration not only of the holiness of the ordinance of conferring the Holy Ghost upon a worthy recipient, but also of God's active approval of the action.

Naturally, ordinances require persons who are authorized and worthy to perform them. And the details of ordaining "priests and teachers" come next (Moro. 3:1). The ordination procedure, too, goes back to the days of the Savior's visit. As in the case of conferring the Holy Ghost, ordaining required prayer by church leaders "unto the Father in the name of Christ" and laying "their hands upon them" (3:2). Such prayer meant that "they ordained [priests and teachers] *by the power* of the Holy Ghost, which was in them" because of their worthiness (3:4; emphasis added). Moroni even records the words that were spoken during such ordinations, thus emphasizing the need of repeating such words: "In the name of Jesus Christ I ordain you to be a priest . . . to preach repentance and remission of sins through Jesus Christ, by the endurance of faith on his name to the end. Amen" (3:3). These words, coupled with God's power, make the ordinance effective.

As we have already seen, the Risen Christ was anxious that His authorized disciples "not suffer anyone knowingly to partake of my flesh and blood unworthily" (3 Ne. 18:28). Now Moroni takes us to the words that invest the sacramental emblems with covenantal power. Mirroring the order that Jesus established for the ordinance—first the bread and then the wine (see 3 Ne. 18:1–3, 8)—Moroni repeats the exact words of the prayers that only "elders and priests" were to respectfully recite over the bread and wine before members of "the church" (Moro. 4:1). As in earlier cases, these prayers repeat the precise words of the Savior, which He had taught during His visit: on that occasion, "they administered [the bread and wine] according to the commandments of Christ" (4:1).

That these ordinances had formed part of the sacred services of the church in Moroni's day becomes apparent in his remark that church members "did meet together oft to partake of bread and wine, in remembrance of the Lord Jesus" (Moro. 6:6). Importantly, the complementing worthiness remained an essential aspect of religious life and appears in Moroni's narrative: "the church did meet together oft, to fast and to pray." Moreover, "they were strict to observe that there should be no iniquity among them" (6:5, 7). The result was that "their meetings were conducted by the church after the manner of the workings of the Spirit, and by the power of the Holy Ghost" (6:9). Such displays of divine influence, of course, formed the proof that God was working in their midst.

Ordinances did not represent the only efforts of the church to influence the lives of individuals, and Moroni reminds us of this fact. After setting out the details concerning ordinances, he makes it clear that people "were not baptized save they brought forth fruit meet that they were worthy of it" and came "unto baptism . . . with a broken heart and a contrite spirit" (Moro. 6:1–2). In their personal lives, candidates for membership were to repent "of all their sins" and, at baptism, take "upon them the name of Christ" after exhibiting "a determination to serve him to the end" (6:2–3). For those who received baptism and were "cleansed by the power of the Holy Ghost, they were numbered," that is, "their names were taken, that they might be . . . nourished by the good word of God, to keep them in the right way" (6:4). Thus, receiving the ordinances was only a part of the new life for worshipers. Fellowship based on mutual, spiritual assistance played an important role in their lives. All of this was brought to an end for church members with the annihilation of the Nephite people. It is Moroni who holds in the light this part of his life of devotion by making an effort to recount the ordinances that he had both received and known to be effective.

ANGELS

More than any other ancient writer, Moroni preserves what angels do and how they interact with mortals.[33] Moroni himself writes little about angels, but his father, on the other hand, writes a good deal that Moroni chooses to repeat. The fact that Moroni preserves his father's words demonstrates the value that he places on knowing about angels. Moroni's only personal notation about angels comes forward in his listing of spiritual gifts when he mentions the gift of "the beholding of angels" (Moro. 10:14). Such a gift, apparently, is not for everyone.

Why do angels appear to mortals? Mormon provides some answers. His first point is that, before the coming of Christ, God "sent angels to minister unto the children of men, to make manifest concerning the coming of Christ." Their early mission was to convince the ancients that "in Christ there should come every good thing" (Moro. 7:22). The result was that "by the ministering of angels . . . men began to exercise faith in Christ; and . . . they did lay hold upon every good thing . . . until the coming of Christ" (7:25).

In the same broad sense, Mormon declares that "the office of [the angels'] ministry is to call men unto repentance." They are also "to do the work of . . . the Father . . . by declaring the word of Christ unto the chosen vessels of the Lord, that they [in turn] may bear testimony of him" (Moro. 7:31). From this passage, it is apparent that angels not only call people to repentance but also, in the specific case of "the chosen vessels of the Lord," such as prophets and apostles, they declare "the word of Christ" to them so that those persons can "bear testimony of [Christ]." It is these individuals who are "of strong faith and a firm mind in every form of godliness" to whom angels come "according to [God's] command, showing themselves unto them" (7:30).

In sum, according to Moroni and his father, among recipients of angelic ministrations are those who receive the gift of "the beholding of angels" (Moro. 10:14), those who became witnesses of "the coming of Christ" before His mortal birth (7:22), those who are called "unto repentance" (7:31), and those "of strong faith and a firm mind" who are "the chosen vessels of the Lord" and are also recipients of angelic visitors "declaring the word of Christ" so that these "chosen" persons "may bear witness of [Christ]" (7:30–31). Undergirding all, an important principle lies at the base of angelic visitations: "it is by faith that angels appear and minister unto men" (7:37). Angels do not make casual, unplanned visits to mortals.

CHILDREN

As in the case of angels, much of what we learn about children comes from Moroni's father. Again we must remember that, because Moroni inserts his father's words into his record, he holds them as his own, laying emphasis on them. We must also keep in mind that Mormon and, hence, his son, "measured civility by how women and children fared" (see Morm. 4:14, 21; Moro. 9:11–14).[34] Moreover, the Savior's memorable interaction with children during His three-day visit raised the consciousness of Moroni's forebears about children's well-being and wondrous potential. Finally, it must have deeply pained Moroni to witness, as his father did, the horrors that children suffered during the final wars between their people and the Lamanites, horrors that may have ended the lives of his own children, thus sharpening his feelings.

The first words about children arise out of events in A.D. 367, when Mormon mentions their helplessness in suffering during times of war. He writes that in that year the Lamanite armies marched "against the city of Teanchum, and did drive the inhabitants forth out of her, and did take many prisoners both women and children, and did offer them up as sacrifices unto their idol gods" (Morm. 4:14). In this instance, the treatment of child prisoners cannot differ more sharply from Jesus' treatment of children during His ministry among their ancestors. But that day of concern and compassion had long been forgotten. Naturally, the Nephite armies, made up of fathers and brothers, responded in anger and force to this mistreatment of children, driving "the Lamanites . . . out of their lands" (4:15). But matters did not end there.

After a respite of eight years, a huge Lamanite army "with all their powers" attacked the border city called Desolation in A.D. 375 (Morm. 4:17, 19). Standing "as an idle witness" to these affairs (Morm. 3:16), Mormon writes that "there was an exceeding sore battle fought in the land Desolation" which forced the Nephites to flee to the nearby city of Boaz where their resistance collapsed, leading to "an exceedingly great slaughter." What is worse, "their women and their children were again sacrificed unto idols" (Morm. 4:19–21). On another occasion, though its date cannot be determined, Mormon writes a letter to Moroni about other atrocities, reporting that after the fall of a tower called Sherrizah wherein "men, women, and children" had taken refuge, Lamanite soldiers "have slain" the men "and they feed . . . the children upon the flesh of their fathers" (Moro. 9:7–8). Mormon's response? It is clear that words fail him as he writes to Moroni: "O my beloved son, how can a people like this, that are without civilization—?" Mormon's thoughts stop. Only after several tries at expressing himself does Mormon shape his thoughts into a damning question because he has no answers: "How can we expect that God will stay his hand in judgment against us?" (Moro. 9:11, 14). It is that very judgment, of course, that Moroni would live to see, leaving him—as far as he was aware—the lone survivor of his people.

At some point during these years of numbing conflict, the riveting concern that Mormon and Moroni shared for children comes out in an earlier letter, preserved in Moroni 8.[35] The central issue concerns baptizing "little children" (Moro. 8:5). News had reached Mormon about "this gross error" directly from Moroni—"after I [Mormon] had learned these things of you [Moroni] I inquired of the Lord concerning the matter" (8:5–7). As mentioned earlier, Moroni carries an ecclesiastical responsibility which allows him to act on his father's behalf, and plainly his father bears overall responsibility for the affairs of the church. The fact that the Lord responds to Mormon also discloses him as the Lord's representative: "the word of the Lord came to me" (8:7). And what does the Lord reveal? His landmark answer comes in two parts, both of which deal with children. First, "little children are whole, for they are not capable of committing sin." The reason is that "the curse of Adam is taken from them in me, that it hath no power over them" (8:8). Therefore, in the words of Mormon, "little children need no repentance, neither baptism" (8:11).

The second part of the Lord's answer is intriguing. He reveals that "the law of circumcision is done away in me." According to the Bible, and presumably also the record on the brass plates, the Lord instituted circumcision as a sign of His covenant with Abraham (see Gen. 17:9–14). But the Lord's answer to Mormon hints that circumcision may have served as a covenant sign as early as Adam, for they seem to be connected: "the curse of Adam is taken from them in me . . . and the law of circumcision is done away in me" (Moro. 8:8). Whether or not this law or sign of covenant goes back to the days of Adam, the immediate effect for Moroni and other church members was that they no longer need feel obliged to circumcise their male infants.

In the end, however, Mormon chooses to focus on the matter of the fundamental innocence of children. For that affects the perceived need to baptize them, a need which some church members felt—probably because infants were dying in war—and which the Lord rejected. Mormon spells out the implications by correctly insisting that "little children are alive in Christ, even from the foundations of the world" (Moro. 8:12). Observing that "many little children have died without baptism," a telling characteristic of his blighted society, he writes: "if little children could not be saved without baptism, these must have gone to an endless hell" (8:12–13). Such a view assumes "that God saveth one child because of baptism" and not another "because he hath no baptism" and is therefore "a respecter to persons" (8:15, 12). This concept riles Mormon to the point that he cries out: "he that supposeth that little children need baptism is in the gall of bitterness and in the bonds of iniquity [and] . . . must go down to hell" (8:14). The companion principle to not baptizing children is that "little children cannot repent." How so? Because "they are all alive in [God] because of his mercy" which grows out of His "atonement . . . and the power of his redemption" (8:19–20).

The concern of Mormon and Moroni for the eternal status of children stands in sharp contrast to the atrocities occurring throughout their general society. It forms an indicator of their deep love and concern. As Mormon writes, "I love little children with a perfect love" (Moro. 8:17). In reality, the day only became bleaker for children as society moved relentlessly toward annihilation.

CONCLUSION

Born Moroni, son of Mormon, he comes into the world as the son—perhaps the only son—of one of the most prominent men of that era. For his father served as the commander in chief of his people's armies for a total of forty-six years and stood at the head of the church. At first, Moroni's life is bathed in the glow of prominence and promise. But his life turns out quite differently, a prey of forces far beyond his control. For his people's general unwillingness both to change their lives and to pursue peace with their enemies sowed the seeds of destruction that within a generation would mature into an incapacitating, self-induced social pestilence and would choke off any avenues for the survival of their civilization. On the side of their enemies, the Lamanites, pursuit of war with Moroni's people finally pays the dividends that they had sought so long—complete annihilation of the hated Nephites, a hatred that like many others went back to an old family quarrel. It was indeed a dark day across the land. Yet from the smoldering, bloody ruins of the entire Nephite people arises the solitary, lonely figure of Moroni. Fiercely loyal to the cause of Christ, he is forced to flee the scene of the last battle, leaving behind the mortal remains of his beloved father and other family members.

Some fifteen years later we glimpse Moroni in his outcast circumstance as he finishes his father's book. To the fore have come concerns that had burrowed deep into his soul during those years, aided and amplified by revelations from the Lord. Those topics have to do with the fate of the record itself, with faith in Christ and, finally, with his enemies, the Lamanites. Then, almost twenty-one years after that, we behold him at the last as he presents the record of the Jaredites, another people who suffered total annihilation because of their unwillingness both to change their lives and to pursue peace with one another. In addition, he sets out for readers the essential ordinances of salvation, holding up a pattern that readers will find in the true church. He ends his record by recording a sermon of his father on the lofty virtues of faith, hope, and charity, and by preserving two of his father's letters to him that touch on the important topics of the fundamental innocence of children and, in stark contrast, the depravities that would rob their society—and ours—of the merciful protections of God. It is as though the memory of what had happened to children in Moroni's society, perhaps even to his own, still burns hot within his heart and he seeks something infinitely better for unborn generations. As he is about to sign off, he turns again to his "brethren, the Lamanites" and implores them to seek after spiritual blessings, including a testimony that what he and others have written in the record is true. With his last words, his thoughts turn to Jerusalem whence his ancestors had departed a thousand years earlier. He pleads for her redemption because, as he knows, when she and the house of Israel are redeemed, the purposes of God will have come to fulfillment.

NOTES TO CHAPTER SIX

1. Mark D. Thomas has recently drawn attention to some of these virtues in "Moroni: The Final Voice," *Journal of Book of Mormon Studies* 12, no. 1 (2003): 88–99.
2. Consult Morm. 4:14, 21–22; 5:5, 7; compare 2:21. The most recent summarizing article is by Byron R. Merrill, "Moroni," *Book of Mormon Reference Companion,* ed. Dennis L. Largey et al. (Salt Lake City: Deseret Book, 2003), 557–60.
3. The notices of Mormon's selection to lead the Nephite armies in A.D. 326, of his retirement in disgust in A.D. 362, and of his return to active duty about A.D. 375 appear in Morm. 2:1; 3:11; and 5:1.
4. The translated expression "the son of . . ." may simply represent an idiom that can mean "a son of . . ." and not point to an only son. But the phrase suggests that Moroni had no brothers.
5. The linguistic heritage of Book of Mormon peoples has yet to be fully explored. Consult Brian D. Stubbs, "Book of Mormon Language," in *Encyclopedia of Mormonism,* ed. Daniel H. Ludlow et al. (New York: Macmillan, 1992), 179–181, and citations. Moroni, who lived about 1,000 years after the earliest generation of his people, may be the only accurate gauge of what his people had inherited linguistically from the past. For later language patterns, see "Was There Hebrew Language in Ancient America? An Interview with Brian Stubbs," *Journal of Book of Mormon Studies* 9, no. 2 (2000): 54–63.
6. Consult Alma 48:11–13, 16–17, for Mormon's tribute to this man.
7. For a different assessment of Moroni's date of birth and age, consult H. Donl Peterson, *Moroni: Ancient Prophet, Modern Messenger* (Bountiful, Utah: Horizon Publishers, 1983), 17–18; and his "Moroni, The Last of the Nephite Prophets," in *The Book of Mormon: Fourth Nephi through Moroni, From Zion to Destruction,* ed. Monte S. Nyman and Charles D. Tate Jr. (Provo, Utah: BYU Religious Studies Center, 1995), 235–37.
8. It is JST, Gen. 17:4–7 that sets out the doctrinal dimensions of the Canaanites' apostasy, including the rejection of "my [God's] precepts" and the adoption of the mistaken belief that "the blood of the righteous Abel was shed for sins." The Canaanites' later actions are chronicled in the biblical books of Judges and Joshua.
9. For the original Nephite settlement, see 2 Ne. 5:6–18; the Nephites were forced from that area about 170 B.C. by a Lamanite invasion, and it fell to the Lamanites. Except for a 50-year period when a group of Nephites took possession of the city of Nephi and made it their home until a treaty forced on them by Lamanites grew intolerable and they fled north to Zarahemla, it remained in Laminite hands. (See Mosiah 9:1–7; 19:25–28; 22:10–13.)

10. For hints about the economic benefits of expanding into the northern territory, consult Alma 63:4–10. Concerning the Lamanite military strategy of controlling Nephites from the north and south—the seas lay on the east and west—see Alma 22:29–34.

11. Mormon also knew of the flight south of some survivors aside from the twenty-four (see Morm. 6:15). It is also possible that some or all of the twenty-four survivors who found one another after the battle, including Mormon and Moroni, and who could flee, traveled south as well (see 6:11, 15). Any such flight would have taken place after the death of Mormon, who apparently died of his wounds (see 6:10; 8:3, 5).

    Such a flight, and the one that Moroni undertook to remain alive for more than thirty-five years after the last battle, raises questions about carrying the record. It seems apparent that he had access to at least the sermon of his father (see Moro. 7), letters from his father (see Moro. 8–9), and the record of the Jaredites until he made the last entries. He must have borne these and the translation aids, as well as his father's edited work (First Nephi through Mormon, chapter 6), wherever he went. Perhaps he owned a beast of burden to assist him, but we cannot say for certain how he carried those records.

12. The last, protracted war began in A.D. 361 after ten years of peace. See Morm. 2:28; 3:1, 7.

13. The clanish character of Lamanite society can be seen in accounts that preserve their names (e.g., Alma 2:2–4), as is the case among Nephites (e.g., Alma 30:59; 31:1–3). For clans in the era before the final battle, see 4 Ne. 1:35–38. For the relief from competing clan interests, see 4 Ne. 1:17.

14. The other reference to "the house of Israel" comes in a plea that "God the Father remember the covenant which he hath made" and plainly includes "our brethren" the Lamanites (Morm. 9:35–37).

15. I have been unable to find studies that discuss this irregular juxtaposition of tone concerning the Lamanites in Mosiah 17. See my reference to it in chapter 4, note 20.

16. See 3 Ne. 16:11–20; 20:10–28; 21:1–13, 20–29.

17. As an example, consult the prayer of Enos on behalf of the record and its influence on the Lamanites (Enos 1:11–17).

18. Moroni's argument follows that of his father; see Mormon's observations in Moro. 8:12, 18.

19. The sense is similar to that expressed in Ps. 102:25–27.

20. Studies that tie Moroni's catalogue and that of Paul's, as well as other scriptural passages, include Sidney B. Sperry, *Book of Mormon Compendium* (Salt Lake City: Bookcraft, 1970), 491–92; S. Brent Farley, "Come Unto Christ (Moro. 9–10)," in *Studies in Scripture, Volume Eight, Alma 30 to Moroni,* ed. Kent P.

Jackson (Salt Lake City: Deseret Book, 1988), 304–12; and Joseph Fielding McConkie, Robert L. Millet, and Brent L. Top, *Doctrinal Commentary on the Book of Mormon,* 4 vols. (Salt Lake City: Bookcraft, 1992), 4:367–69.

21. A number of studies have explored these principles. See, for instance, Sidney B. Sperry, *Book of Mormon Compendium,* 487–88; Monte S. Nyman, "Hope, Faith, and Charity (Moroni 7–8)," in *Studies in Scripture, Volume Eight, Alma 30 to Moroni,* 293–303; Alvin C. Rencher, "Unity through the Power of Charity," in *The Book of Mormon: Fourth Nephi through Moroni, From Zion to Destruction,* ed. M. S. Nyman et al., 263–275; McConkie, Millet, and Top, *Doctrinal Commentary on the Book of Mormon,* 4:342–47.

22. For the account of the miracle at the prison where Nephi and Lehi were held, see Hel. 5. For the miraculous collapse of the prison where Alma and Amulek were held, see Alma 14:27–28.

23. Modern studies about Paul's treatment on charity, most likely an early Christian hymn (see 1 Corinthians 13), generally conclude that Paul is its author. See Gordon D. Fee, *The First Epistle to the Corinthians* (Grand Rapids, Mich.: Eerdmans, 1987), 625–26.

24. There are a few other dimensions of Mormon's sermon which plausibly go back to Jesus' words, but they need careful review. (The revelation that Moroni receives wherein the Lord refers to "faith, hope and charity" [Ether 12:28] comes after the death of Mormon and therefore too late to serve as a source for Mormon's sermon.) Mormon's principal early theme is good versus evil (see Moro. 7:5–10, 12–17, 19–20), measured against the actions involved in giving (Moro. 7:6–8, 10), praying (verses 6, 9, 48), discipleship (verses 11, 48), and judging (knowing good from evil, in verses 14–19). The Resurrected Jesus discussed all of these concepts in his sermon:

    Good and evil (3 Ne. 14:11, 15–20)

    Giving (3 Ne. 14:9–11)

    Praying (3 Ne. 13:5–13)

    Discipleship (3 Ne. 13:24)

    Judging (3 Ne. 14:1–6)

    In this light, I would deem that Moroni 7 consists of Mormon's reflective homily on the words of the Risen Jesus, chiefly those in his sermon at the temple on day one. There are indicators that Mormon, and even Moroni, relied on memory for many quotations. Even so, the level of reflection on Jesus' words is profound and far-reaching. For example, Moro. 7:5 almost quotes 3 Ne. 14:16 and 20. Moro. 7:6 and 8 both echo 3 Ne. 14:9–11 and 14:15–19 (a false prophet [verse 15] prays without result); Moro. 7:11 echoes 3 Ne. 13:24 (God and Mammon); and Moro. 7:18 almost quotes 3 Ne. 14:2 (measure of judgment). There are other near quotations, but these will suffice.

25. A good summary about these three Nephite disciples is that by William A. Wilson, "Three Nephites," *Encyclopedia of Mormonism,* 1477–78, and citations.

26. The best discussion of Moroni's three endings and their significance is that of Thomas, "Moroni: The Final Voice," 88–99.

27. The worry is expressed in slightly different terms, but amounts to the same thing. Moroni notes possible "imperfections" in the record that might form a deterrent to a warm reception (see Morm. 8:12, 17; 9:31).

28. Consult the study of John Gee, "Limhi in the Library," *Journal of Book of Mormon Studies,* 1, no. 1 (1992): 54–66.

29. The references to "the Gentiles" occur in Ether 12:35–38.

30. On the pining for Jerusalem and the land of promise, see S. Kent Brown, *From Jerusalem to Zarahemla: Literary and Historical Studies of the Book of Mormon* (Provo, Utah: BYU Religious Studies Center, 1998), 12–17.

31. For these covenantal terms, see Gen. 12:2, 7; 13:14–16; 15:5, 18; Abr. 2:6, 11.

32. For the influence of the Book of Mormon, and of Moroni in particular, on the practices of the Church, consult Scott H. Faulring, "The Book of Mormon: A Blueprint for Organizing the Church," *Journal of Book of Mormon Studies* 7, no. 1 (1998): 60–69; also Peterson, *Moroni: Ancient Prophet, Modern Messenger,* 61–65. A summary discussion of the ordinances appears in Robert E. Parsons, "The Practices of the Church (Moroni 1–6)," in *Studies in Scripture, Volume Eight, Alma 30 to Moroni,* 282–92.

33. One of the important reviews of the ministering of angels is that of Dallin H. Oaks, "The Aaronic Priesthood and the Sacrament," *Ensign,* Nov. 1998, 37.

34. The quotation is from Phyllis Ann Roundy, "Mormon," *Encyclopedia of Mormonism,* 933.

35. The Printer's Manuscript of the Book of Mormon exhibits the following line before the beginning of Moroni, chapter nine: "The second epistle of Mormon to his son Moroni." This statement, if written by Moroni, would date the letter quoted in chapter nine after the one cited in chapter eight. See Royal Skousen, ed., *The Printer's Manuscript of the Book of Mormon,* 2 vols. (Provo, Utah: FARMS, 2001), 2:970.

CHRONOLOGICAL CHART OF APPROXIMATE DATES (185–70 B.C.)

DATES (B.C.)	NEPHITES/PEOPLE OF ZARAHEMLA	NEPHITE COLONY (ZENIFF)	ALMA'S COLONY	LAMANITES
185	Coronation of Mosiah (c. 185 B.C.) *Omni 1:12*			
180				
175	Flight from land of Nephi (between 175 and 170 B.C.) *Omni 1:12–13*			King Laman drives out Mosiah (between 175 and 170 B.C.) *Omni 1:12–13*
170	Colonists under Zeniff go back (between 170 and 165 B.C.) *Omni 1:27–30; Mosiah 9:1–6*			
165		Zeniff reigns (c. 165 B.C.) for more than 22 years *Mosiah 10:3*		King Laman negotiates with Zeniff and withdraws from city of Nephi (c. 165 B.C.) *Mosiah 9:6–8*
160				
155	Coronation of Benjamin (c. 155 B.C.) *Omni 1:23*			
150		Nephites respond successfully to invasion, and rearm (c. 152 B.C.) *Mosiah 9:15–10:1*		King Laman stirs people to war in 13th year of Zeniff's reign (c 152 B.C.) *Mosiah 9:11–14*
145		Nephites respond again to invasion (c. 143 B.C.) *Mosiah 10:9–10, 20*		King Laman coronated in 22nd year of Zeniff (c. 143 B.C.) *Mosiah 10:6*
140		Coronation of Noah (c. 140 B.C.) *Mosiah 11:1* Noah responds to Lamanite harassment (c. 140–138 B.C.) *Mosiah 11:18–19*		Lamanites prepare for war and attack colony (c. 143 B.C.) *Mosiah 10:6–8* Lamanites create tension with colony soon after Noah's coronation (c. 140–138 B.C.) *Mosiah 11:16–17*
135				

CHRONOLOGICAL CHART OF APPROXIMATE DATES (185–70 B.C.), CONTINUED

DATES (B.C.)	NEPHITES/PEOPLE OF ZARAHEMLA	NEPHITE COLONY (ZENIFF)	ALMA'S COLONY	LAMANITES
130		Abinadi appears the first time (c. 130 B.C.) *Mosiah 11:20* Abinadi appears the second time and is tried and executed (c. 128 B.C.) *Mosiah 12:1; 17:5–20*	The 450 people of Alma flee Noah's army (c. 127 B.C.) and settle in the land of Helam *Mosiah 18:34–35; 23:1–5, 19*	
125	Coronation of Mosiah (c. 124 B.C.) *Mosiah 6:3* Benjamin dies (c. 121 B.C.) *Mosiah 6:5*	Noah is toppled by Lamanite attacks; coronation of Limhi (c. 121 B.C.) *Mosiah 19:6–11, 23, 26*		Lamanites attack Noah and then make covenant with Limhi (c. 121 B.C.) *Mosiah 19:6, 26*
120	Mosiah sends 16 soldiers to find Nephite colony (c. 118 B.C.) *Mosiah 7:1–3* Colonists of Limhi reach Zarahemla (c. 118 B.C.) *Mosiah 22:11–14* Colonists of Alma reach Zarahemla (c. 118 B.C.) *Mosiah 24:18–25* Assembly of national unity (c. 118 B.C.) *Mosiah 25:1–20*	16 soldiers reach colony (c. 118 B.C.) *Mosiah 7:4–7; 21:22–24* Colonists flee to Zarahemla (c. 118 B.C.) *Mosiah 22:11–14*	Amulon takes charge of Alma's colony (c. 118 B.C.) *Mosiah 23:39* Colonists flee to Zarahemla (c. 118 B.C.) *Mosiah 24:18–25*	Lamanites attack Limhi's people because of broken covenant (c. 119 B.C.) *Mosiah 20:7* King Laman allows harassment of Limhi's colonists (c. 118 B.C.) *Mosiah 21:2–3*
115				
110				Ishmaelite king coronated (c. 110 B.C.) *no record*
105				
100				
95	Sons of Mosiah depart on mission (c. 94 B.C.) *Mosiah 28:9*			Sons of Mosiah arrive in Lamanite lands (c. 94 B.C.) *Alma 17:13*

CHRONOLOGICAL CHART OF APPROXIMATE DATES (185–70 B.C.), CONTINUED

DATES (B.C.)	NEPHITES/PEOPLE OF ZARAHEMLA	NEPHITE COLONY (ZENIFF)	ALMA'S COLONY	LAMANITES
93	Mosiah and Alma die (c. 91 B.C.) *Mosiah 29:45–46* Alma the Younger inaugurates era of judges (c. 91 B.C.) *Mosiah 29:42* Trial and execution of Nehor (c. 91 B.C.) *Alma 1:2–15*			Ishmaelite king meets Ammon and Aaron (c. 91 B.C.) *Alma 20:8; 22:1*
90	Amlici leads unsuccessful effort to restore monarchy (c. 86 B.C.) *Alma 2:1–38*			
85	Nephihah succeeds Alma as chief judge (c. 83 B.C.) *Alma 4:11–17*			Anti-Nephi-Lehi coronated (c. 81 B.C.) *Alma 24:3*
80	People of Anti-Nephi-Lehi arrive and move to Jershon (c. 80 B.C.) *Alma 27:14–26* Ammonihah destroyed by invading Lamanites (c. 80 B.C.) *Alma 16:1–3*			Lamanite civil war; new king chosen (c. 80 B.C.) *Alma 24:20* People of Anti-Nephi-Lehi migrate to land of Zarahemla (c. 80 B.C.) *Alma 27:14, 26* Lamanite army destroys Ammonihah (c. 80 B.C.) *Alma 16:2–3; 25:2*
75	Lamanite invasion of west (c. 73 B.C.) *Alma 49:1–27*			Lamanite king assassinated by Amalickiah (c. 74 B.C.) *Alma 47:24* Amalickiah sends Lamanite army to attack the western Nephite area (c. 73 B.C.) *Alma 48:1–6; 49:1*
70